AF540507

PROFESSIONALISM IN TEACHER EDUCATION

About the Editors

Prof. P.K. Sahoo is Professor and Head in the Department of Education, University of Allhabad, Allahabad. He was also the Director of the Institute of Correspondence and Continuing Education, University of Allahabad and Director, Academic at Kota Open University, Kota, Rajasthan. Born in Orissa Prof. Sahoo studied in the M.S. University of Baroda, for his doctoral degree in Education. He has owned the distinction of IATE National Eminent Teacher Edicator Award, 2009 UGC Visiting Associate 1997-99, AAOU UNESCO PROP AWARD, 1998, University Medal for Ist Rank in MA Examination and UGC Research Fellowship of CASE, M.S. University of Baroda, Vadodara. To his credit Prof. Sahoo has authored three books viz. Educational Technology in Distance Education (1999), Open Learning System (1994) Higher Education At-a-Distance (1993) and co-authored two books viz- Futurology in Education (1989) and Futures Studies (1991). His areas of interest are Open and Distance Education, Futuristic Education, Educational Technology and Development. Prof. Sahoo has published around 190 Research Papers in national and international journals and books. He was the General Secretoary of Indian Association of Teacher Educators.

Dr. Dhananjai Yadav is Reader in Education, Department of Education, University of Allahabad, Allahabad. Born in UP Dr. Yadav studied in University of Allahabad for his doctoral degree in Education. He has owned the distinction of being UGC Research Fellow in the University of Allahabad for his doctoral research. His areas of Interest are ICT in Education, Educational Technology and Concept Analysis. He has authored a book on Philosophy of Wittgenstein. He has published around 50 research papers in national and international journals and books.

Dr. B.C. Das is Lecturer in Education in the Department of Teacher Education, Rani Bhagyawati Devi Women's PG College, Bijnor under M.J.P. Rohilkhand University, Bareilly, UP, India. He is also the Programme In-charge of IGNOU B.Ed. Programme Study Centre, Bijnor. Born in Orissa, Dr. Das studied in the University of Allahabad for doctoral degree in Education. He has owned the distinction of being a Research Fellow of Ministry of Tribal Affairs, Government of India at his doctoral stage of research. To his credit Dr. Das has published around 20 research papers in reputed journals and books of India and abroad. His areas of interest are Tribal Education, Educational Technology and Development. He has authored a book titled Tribal Eeducation Trends and Future Scenario.

Professionalism in Teacher Education

Contemporary Perspectives

Edited by
P.K. Sahoo
D. Yadav
B.C. Das

CONCEPT PUBLISHING COMPANY PVT. LTD.
NEW DELHI-110 059

ISBN-13: 978-81-8069-706-7

First Published 2010

Published and Printed by

Concept Publishing Company Pvt. Ltd.
Regd. Office:
A/15-16, Commercial Block, Mohan Garden
New Delhi-110059 (India)
Phones : 25351460, 25351794, *Fax* : 091-11-25357109
Email : publishing@conceptpub.com,
Website : www.conceptpub.com

Editorial Office:
H-13, Bali Nagar, New Delhi-110 015, India.

Dedicated
In Memory of
Professor M.B. Buch
The Eminent Teacher Educator
of Twentieth Century

प्रोफेसर आर० जी० हर्षे
(प्रो० राजन हर्षे)
कुलपति
इलाहाबाद विश्वविद्यालय
सीनेट हाउस
इलाहाबाद–211 002 उ.प्र.
(भारत)

Prof. **R.G. Harshe**
(Prof. Rajen Harshe)
Vice-Chancellor
University of Allahabad
Senate House
Allahabad-211 002 U.P. (INDIA)

Foreword

India needs adequately qualified and competent teaching professionals in order to provide quality education at different stages of learning. This objective would be achieved through incessant collective and well coordinated efforts of devoted educationists, experts, researchers and policy-makers. This book entitled **Professionalism in Teacher Education** is quietly an unprecedented endeavour in bringing out the contemporary perspectives on teacher preparation.

In fact, new generation of teachers could be trained in the context of all pervasive and permeable paradigm of information and communication technology (ICT). In its turn, ICT has been stimulated by the dominant trends such as globalization, liberalization and privatization of the world economy. Empowerment of teachers in ICT appears to be a sine qua non condition towards the preparation of new generation of teachers.

As a corollary, teacher preparation is also to be viewed in the context of significant developments in open and distance learning mode. Teaching learning system has witnessed a paradigm shift from teacher-centeredness to learner-centeredness. The shifting roles of a teacher are being recast in terms of facilitating a reciprocal process of learning by teacher as well as the taught a stance that opens up the possibilities for innovation involving constructive learning. Evidently teaching professionals must possess appropriate professional ethics, self appraisal practices and positive attitude towards teaching profession. Similarly a value integrated curriculum must be given serious attention in the shifting agenda of teacher preparation.

Moreover, quality assurance is being regarded as the most significant component of education system which is contingent upon the quality of on-going teacher education programmes. The quality assurance bodies like National Assessment and Accreditation Council (NAAC), National Council for Teacher Education (NCTE), Rehabilitation Council of India (RCI) and Distance Education Council (DEC) have come out with definite quality assurance strategies for quality assessment in teacher education programmes.

Recent report of 'The Committee to Advise on Renovation and Rejuvenation of Higher Education' chaired by Prof. Yashpal has recommended for the constitution of a National Council for Higher Education and Research (NCHER) as the single regulatory and quality control body of Higher Education indicating relevant structural and functional transformations in teacher education programmes. Major transformations are expected from quality assessment bodies in view of accreditation and quality assurance of such programmes in the future.

The attempt made by Prof. P.K. Sahoo, his editorial team and the distinguished educationists, experts and researchers is laudable and deserves all appreciation. I am sure; this is a significant contribution to the rejuvenation of teacher education programmes and professional development of teachers in the global context.

Yours sincerely,

(R.G. Harshe)

Preface

Teacher is a major input of education system and so is teacher education. Teaching has been one of the oldest and most respected professions in the world. A profession is characterized with involvement of people practicing a socially valued vocation with background of specialized knowledge, possession of competencies, skills and value orientation. Professional development of teachers aims at refinement of well defined area of knowledge concerning education in general and teaching-learning in specific, training on competencies and skills associated with teacher performance in school system and development of humane and social values. Formal efforts in strengthening the base of professional development of teachers have almost a century old history in India. With the emergence of knowledge society, where education for all is recognized as a motto of the nation, meaningful efforts need to be made in broadening the horizon of education of teachers and making it relevant and purposeful. Of late, the report of the Committee to Advice on Renovation and Rejuvenation of Higher Education (2009) under the chairmanship of Professor Yashpal proposed to constitute National Council for Higher Education and Research (NCHER) as a single body in the field of higher education to treat all area in an integrated manner and work towards convergences with regulatory powers. The committee has made two significant observations concerning teacher education. One, the preparation of teachers for all levels of school education should be the responsibility of institutions of higher education......it is also necessary to enhance quality of teacher education within higher education, Two, jurisdiction of NCHER shall also cover the subject of teacher education which are currently under direct control of various regulatory bodies like NCTE, UGC, RCI and DEC. Yet the major focus concerning teacher education remains on structural and functional transformation of teacher education taking into account complex contextual realities and global vision. This book which is a compendium of 33 papers depicts the present status and future scenario of teacher education on various areas like curriculum, global context, open and distance learning, professional ethics and values, ICT and context specific competencies and quality assurance in teacher education. The discourses concerning themes by eminent educationists and researchers in the field of education broaden the scope for reflections on development of teacher education in the country in the context of globalization.

It is hoped that this book will be a relevant reference material for researchers, education experts, planners, policy-makers and students in the field of Education. The editors express gratitude to all the authors who contributed their ideas, experiences and studies to this volume. Specific thanks are due to Prof. Mohammad Miyan, President, Indian Association of Teacher Educators (IATE) and Prof. Ramesh Ghanta, the Former President of IATE for their encouragement and guidance for this publication. The editors express heart full thanks to Prof. R.N. Mehrotra, the octogenarian educationist of the country and Professor Mohan B Menon, a leading international expert in the area of teacher education for their valuable guidance and co-operation. The editors are grateful to all the well-wishers and friends who extended their help directly or indirectly in bringing out this volume. Some of their names that need specific mention are: Prof. Janak Pandey, Prof. Shyam B. Menon, Prof. L.C. Singh, Prof. D.N. Sansanwal, Prof. S.P. Malhotra, Prof. R.S. Pandey, Prof. M.S. Sodha, Prof. P.C. Saxena, Prof. Vidya Agarwal, Prof. J. Mohanty, Prof. N.K. Dash, Prof. M.K. Das, Prof. U.C. Vashistha, Prof. Girijesh Kumar, Prof. N.N. Pandey, Prof. D.R. Singh, Dr. C.S. Shukla, Prof. M. Verma, Prof. H.S. Bajwa, Prof. G.N.P. Srivastava, Prof. Subhash Gakhar and Prof. R.P. Singh.

We are also thankful to the emerging researchers, teacher educators and experts who made significant contributions to this volume, such as Dr. K.C. Sahoo, Dr. S. Kumar, Dr. Chenna Reddy, Dr. P. Sahu, Dr. Priya Khanna, Dr. Gaurav Singh, Dr. B.C. Mohapatra, Dr. Kaushal Sharma, Dr. Sutapa Bose, Dr. J. Sthapak, Dr. S.S. Dahiya, Dr. J. Amin, Dr. R.L. Madhavi ,Dr. Tara Sabapathy, Dr. Namita Sahoo, Dr. M.B. Shrestha, Dr. P. Mallick and Dr. M.T.V. Nagaraju. We also thank the research scholars Shri Dinesh Kumar, Mr. Surendra Kumar, Ms. Reena Singh, Mrs. Bhavana, Mrs. Rama Gupta, Mr. Prashish Khare, Mr. Rajesh Kumar Yadav and Mr. Dinesh Kumar Gupta in this connection.

P.K. Sahoo
D. Yadav
B.C. Das

Contents

V. QUALITY ASSURANCE

The Contributors

B.C. Das, Lecturer, Department of Teacher Education, R.B.D.Women's PG College, Bijnor, U.P., India.**Sutapa Bose,** Reader, School of Education, IGNOU, New Delhi, India.

B.C. Mohapatra, Former Lecturer in Education, M.P. Bhoj Open University Bhopal, M.P., India.

Chenna Reddy, Head and Dean, Department of Education, S.K. University, Ananta Pur, A.P., India.

C.S. Shukla, Head, Department of Teacher Education, Vardhaman P.G. College, Bijnor, U.P. India.

D.N. Sansanwal, Former Head and Dean, School of Education, D.A.V.V., Indore, M.P., India.

Dhananjai Yadav, Reader, Department of Education, University of Allahabad, Allahabad, India.

G.N.P. Srivastava, Head, Department of Education, RIE, Bhopal, M.P., India.

Gaurav Singh, Lecturer in Education, RBTT Institute, Bareilly, U.P., India.

Girijesh Kumar, Head, Department of Education, MJPR University, Bareilly, U.P., India.

H. Dinker, Lecturer, M.P. Bhoj Open University Bhopal, M.P., India.

H.S. Bajwa, Professor, Department of Education, Punjab University, Chandigarh, India.

J. Sthapak, Lecturer, in Education, M.P. Bhoj Open University Bhopal, M.P., India.

Jyotsna Amin, Lecturer, Department of Education, MS University of Baroda, Vadodara, Gujarat, India.

K.C. Sahoo, Reader, Faculty of Education, Shanti Niketan, W.B., India.

Kaushal Sharma, Former Lecturer in Special Education, M.P. Bhoj Open University Bhopal, M.P., India.

L.C. Singh, Former Head, Department of Teacher Education, NCERT, New Delhi, India.

Mohan B. Menon, Former Education Specialist, COL, Vancouver, Canada. Currently working as Chief, Education Specialist, UNRWA HQ (A) P.O.BOX 140157 Amman 11814 Jordan.

M.S. Sodha, Former Vice Chancellor,Devi Ahilya Vishwavidyalaya, Indore, Barkatullah Univeristy, Bhopal and University of Lucknow, Lucknow, U.P., India.

M. Sthapak, Lecturer in Education, Department of Technical Education, New Delhi, India.

M.T.V. Nagaraju, Reader, Department of Education, SPM Vishwa Vidyalaya, Tirupati, A.P. India.

M. Verma, Professor, Department of Education, University of Lucknow, Lucknow, India

Min Bahadur Shreshtha, Sr. Lecturer, Central Department of Education, Tribhuvan University, Kathmandu, Nepal.

Mohammad Miyan, Dean, Faculty of Education and Director, AIIODL, Jamia Millia Islamia, New Delhi, India.

N.K. Dash, Professor of Education, School of Education, IGNOU, New Delhi, India.

Namita Sahoo, Lecturer in Education, K.P. Training College, University of Allahabad, Allahabad, India.

P.K. Sahoo, Head, Department of Education, University of Allahabad, Allahabad, India.

P. Mallick, Sr. Lecturer, Department of Education, Tulsi Womens College, Kendrapara, Orissa, India.

P. Sahu, Reader in Special Education, RIE, Bhubaneshwar, Orissa, India.

Priya Khanna, Faculty of Education, AIIODL, Jamia Millia Islamia, New Delhi, India.

Purnima K., Principal, Gold Field College of Education, Kolar, Karantaka, India.

R.L. Madhavi, Lecturer, Department of Education, MS University of Baroda, Vadodara, Gujarat, India.

R.N. Mehrotra, Former Head and Dean, Department of Education, CIE, University of Delhi. Currently working as Advisor, Dayal Bagh Education Institute, Dayal Bagh, Agra, U.P. India.

S. Kumar, Professor, Department of Education, University of Lucknow, U.P., India

S.K. Joshi, Lecturer Department of Teacher Education, Vardhaman P.G. College, Bijnor, U.P. India.

S.N. Sahoo, Vice Principal, SVM, Angul, Orissa, India.

S.S. Dahiya, Head, ICT Center, CR College of Education, Rohtak, Haryana, India.

S.P. Malhotra, National Fellow, NUEPA, New Delhi, India.

Saroj Pandey, Reader, Department of Teacher Education, NCERT, New Delhi, India.

Shyam B. Menon, Vice Chancellor, Ambedkar University, Dwarka, New Delhi, India.

Subhash Gakhar, Former Chairman, Professor, Department of Education, Punjab University, Chandigarh, India.

Sutapa Bose, Reader, School of Education, IGNOU, New Delhi, India.

Tara Sabapathy, Reader, Department of Education, Bangalore University, Bangalore, India.

U.C. Vashishtha, Former Head and Dean, Department of Education, University of Lucknow, Lucknow, India.

Introduction

P.K. SAHOO

The major focus of Global Society remains on "basic education for all," "core work skills for all" and "life long learning for all". Globalization is linked with promotion of processes of continuous learning over the life time by each and every member of society thereby highlighting the skills of "learning to learn". In a knowledge society where access to information continues to grow exponentially and knowledge and skills required for leading new kind of life keep on changing fast, various alternatives are explored to impart quality education for all. Global changes keep on pressurizing all groups to acquire and apply new skills in every sphere of life. Such phenomena must be well accomplished in the educational system. Encouraging opportunities for multidimensional context specific learning situations remain as a key issue for education of the day. Moreover the opportunities for stimulation for knowledge creation, sharing of knowledge and dissemination process enlarge the scope of teaching learning system. In this context, it is very much significant to visualize changing role of teachers and teaching profession in a learning society.

Teaching is considered as one of the oldest professions in the society. As a profession it fulfills the criteria of specific orientation into well defined area of knowledge concerning education, profession of highly specialized competencies and skills of pedagogy with sound theoretical frameworks and adherence to certain codes of ethics. Professionalism in teacher education focuses on the quality of teaching profession and quality mechanism adopted in preparation of teachers for different stages of education covering pre-primary, primary, secondary, tertiary and quaternary stages. As basic criteria of teaching profession, professional ethics are evolved through continuous deliberation of specific guild of teachers and teacher educators keeping in view the contextual realities as well as global characteristics of teaching profession. That is how the role of professional bodies like Indian Association of Teacher Educators is considered significant to shape quality of teaching profession in the context of knowledge, competency and value dimensions.

Teacher education system encompassing various kinds of teacher preparation and empowerment activities is very much integrated with the school (including higher education) system. Changes incorporated in the ideology and curriculums of school system dictate the nature and functioning of teacher education. For instance, policies concerning national curriculum framework at school level delineates the role of teacher preparation system. It is also most significant that teacher preparation must take note of internal dimensions of school system as well as the socio-cultural milieu in which the system operates. In this context, developments taking place in the field of knowledge and skills, the process involved in acquisition of knowledge, criteria governing the required knowledge to be developed among learners and pedagogic principles and practices influence the forms and processes of teacher education. While relevance of teacher education is examined in the context of meeting developmental needs and expectation of school system, its value is also determined in term of its role in influencing the nature and functions of school system. The extent to which required knowledge, competencies and values imbibed by a teacher through quality teacher education programmes indicate professionalism in teacher education system.

As a matter of fact there has been a tremendous change in the knowledge system and the process of acquisition of learning experiences in the age of ICT and globalization. Such changes are not only significantly witnessed at apex level but also it has been pervasive at grass root level of education. In one or the other form, liberalization has penetrated into different walks of life in Indian soil including the school system. The nature of schooling, curriculum, pedagogic practices, and technological intervention and management practices has triggered a plethora of challenges for teacher preparation in the country. As a major development the NCERT has come out with national curriculum framework highlighting the contextual multiplicity of schooling with due emphasis on global developments. It focuses on developmental perspective of quality education at learner level as well as making it potential for global challenges thereby requiring a new role of teacher education. Significant developments have taken place by interventions of corporate sectors like Intel India Ltd. in using ICT as a major tool through collaborative efforts with NCTE and leading university teaching departments of education in India.

Another development that has been witnessed in the field of teacher education is in the form of renewal of teacher education curriculum at NCTE level. It intends to make structural and procedural changes in teacher education curriculum with wider perspective. However, major focus remains on preparation of pre-service teachers in face-to-face traditional mode of transaction. Enough remains to be worked out in the direction of integrating initial teacher preparation with continuing professional development of teachers with a holistic perspective.

With liberalizing economy as a backdrop there needs to be provisions of multiple entries and multiple exits and for bridges with other courses along with continuing educational practices for teacher trainees. In the age of ICT gradually the distinction between traditional face-to-face mode and open and distance learning mode of teacher education is going to be blurred. There is possibility of adopting network based learning opportunities in face-to-face mode of teacher education thereby making the presence of open and distance learning in an integrated form. Hence, the future scenario is visible in multi-mode, multi-side and modular forms of teacher education in Indian soil.

It is high time to develop holistic framework of teacher education and its relevance in shaping the future scenario of school system. Professional values of teachers (including teacher educators) need to be focused in the changing perspectives. Accordingly suitable pathways can be explored through experience based and research supported evidences. The above issues have been discussed in detail in this book through the contributions of eminent educationists and teacher educators on five themes:

- Curriculum Framework
- Globalization, Knowledge Economy and ODL Contexts
- Professional Ethics and Values
- ICT and Context Specific Competencies
- Quality Assurance

While discussing the nature of curriculum for teacher education it is significant to throw up light on structure of teacher education in a holistic form. Prof. R.N. Mehrotra highlights the significance of teacher education being integrated with the **mainstream of academic life of the universities.** Moreover, he emphasizes on teacher educators helping the prospective teachers "to understand education in all its parameters, to attain skills of classroom teaching and to build up professional attitude." To him teacher education at all levels to be taken over by higher education frameworks would be intended to strengthen pre-service and in-service education of teachers incorporating pre-primary, primary and secondary stages. Open and distance learning system in teacher preparation has its history of more than four decades in India. Keeping in view the nature of teacher education curriculum and the scope of technology intervention in distance education, innovations have taken place in designing ODL curriculum and making it more relevant to school system. Prof. M.B. Menon while discussing the teacher education curriculum in a global context suggests constructivist approach to curriculum design. He insists "the cases, problems etc would be designed and developed in such a way that the trainees while going through them can be able to take appropriate decision, perform relevant activity, experience in real situations and /or an audio-video episode, recall prior experiences, read a relevant theoretical writing or factual information and/or reflect on the issue either individually or collaboratively in face- to –face or technology mediated human interaction."

Education system functions in its own environment being influenced by socio-political expectations. It also influences changes in external environment by providing new directions to development processes. Highlighting society and school linkage in shaping curriculum Dr. Chenna Reddy states "Educators and the public need to understand why society would be better served if schools clarify their purposes, and expects students to demonstrate knowledge and skills required for success in life." Reddy has classified different categories of expected curricular outputs in above context and has discussed in detail the above implications of such analysis for school system in general and teacher education in specific. On a similar line Dr. Saroj Pandey has talked about the role of education "as the vehicle to promote a cohesive society by taking into consideration the diversity of individuals and groups and by ensuring that the education system itself doesn't contribute to social exclusion." Pandey further adds that " preparing teachers for a cohesive society calls for a global perspective in teacher education programmes which takes into account the diversity and multi-cultural contexts, encourages aesthetic and cultural sensibility, promotes reflective thinking, generates awareness of human rights and fundamental duties among teachers...." In her paper she has discussed in detail about social goals of teacher education like equipping teachers to resolve conflicts, promoting religious tolerance, preparing global citizenship and helping teachers to become reflective practitioners. She also throws up light on curriculum practices incorporating content integration, knowledge construction processes, prejudice reduction, equity and pedagogy in empowering school culture.

Besides critical analysis of theoretical framework of school curriculum vis-à-vis teacher education system empirical studies reveal provision of professional development practices in existing teacher education curriculum. One such study conducted by Dr. P. Sahu has revealed dismal picture about one year as well as two year B.Ed. programmes. Sahu has concluded that none of the courses under two year B.Ed. programme were concerned with different sub-variables like: period and training, accountability, professional code of ethics and professional developments. However one year B.Ed. programme incorporated practices leading to professional code of ethics and professional development.

Co-curricular activities constitute a significant component of any effective teacher education curriculum. Participatory experience based learning has been emphasized by Dr. K.C. Sahoo, Dr. S. Kumar, Prof. U.C. Vashistha and Prof. M.S. Sodha in their paper on teacher's role in co-curricular activities. Different papers covered in section one have focused on contextual realities at macro as well as micro level playing major role in evolving curriculum framework for teacher education.

The papers included in Section II of this book intend to visualize alternative opportunities of teacher education in the era of globalization. Globalization is visible in every society. It has influenced market output as a matter of private return. Prof. S.P. Malhotra, in his paper, has emphasized the link between economic performance and applicability of ideas generated by universities in the world of work. "The knowledge based business is now recognized to be key drivers at all levels in proportion to other business." In this context the author highlights the need for expansion of relevant teacher education programmes in the private sector. Entrepreneurship, networking, knowledge based skills and research and development are some of the key features of such system. Specialized skill training is essential in quality teaching, quality assessment and quality guidance. Such issues have also been discussed by Dr. S.N. Sahoo in his paper highlighting the special role of teachers as learning facilitators, helping students to select and grasp appropriate information, making best use of ICT etc. Likewise, to make teacher preparation responsive a comprehensive debate has been surfaced by Dr. Dhananjai Yadav relating the nascent demands of learners and schools as the major determinants of designing teacher education programmes. While discussing political dimensions of globalization and education, Dr. M.T.V. Nagaraju has focused on "schools being expected to carry much of the burden of national reconstruction". He has stressed that relations between education and citizenship and teacher education programmes rendered by the universities have posed some paradoxical consequences. Liberal tradition of teacher education promoting openness and adaptability to different learning situations is projected to be more relevant than study of theoretical bases of teacher education.

As discussed above Open Distance Learning System (ODLS) has emerged as a complimentary mode of teacher education. Research in ODL system is very much significant from the point of views of "generating knowledge concerning pedagogic principles involved in DE mode and development of appropriate teacher education programme through experience based interventions." Various issues concerning research in teacher education in ODLS have been discussed in papers of Prof. P.K. Sahoo and Prof. N.K. Dash. Researches concerning teacher competencies, methods, media and strategies, human resource management and evaluation strategies are some of the areas which draw special attention. Reviews of studies in these areas prepare a sound base for exploring further studies in ODLS. Prof. N.K. Dash explores possibilities of networking among distance teacher education institutions in a well knitted model taking into account national open university, state open universities and traditional universities. While stressing on the need for sound support services in ODLS Dr. B.C. Mohapatra and Dr. K. Sharma have highlighted re-engineering of the system with Information Communication System (ICS). They have shared the experiences of different sources of ICS like EDUSAT, *Vartalap, Matrubhasha* and *Bharateeya* Open Ofiices, etc.

Section III of this book is devoted to discuss nature of professional ethics and significance of value education as components of teacher preparation. The concept of education is itself a kind of value expression. Values are concerned with guiding forces for determining directions of life and choosing desirable behaviour in society. Education leads to attainment of values. More specifically teacher education plays a vital role in sensitizing teachers about different kinds of learning experiences directly associated with value development. Prof. P.K. Sahoo has emphasized upon constructivist approach to value development where the role of teacher educator is significant in assisting learners to build constructive environment. Prof. G.N. Prakash Srivastava has dealt with clarification of nature of values and guiding principles associated with cultivation of values. Prof, Bajwa has been very much critical about value orientation in existing practices of teacher education. While criticizing the de human nature of IT he insists on teacher's role in development of values with humane touch. He has evolved a model of value oriented teacher education programme and is optimistic about the role of NCTE. In this regard, Dr. C.S. Shukla and Dr. S.K. Joshi in their paper have also justified the significance of value education curriculum as a component of teacher preparation. They have dwelt on sociological issues concerning nature of values and value education. Prof. Mohammad Miyan and Dr. Priya Khanna have emphasized on interpersonal relationship as an indicator of institutional development. Organization theories concerning interpersonal relationship need to be applied in preparation of teachers. They state " improvement of interpersonal relationship is an essential aspect of performance management, a process which involves supporting, improving and monitoring teachers' performance both as individuals and as members of the team. It promotes professional growth among teachers by encouraging them to be fully engaged in school planning and to control the effectiveness of their own work."

Section IV covering ICT and context specific competencies has taken into account the role of ICT in making teaching learning in general and teacher training in specific, effective and efficient in the context of face-to-face as well as distance education mode institutions. Describing the nature of innovations in ICT and its applications in teacher education

Prof. D.N. Sansanwal has made comparision between web-based instruction and traditional instruction. He has dwelt on different applications of ICT in curriculum development, instructional design, learner evaluation and research. Prof. L.C. Singh and Dr. S.S. Dahiya's paper also analyses various uses of ICT with critical review of developments taking place in India and abroad. Dr.J. Amin and Dr. R.L. Madhavi have discussed in detail different factors of empowerment of teachers, such as decentralization, democratization, inversion of hierarchy, enablement and professionalism. ICT needs for teachers have been examined by them in the context of training needs, access to ICT, and support and advice.

Two empirical studies have been reported on ICT awareness and attitude of teachers towards ICT. In her study, Dr. Tara Sabapathy found that there existed high negative relationship between attitude of teachers towards ICT and their ICT anxiety scores. Different background variables like gender, type of school management, subject specialization and teaching experience did not have significant effect on teachers' attitude towards ICT. Dr. Namita Sahoo and Dr. B.C. Das have reported about inadequate facilities of ICT in teacher education institutions. The teacher educators and pupil teachers were aware of the uses of ICT to some extent. As a whole, their competencies were poor with regard to various skills of using ICT in educational practices.

Dr. Sutapa Bose has highlighted different measures for integrating ICT with teacher education programmes at different stages. Besides ICT based interventions in teacher preparation, other kinds of experiences concerning teacher empowerment have been covered in two papers viz. Van Hiele Model of thinking in developing teachers' competencies in teaching of Geometry by Dr. M.B. Shrestha and empowerment of teachers in tribal education by Dr. B.C. Das.

Section V of this book sketches out quality issues in teacher education. Prof. Shyam B. Menon highlights different assumptions of teacher education, such as dependence on the expectations of school education, assumption of content mastery leading to training in curriculum transaction and the value of certification in job market. He discusses different context specific parameters of quality assessment and insists on major transformations in existing measures adopted for assessment of teacher education programmes. Prof. Subhas Gakhar has expressed his concern about existing system of teacher education and has suggested various measures of quality assurance and insists on major transformations in existing measures adopted for assessment of teacher education programmes. Prof. M. Verma and Dr. P. Mallick have been optimistic about the role of NCTE and NAAC in enhancing the quality of teacher education. Dr. Purnima has discussed about teacher-taught relationship, staff recruitment, development policies and educational management, school community relationship and provision for empowerment of teachers as some of the quality indicators of teacher education.

The issues discussed regarding teacher education through contributions of different authors are associated with the dynamics of teacher education and school system in a global society. The meaningful contributions of teaching community for knowledge generation and its transmission in a societal framework have gone beyond the boundaries of school system. The values governing teachers' role, school curriculum and education system are reflections of social, political, economic and technological perspectives. The discussions taking place about changing scenario of comprehensive models of teacher education, its curriculum, alternative models and technological interventions throw up light on plausible reforms in teacher education system. Quality concerns in school education in general and teacher education in specific have been highlighted in different papers with alternative approaches of quality assessment. The roles of national level bodies and institutional level initiatives along with networking of different kinds of institutions have been highlighted in this book. Implications of these discourses shall project a holistic scenario of teacher education in the Indian sub-continent. This will act as a seminal source of reflection to scholars, teacher educators, experts, planners, policy-makers and evaluators, concerning professional development of teachers.

I

Curriculum Framework

1

Teacher Education in My Dreams

R.N. Mehrotra*

Let me share with you some of my dreams. I think that they are prompted by the recent phenomenon of integrated Law education and opening of Law colleges. In my dreams, I see large-sized beautiful campus-based teacher education institutions in different towns all over the country. I often see open, green Campuses of Education with impressive buildings including residences for staff and hostels for students with vibrant youngsters moving around merrily and with scholarly seriousness.

My dreams further include a few Indian Institutes of Education (I.I.Es.) which attain the reputation and status of the IITs and IIMs. Besides, there are a large number of reputed regional Institutes of Education, National Institutes, State Institutes of Education, reputed University Faculty/Department of Education, DIETs with enhanced functions at all levels. The private sector has entered in a big way. There are Tata Institute of Fundamental Education, Birla Institute of Education and so on. Some are constitutionally autonomous.

I dream that there is great demand for joining teacher education courses—the talented school leavers get attracted to teaching profession and seek admission to these courses. As a result, the coaching sector is in it actively. The popular coaching institutions, the FITJEE, The Brilliant Tutorials, the Bansals are preparing for admission to education courses. The Kota town is full of education applicants.

There are campus placement interviews and the students are offered jobs in private, aided and state schools before their passing out. An annual package between Rs. 6-12 lakhs is offered to their toppers. The scales of pay are the same at all levels of education. The similarly qualified get the same scale whether they teach in a nursery or primary or secondary school.

In my dreams, I perceive the immediate and distant vision of these institutions which have achieved excellence in (1) study of Education and (2) education of teachers. They are vibrant organisms constantly generating scholarship and its application. Quality is the hallmark of their activities. They are a source of inspiration to coming generations, inciting their imagination, provoking among them thoughtful reflection and creative thinking on both the concept and the praxis of education in all its multitudinous dimensions and parameters. They have developed multifaceted links with formal and informal, appropriate structures and mechanisms between the University, the Faculty, the Departments, the educationists, the teacher educators, the student teachers, the school practitioners, the schools and the society.

The faculty of the institutions of teacher education have matured into such an expert body that it and its individual members are looked into and sought for ideas about educational policies and strategies at the micro, meso and macro levels. Their products are valued in schools, in teacher education institutions, in international and national professional educational organisations as experts in curriculum development, textbook writing, and as institutional planners, researchers and such other professionals in education.

These are my dreams—always in early morning, which, it is said, prove to be realistic and fulfilled in future.

How do we realise the Dreams?

Teacher Education should clearly define its mission, compatible with this vision and accordingly lay down its objectives to be transformed into specific attainable goals and programmes and their transaction.

The Concept of Excellence of an educational institution includes visible demonstrated performance. Its products are recognised and valued highly locally, nationally, internationally. It is built into the following internationally accepted Education Criteria/Quality indicators:

1. Visionary Leadership
2. Learning centred education
3. Organisational and personal learning
4. Valuing faculty, staff and partners
5. Agility
6. Focus on the future
7. Managing for innovation
8. Management by fact
9. Social responsibility
10. Focus on results and creating value
11. Systems perspective

Globalisation and Teacher Education

I begin with the present favourable practice among academics to refer to Globalisation. I submit to the notion that a Lecture is incomplete if it does not talk of Globalisation. I base my ideas on a document called Helsinki Process. Globalisation contains forces for both good and ill. The world today faces both opportunity and threat-opportunity to come together to pursue a common goal or break into opposing groups based on differences in race, faith, interests or income. These create tensions, the worst of which is the sense of increasing inequality in an already unequal world. A minority is growing in astronomical richness while billions of human beings live in abject poverty and their number is increasing. Humanity has to meet this major ethical challenge. Inequality goes with lack of democracy, loss of dignity and freedom of the individual, societies and nations. It may result in economic and cultural colonialism with the few powerful dominating the weak and this filters down at all levels—international, national and local.

Gloculisation

(Recently, I came across a term Gloculisation—a hybrid, fusion between Global and Local—so Think Globally, act locally—is expressed by Gloculisation). There is need to reflect on transformational actions, reversing some of the current trends and forces. The change agents will essentially have two components,viz., (i) value based ethical principles binding actors to common purposes and (ii) instrumental, which involves individual, institutional and corporate efforts. Responsibility for human solidarity rests with each of us as a citizen, of our community, state or globe—local, national and public institutions.

Three major engines of change in society which have to work together to move the society forward are (i) the state, (ii) the private sector and (iii) the civil society. It is the synergy, the simultaneous, substantial efforts of these three which will give global society a new sense of itself as just, open and fair. The complementary rather than competitive relationship among these three, with all their institutions, will give results in education, health, gender equality, poverty reduction and environment.

Any agenda in this direction will include an important role for *education.* Education implies great responsibility on *teachers.* Whenever teachers are the actors, *teacher education* gets a place of honour and of accountability.

Globalisation has opened the gates for hyperactive international managers of education. Education as a market commodity has brought in very sharp salesmen, with expertise in opening chain malls (campuses) and selling their wares (courses). The Educational Fairs of Australia, Britain, USA and other countries are enticing our youngsters with their campuses, degrees and job prospects. Courses in Management, Engineering and Medicine are the commonly flaunted goods. Fortunately, they have not intruded into teacher education yet. Therefore, there is still time for us to sit up and build strong, safe security walls of quality curriculum, excellent programmes and effective teacher education. How?

Present State of Teacher Education

Some of the disturbing features of the present state stare me in the face. The teacher education has low credibility. There is general dissatisfaction. General ambience in the teacher education community is that of pessimism. Proliferation of substandard B. Ed. institutions and rank commercialisation are disturbing concerns. A gloomy feeling of helplessness is pervasive. Many institutions function only for admission, examination (without the students going through the prescribed courses) and award of degrees. Secondly, in our long-due campaign for removal of illiteracy and 'all children in school', we have taken certain measures which compromise with quality, infrastructure and teacher's qualifications. Teachers with low level of general education, no pre-service teacher education qualifications—popularly called 'para-teachers', with very attractive nomenclatures like *Shiksha-Mitra, Saraswati-putra,* have been employed in very large number for a very large number of primary schools. Even for regular teaching jobs in elementary schools, persons not trained for that level, are being employed. The long existing evil of the B.Ed's, which degree provides preparation for secondary education, being recruited for the elementary schools, with or without some nominal orientation to elementary stage, continues.

Action Plan

Teacher education fraternity is an intelligent and committed group of professionals. Fortunately, a very large number of teacher educators are devoted to their duties and are conscientious workers. In their sincere and dedicated work habits lies hope for the future. Nothing much is lost yet. There are many institutions which are performing their task in a disciplined, regular and efficient manner.

My dreams can possibly be explained by my psychologist friends as expression of my unfulfilled conscious, subconscious and unconscious desires. So be it. But I believe that they are not in the realm of impossibility of realisation. With vision, mission and action, they may prove real one day, may be, hopefully, even in my life-time.

We need to think and reflect on the steps to be taken so that my dreams are realised. We need to open out and expand our mental horizons and carry out our vision and mission enthusiastically.

I wake up to the real world. I suggest that we should think big and act big.

I suggest the following for your consideration.

1. We plan for large sized Comprehensive Colleges of Education.
2. Integration be the focus, our *Mantra*—there be integration of (a) general and professional education (b) of teaching for all levels of schooling-specialisation and integration (c) of content and pedagogy. The dichotomy of the discipline and pedagogy must go. The same teacher educator in a school subject should handle both the content and the methodology.
3. Teacher education at all levels be taken over by higher education.
4. Specialisation in a stage of education be strictly accepted and enforced. Teachers with pre-service courses for a particular level of education only teach that level.
5. Private-Public collaboration—We should adopt private-public partnership model. The private enterprises be accepted with open hearts but with care and assurance that their motives and attitudes be more altruistic,philanthropic and social, rather than profit-making.

   In this context, with some trepidation, I draw your attention to a phenomenon in the international academic culture. There is a trend among academics in universities like Oxford, Cambridge and Harvard, to become entrepreneurs, cashing on their research work. The inhibition that we should not 'stoop down' to make money is disappearing. The feeling is 'we sweat out in our institutions while clever businessmen make money out of our expertise'. Why should some of us not be entrepreneurs, after retirement and in-service, instead of giving the businessmen advice/consultancy on a pittance, or membership of their managing committees. Let us not dismiss the idea that serious academic work and business could not go together or that it involved too many ethical compromises. As long as we do maintain our passion for normal teaching and research work, we do not 'sell our soul', we may market and cash our ideas, innovations and expertise in building good schools, good teacher education institutions.

6. Teacher education be considered an individualised course; teach the individual rather than the class average.
7. **Very Important:** Take measure to strengthen the preparation of a Teacher-educator. Restructure M.Ed. course.

Allow me to elaborate two of these points—(i) The restructuring of the initial under graduate teacher education courses and (ii) the education of Teacher Educators.

I. Presently the following two ideas have emerged with universal consensus among academics and practitioners in teacher education all over the country

(a) Teacher education be **'brought into the mainstream of the academic life of the universities',** that is, teacher education programmes at all levels—pre-primary, elementary, secondary and postgraduate be part of the higher education system.

At present, only preparation of teachers for secondary education is within the purview of universities. Teacher education for elementary education is looked after by state education departments through bodies like State Council of Educational Research and Training. Pre-school teacher education is generally in private hands.

(b) Introduction of 4-year integrated courses of general and professional education in universities/colleges of teacher education to be pursued concurrently after the completion of 10+2 level of school education.

1. A 4-year Bachelor of Secondary Education—B. Sec. Ed. or B.A./B.Sc./B. Com. B.Ed.
2. 4-year Bachelor of Elementary Education—B.El.Ed. or B.A./B.Sc./B.Com., B.Ed. (Elementary).
3. 4-year Bachelor of Pre-Primary Education—B.Pr.Ed. or B.A./B.Sc./B.Com., B.Ed. (Pre-School/Pre-primary).

(c) The present main flagship of teacher education—B.Ed.—play a low role and be gradually phased out. It may continue to be offered only to postgraduate degree holders (in some school subject). It also may be diversified as B.Ed. (Secondary), B.Ed. (Elementary) and B.Ed. (Pre-primary). This suggestion and other alternatives may be considered at a later stage, after the 4-year integrated courses gets stabilized. In course of time, may be, one-year course is abolished.

II. An essential implicaton of the above is to establish large-sized teacher education institutions, catering to 600-1000 students (with an intake of, for example, only 50 for each year, there will be 200 students in each level) for a 4-year course.

This policy will be in line with other professional courses like Law, Engineering, Medicine etc.

The proposals for integrated programme of teacher education of 4/5 years catering to all stages of teacher education made off and on in the past and implemented and given up in some institutions and now presented to the nation by The National School Curriculum Framework, 2005 and its Focus Group on Teacher Educatiion need to be seriously pursued. The large-sized colleges will be on the lines of Comprehensive Colleges of Teacher Education as conceptualized in the Secondary Education Commission (Mudaliar Commission) long back in 1952 and have been paid lip-sympathy again and again.

Education of Teacher Educators

Teacher Educator has a crucial role in quality assurance in teacher education. A cursory job-analysis of a teacher educator reveals that he is required to teach theory, to supervise student teaching, to facilitate exposure and adjustment to school situations, to provide individual guidance, to counsel in personal and professional problems. He is the philosopher, friend and guide to the prospective teacher. As a teacher, he tends to become a model—ideal, good or bad, to be copied. His conduct and style, his interest in the school subjects, his ways of relating to student-teachers mould their outlook and behaviour as teachers. His visible approach to his duties, spirit of sincerity, sense of seriousness, relations with colleagues and school teachers are seen and effortlessly learnt by student-teachers. He, thus, is expected to help them understand education in all its parameters, to attain skills of classroom teaching and to build up professional attitudes. He also should stimulate curiosity and assist in generating knowledge.

Besides, he should extend his services to the school system. He also conducts and guides research. Considered an educationist and an expert on educational matters, he is often consulted and he participates in policy-decisions and administration.

Equipment of Teacher Educator

To ensure good performance in these various job-oriented activities, a teacher educator should be adequately equipped in the beginning of his career and remain so throughout his working life. He should be saved from obsolescence, routinisation and burn-out.

Is the teacher educator adequately equipped when he begins his career to perform well? How has he been prepared for his responsibilities? How does he continue to maintain and improve upon what he began with? How does he avoid becoming a worn-out machine?

It is my perception that neither by pre-service education nor by experience, our teacher educators are well equipped for effective teacher education.

With respect to his academic preparation he has a long period of general education followed by or integrated with professional courses. Generally, at all the levels of teacher education, teacher educators possess a Master's Degree in a school subject and have also obtained a research degree—M.Phil or Ph.D.

We should design a pre-service course which prepares teacher educators for *specialization* in any one or two aspects and areas of teacher education. It would need offering a comprehensive course in each area—whether it be (i) theory/ foundation areas like philosophy/psychology/history/sociology or (ii) in levels of education like secondary, elementary, pre-primary, or (iii)in pedagogy of school subjects like methods of teaching History or Physics or (iv) in areas like evaluation, guidance, administration or modes of Teacher Education—Face-to-face, Distance Education and so on. If the idea of a specialization-based M.Ed. be accepted in principle, details can be worked out.

The M.Ed. should also include teacher education related practical work including practice-teaching to student-teachers in teacher education institutions.

In-Service

With the passage of time, the teacher educator becomes routinised, status quoist and conservative. He goes on repeating and replicating year after year—even the same anecdotes, same quotes, and same jokes. Most cease to reflect, read, write or research.

Much more can be done to improve the teacher educator's competence, knowledge and expertise by in-service programmes conducted through multifarious strategies, including distance education.

Distance Education

Distance Educaton may be used to provide in each specialization area the following instructional materials in different forms, periodically and regularly:

(a) *Innovations*: Innovative practices and success stories at home and abroad may be brought to teacher educators' notice. Discussions may be held as to how they can be introduced in practice by them.
(b) Information about articles, journals, books, monographs in their relevant areas.
(c) Skill in Communication Strategies.
(d) Learning Relationships.
(e) Skills of Guidance and Counselling.
(f) Dissemination of Research findings relevant to teacher education with suggestions about how they can be adopted into the system.

Research

Search for knowledge about *'teaching how to teach'* and teaching (the two are *per se* different) will perennially provide themes for research in an institution which is involved in teacher education programmes. Besides, the teacher educator will do well to get into action-based research to continue research endeavour with real world involvement and action. The outcome would be generation of knowledge which would improve the standard of teacher education, the quality of life of the individuals and the society, of which education is a sub-system.

Self/Peer Learning

Like all professionals, some teacher educators grow with experience. Some develop specialization by self-steady or experience of teaching, publication or research in the area of their interest. Most academics, with the passage of time, become specialists in some aspect of their discipline. Unfortunately, in teacher-education, we do not develop such specialized interests. As research guides, we are ready to supervise a doctoral student in any area!

Academics go on learning by interaction with peers. In Education though prolific seminars/workshops are organized but unfortunately those in which issues are analysed in depth are rare. The Academic Staff Colleges in our Universities have made only small dent, by way of orientation or refresher courses.

Institutional Culture

Teacher education succeeds in a healthy humane ambience. An effective teacher education is an individualized and a personalized programme. Each student teacher has different educational and socio-economic background, understandings andpotentialities. Therefore, a teacher educator has to have the values of respect for an individual, patience, compassion, tolerance and readiness to work hard for individuals. How he relates with his students makes all the difference in creating a healthy teaching-learning culture. A teacher educator should be easily approachable and be available as and when a student needs or wants and vice versa. This necessitates full day physical presence of both the teachers and the students in the institution. This necessitates habits of regularity, dissatisfaction with mediocrity, non-acceptance of slip-shod assignments and urge for depth, seriousness and integrity.

In Distance Education also, regular contact with the target learner is essential. As the Distance Education learner is studying in his own time, over and above his usual daily personal and professional life, he has to goad himself and find energy and motivation to sit down to his learning. He, therefore, needs to have the facility of easy interaction with the Distance Education counselors, teachers, material writers, evaluators, supervisors and student services administrators. These facilities and contacts should be available to the learner as and when he needs them.

Self-Realisation

The overall pervading impact of long hours of sustained work in itself builds capacity in the teacher educator and the teacher. Further, self-actualization and self-realisation lead to conscientious performance of duties. Spiritual angle to his evolution is an added and highly important ingredient. The outcome is awareness and devotion to his work, sensitivity and warmth of interpersonal feelings, humaneness and congenial relationship with all he comes in contact with—his discipline, students, colleagues, peers, community, society, humanity. All these qualities of hand, mind, heart and spirit make him a worthy teacher educator.

Role of the Universities

In the restructuring of the pre-service teacher and teacher educator preparation courses, the universities have to play a leadership role. The Faculties and Departments of Education in the universities will have to initiate the relevant action. The suggestions may be discussed intensively and extensively in principle and later in detail within each institution among all concerned. I may add that we in the universities need not wait for the NCTE to take some steps. After all, the universities have had their rules, regulations, norms, standards for teacher education courses extensively for several decades. NCTE has been in existence only for a decade.

In the meantime, to my dreams will be added—meetings and deliberations on the integrated courses for all levels and for teacher educators being held seriously in the universities. I will dream strong brain-storming sessions—in the beginning with strong opinions for and against any change, but ending with consensus-building, harmonious understanding and willingly accepted enthusiastic plans for smooth transition to the revolutionary transformation of teacher education in the country, on the lines, pleaded by me. Then, will start the task of working the details of courses, curricula, syllabi, semester and year wise division, evaluation etc.—the nitty-gritty of any educational programme. We need to be bold, take initiative and be innovative and creative.

Development of Institutions of Education on the pattern discussed above—Phases and Approaches

Used and conditioned for long as we are to the present system of teacher preparation programmes, it would take some time for us to accept the policy of the suggested 4-year integrated general-cum-professional programmes for all levels in a single institution.

I concede that establishement of such institutions will require intensive planning for resources, infrastructure, equipments, staff and other components.

To achieve the target, I visualize the following approaches:

1. NCERT's Regional Institutes of Education, some DIET's and some of the long established reputed institutions and University Departments may be transformed into such institutions.
2. Proposals for any new private or government institutions of Education be of this pattern.
3. The existing Degree Colleges may introduce teacher education courses integrated with their Arts/Science/ Commerce undergraduate courses. [The 4-year Bachelor of Elementary Education (B.El.Ed.) courses conducted in several Delhi University Colleges for the last 6/7 years present a Model]. Many degree Colleges in the country have Departments of Education also offering B.Ed./M.Ed./research courses. They need to be integrated with General Education courses and include elementary and pre-school teacher preparation also.
4. While these suggestions may take some time to materialize, the following approaches may be considered by the one-year B.Ed. institutions to start their journey on the road to ultimate full-fledged 4-year courses.

(a) The present B.Ed. for graduates is a B.Ed. (Secondary). On the same pattern, introduce one-year specialised B.Ed. (Elementary) and B.Ed. (Pre-primary/Nursery).

(b) Alternatively or simultaneously, introduce:
   (i) Diploma in Education (D.Ed.)—a 2-year Elementary Teacher Education course for the Class XII/Intermediate/Senior Secondary passed.
   (ii) Certificate in Education (C.Ed.)—a 2-year Pre-primary Teacher Education course for the High School (Class X) passed.

With these two, the existing B.Ed. Colleges may be equipped to offer three teacher preparation courses leading to B.Ed., D.Ed. and C.Ed.

Their introduction should not face much difficulty. The intake numbers may be decided according to local conditions and resources. Both of them are NCTE approved courses with prescribed Norms and Standards. It may be taken as an experimental initiative a 'try-out', 'seeing-our-way' to the lower levels of teacher education. With this experience, B.Ed. institutions may grow into a full-fledged Institutions of Educational Studies.

2

Teacher Education and Development

MOHAN B. MENON

Education is a component of development and also is means to achieving development. It creates choices and opportunities for people, reduces the burdens of poverty and diseases, as well as empowers them to have ones own choices of livelihood and gives a stronger voice and status in society. For nations it creates a dynamic workforce and well-informed citizens able to compete and co-operate globally—opening doors to economic and social prosperity.

The 1990 Conference on Education for All pledged to achieve universal primary education by 2000. But in 2001, over 100 million school-aged children were still not in school, 57 per cent of them girls and 96 per cent were in developing countries—mostly in South Asia and Sub-Saharan Africa. The Dakar EFA goals and the Millennium Development Goals (MDGs) set a more realistic, but still difficult, deadline of 2015 when all children everywhere should be able to complete a full course of primary schooling. While MDGs 2 and 3 state the goals of UPE and Gender equity in Education, human resource development through education and training is the major focus of all other MDGs. That's how education and training of teachers and all other facilitators involved in education and training within all sectors of development including poverty reduction and livelihood, health, environment, and governance attains such significance in the achievement of Millennium Development Goals. Can we confidently say today that our teacher/facilitator education system—pre-service, in-service and on-going professional development have the potential to do that.

Indian Education and the Commonwealth

The education sector in India witnessed a state of flux in recent decades, thanks to more than required poliitical interference in education. As a body of teacher educators this has been disturbing us. I had the good fortune to be out of this context geographically but couldn't be out of it mentally and professionally reinforced by the requirement to work closely with several organizations in India, representing a multi-lateral organization viz., Commonwealth of Learning (COL). I enjoyed the last 4 and half years of work with COL, a small but vibrant organization and I had the good fortune to be responsible for all its school and teacher development related initiatives in 53 countries in the Commonwealth, of which 48 are developing countries. While working with other countries of the Commonwealth, especially in Sub-Saharan Africa and South Asia I had the chance to examine Indian achievements and failures in its education system with much more objectivity. Many countries in the developing world feel that India with its own unique problems and challenges in its education system has evolved solutions and models which work after all. Mark Tuli in his book 'India in slow motion' compares India to an elephant which moves very slow, but moves never the less. But today the elephant has accelerated its speed and is slowly becoming a model to replicate/adapt for many developing countries. Indian experiences in the education sector,whether it is the IITs or IIMs, the Open School or the Open University are considered success models elsewhere in spite of its problems and issues. I was pleasantly surprised to hear four participants out of about 30, in a half-day Seminar organized in the House of Lords in London by the Department for Educaton and Skills (DES) on Higher Education in Africa, where I was representing COL, referring to Indian success models in education better suited for African countries than their own 'Rolls Royce' models. It is true that many countries of the Commonwealth Africa look forward to India for support in dealing with their critical problems of access to education and quality and ongoing professional development of teachers. Recent signing of MOU between India and NEPAD to make available the EDUSAT transponders for African education is well received. But do we have models of effective teacher development to offer to other developing countries? This might be debatable.

Teacher Education using Open and Distance Learning

In the last two decades teacher education/training through ODL has evolved along four dimensions.

1. Expanding the purpose and target audience of distance teacher training programmes;
2. Improving the design and effectiveness of instructional systems, materials and learner support;
3. Using steadily more sophisticated ICTs; and
4. Extending the variety of courses and the diversity of participating teacher.

Expansion of Purpose and Audience

In the 1980s the key government concerns in the developing countries of the Commonwealth were to ensure that practicing teachers could obtain further training (preferably a diploma or degree) and to respond to a growing demand for initial training from potential teachers. Sadly, however, many of the diplomas and degrees conferred through correspondence programmes in dual mode universities (e.g. Nigeria) were of dubious quality. Both countries later reformed these programmes.

Case studies by UNESCO showed that the purposes of distance teacher training diversified during the 1990s. To the initial training for qualification (e.g. National Teachers' Institute, Nigeria) were added the continuing education of teachers (e.g. IGNOU, India; UNISA, South Africa) and special training for curricular and pedagogical change (e.g. OLSET, South Africa). This diversification has continued in recent years, with even more emphasis on continuing education and professional support. Contemporary Commonwealth examples are the Learning Schools Programme and DEEP (Digital Education Enhancement Project) offered by the UKOU; the Green Teacher programme of the Centre for Environmental Education, India; Training of Special Education Teachers by Netaji Subhas Open University, India and the International MA in Teacher Education by OUSL, Sri Lanka. Other programmes under development are the TESSA Consortium led by the UKOU in Africa, the PG Diploma in Guidance and Counselling by NCERT, India and the Teacher Education Programme of the African Virtual University.

Improvement of Design and Effectiveness

Early teacher training programmes offered at a distance were similar to other correspondence programmes. Courses lacked appropriate instructional design, materials were written as 'lessons' with little attention to the needs of self instruction, and learner support was limited to short contact classes and written assignments without proper feedback. There was little possibility for human interaction and almost no use of school-based experience. Things began to improve in the 1980s and 1990s as open universities and other DE institutions developed capacity for instructional design, the development of self-instructional materials and managing effective learner support systems.

Courses developed in recent years show new learning designs and innovative forms trainee support with a focus on school-based activities and the encouragement of the collaborative reflective practice that favours the development of teaching competencies. Commonwealth examples of such developments include the situated learning design and learner support adopted in the International MA in Teacher Education by OUSL, Sri Lanka; the Primary Teacher training programme of the University of Forte Hare, South Africa; and B.Ed. programme of IGNOU, India and the proposed TESSA consortium in Sub-Saharan Africa. Particular effort is being made to assure quality in teacher training by distance education, for example the Quality Indicators being developed by the National Accreditation and Assessment Council (NAAC), India and COL.

Application of Information and Communication Technologies

The third evolutionary trend in teacher training at a distance is the use of Information and Communication Technologies (ICTs). The 1980s saw extensive use of audio and video programmes and television to support or supplement the print-based learning design (UKOU, IGNOU, etc.). Telephone tutoring was also popular in countries with the necessary infrastructure and was followed by audio-conferencing and broadcasting with audio talk-back arrangements. The 1990s saw satellites being used for programme delivery in the South Pacific and the Caribbean and the introduction of one-way video and two-way audio conferencing by IGNOU for its teacher training programmes at all levels. In the same period in South Africa OLSET began using Radio for improving classroom interaction for English teachers and interactive radio (radio broadcast with-talk back) was deployed for in-service teacher training in some Indian states.

In the present decade reading materials prepared in self-learning style are being made into CD and presented offline and online for better distribution. An example is the STAMP 2000+ materials developed with COL's help by eight southern African countries. As World Space radio (Satellite Radio) becomes popular in Africa and Asia, it is being used for distributing material digitally, for example by the Kenya Institute of Education in providing ongoing professional support to in-service teachers.

Computer use, both offline and online, is growing fast even in developing countries thanks to the increasing availability of hardware and courseware. The DEEP project of the UK Open University in South Africa has been a success story in which model classroom tasks integrate ICT with a range of other approaches. This approach is used in the new Teacher Education in Sub-Saharan Africa (TESSA, 2005) consortium now being implemented in South Africa, Tanzania and Nigeria. Institutions are also starting to use Learning Management Systems (LMS) to offer courses though the Internet. Cost-effective versions of LMS suitable for varied student numbers are available in countries like India.

The African Virtual University is in the process of developing a teacher training programme which will be offered online and offline in collaboration with universities in ten countries in East Africa and Southern Africa. Linkage between governments and the corporate sector is appreciated for making hardware more readily available and accessible to teachers. The challenge now is to develop content with a learning design that is conducive to effective teacher development. COL is facilitating the development of learning object repositories for such content and supporting the creation of electronic platforms for e-content development and delivery in teacher education through a consortium of content providers, instructional designers and software programmers (e.g. I-CONSENT and Learning Initiatives in India).

Extending the variety of courses and the diversity of participating teachers

The number of courses offered by ODL and number of teachers enrolled in them now show a strong upward trend in the Commonwealth countries after a hiatus in the 1990s. In the mid-1990s India's National Council for Teacher Education banned mass enrolment in low quality initial teacher training programmes though correspondence education offered by some dual mode universities and Nigeria imposed a ban on teacher education colleges offering correspondence courses.

This caused an immediate drop in enrolment but subsequent improvements in the quality of materials and learner support led to an upturn in enrolments that continues.

Nigeria's National Teachers Institute now has over 100,000 in-service teachers on its rolls and many institutions in several African countries also have large enrolments in ODL courses (e.g. in Kenya, Lesotho and Uganda). The Open University provided training in the use of computers in teaching to over 150,000 teachers in UK schools of UK over a two-year period through the Learning Schools Project. In India, under the Distance Education Programme of *Sarava Siksha Abhiyan* over one million teachers use self-learning print and audio-video materials and get the benefit of teleconferencing on an ongoing basis. By and large, there is an upward trend in the number of institutions, courses and enrolments in teacher training courses and in in-service training and ongoing professional support to teachers and other personnel in the school system.

Commonwealth of Learning

Commonwealth of Learning set up in 1988 is an intergovernmental organization created by Commonwealth Heads of Government to encourage the development and sharing of open learning/distance education knowledge, resources and technologies. COL is helping developing nations in improving access to quality education and training. Headquartered in Vancouver, Canada, COL is the world's only intergovernmental organisation dedicated solely to promoting and delivering distance education and open learning, and is the only official Comonwealth agency located outside Britain. COL's Mission statement reads *Recognising knowledge as key to cultural, social and economic development, the Commonwealth of Learning is committed to assisting Commonwealth member Governments to take full advantage of* ***open, distance and technology-mediated learning strategies*** *to provide increased and equitable access to* ***education and training*** *for all their citizens.*

Curriculum and Curriculum Transaction

Curricular needs and demands of school education have become extremely varied and complex caused by various trends in the larger societal system, including knowledge explosion, globalization and liberalization, developments in information and communication technology and concerns such as sustainable development and impact of HIV/AIDS pandemic. Similarly, in the educational system too there have been changes such as the shift in the teaching-learning process from teacher centred to learner centred approaches in curriculum organization and transaction. Humanistic and Constructivist learning models find more professional acceptance today and their implication on curricular organization and transaction for both school education and teacher education is very significant. The emerging fast developments in the socio-economic and technology sectors and in the understanding of human learning have put forward immense pressures on the educational system. Curriculum is no more being looked at as a body of knowledge to be communicated to a specific group of students or a fixed set of learning objectives to be achieved through a pre-decided sequence of learning experiences. Report of Teacher Education Curriculum, National Focus Group on Teacher Education for Curriculum Renewal (2005) does endorse this perspective. The shift is from rigid and fixed curricular content and experiences to flexible, learner-negotiated objectives and content, and learner-controlled and individually paced and sequenced learning experiences to be assessed by criterion-referenced rather than norm-referenced testing procedures. One can go on with the discussion on these developments that have been happening in the last couple of decades. While, there could be general agreement on this perspective of curriculum and instruction, these ideas have not percolated enough to practices of curriculum development and transaction in the school system, in most countries. Models of workable practices and classroom processes based on constructivist and humanistic theories are available (such innovations are available in India) which may work in small groups and when the teachers are well oriented to it. However, these models become increasingly difficult with the classes becoming larger and more heterogeneous.

Innovative ways of curriculum development and transaction would obviously have their implication on the nature of competencies required by the teachers and the content and organization of the teacher development curriculum. With more and more teachers to be trained on a recurrent basis and ongoing professional support to be provided to them, most countries find it imperative to use Open and Distance Learning (ODL) including Information and Communication Technologies (ICTs) for in-service teacher development. How could one combine the constructivist models of curriculum organization and transaction with the methodology and technologies adopted in in-service teacher development is a major challenge. I would examine here a few issues and relate some experiences in adopting the philosophy and practices of a constructivist paradigm applied to the development and delivery of teacher development programmes by open and distance learning.

Transactional Processes for Professional Development

The occupation of teaching is slowly emerging as a profession influenced positively by several factors. What is important for an area of occupation is not attaining the status of a profession but moving towards manifesting higher and higher levels of professionalism. Professions may be at different stages of their development and therefore they may have attained the characterizations of a profession to different degrees. These include the increasingly better understanding of the complex processes involved in teaching and theoretical explanations behind them; application of innovative techniques and technologies; developments in the formulation and organization of programmes of professional development, and the gradual' emergence of a body of personnel carrying out teaching.

The training environment should be such that the transactional processes involved in the training situations should facilitate teachers to develop better insights into the classroom practices. The training experiences gained in the pre-service and in-service professional development programmes should be able to prepare teachers for dealing with the complex realities of the classroom and the school, and their interface with the community.

The reality of classroom teaching would most times involve a single teacher placed in a classroom full of students. This occurs in many schools in the developing countries creating multi-level or multi-grade situations. The teacher's job has been to move students through the curriculum and, to the highest extent possible, practice struggling to deal with challenges developed in that environment. These struggles force teachers to assimilate and accommodate as they seek more effective classroom strategies. When teachers are successful in their classroom settings, they gain new experiential insights that build their professional knowledge base. When incidents are unresolved, they persist in the mind of the educator. During such experiences, teachers question their pedagogic abilities and efficacy. If honest, all teachers would admit that they have had such episodes. These unsettling attempts might involve an unruly student, an intimidating parent, or systemic challenges.

Theory-based Teacher Education Curriculum

Teacher development is seen here as the entire process of developing and maintaining professional competence in teachers including pre-service training, induction training, in-service training and on-going professional development of teachers. There have been criticisms of teacher development courses and programmes being very theoretical and irrelevant to the real situations in the classroom. Competencies required for the transacting curriculum in complex situations are often not developed in the teachers putting lot of pressure on them when they enter schools. They do learn a lot on the job but remain ill equipped to a large extent. It has often been argued that what a teacher requires is to deal with classroom and situations and take decisions and manifest competencies in dealing successfully with those situations. However, the teacher education curriculum has remained theoretical with an assumption that if they are taught theory and show its applications in selected situations they would be able to extend that to other situations even if the context changes. Such a theory-based approach to training has been the norm in most face-to-face teacher education courses.

Most teacher education curricula tend to take a theory-oriented approach with the assumption that an understanding of foundational and pedagogical theory and their applications in a few school or class situations will equip the teachers to deal with the complexities of the real situation. They may initially formulate the curriculum objectives based on the roles of teachers and the competencies required but when it comes

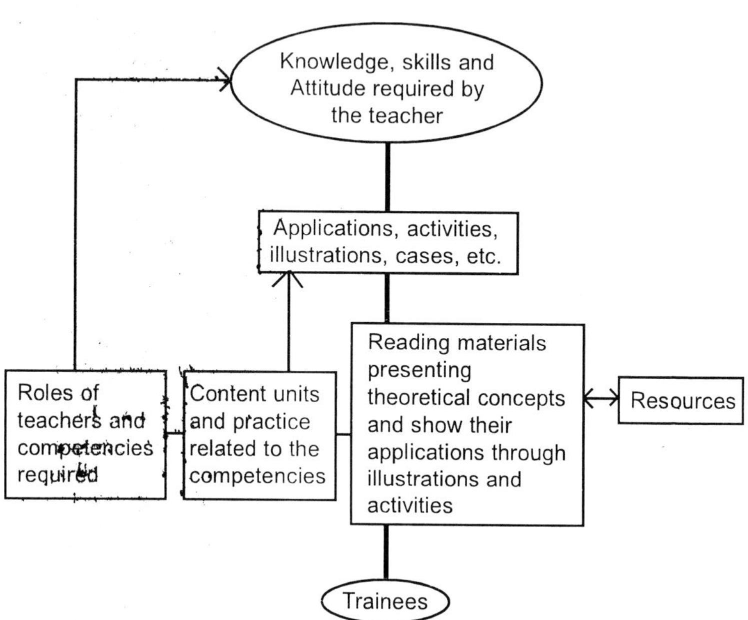

Fig. 2.1: Theory-based Approach to Curriculum Design

to curriculum outlines and transaction, tend to take a theoretical approach. Unfortunately the same approach is largely followed in teacher education courses by distance mode too. Almost all teacher education courses by ODL in India follow more or less the same approach. Although there have been lot of debate in India about quality of "distance teacher education", almost always the debate has been on the adequacy of human interaction and need for self-instructional materials, rather than the nature of curriculum organization or the design of materials or the processes involved in the face-to-face contact sessions. Hence, even the so called "good" courses of teacher education by ODL in India and many other countries remained highly theoretical being derived from a discipline based curriculum development process.

Emerging Transactional Processes

Is it possible to adopt a field and situation based curricular organization and transaction instead of a theory-based approach? Can the training interventions take into account and utilize such episodes and experiences for discussions and reflections? Can case studies and simulations be developed basing on these experiences? According to the theory of *Constructivism,* individuals build their own theory of the nature of the world, from their own perceptions and experiences. It is grounded in the idea that "people learn by actively constructing new knowledge, rather than having information poured into their heads". Many argue (Bates, 1999; Jonassen, 2000) that learning within the constructivist environment promotes meaningful learner engagement and critical, creative and complex thinking by learners. Let us examine a couple of training and educational practices adopting a constructivist environment.

Cady (1998) highlights the effectiveness of Reflective Practice Groups in induction training of teachers. The groups followed a ten-step, reflective process that connected theory to critical incidents of practice. Shared reflective practice was found to be an important element in creating a supportive professional environment for all participants—new teachers, experienced teachers, administrators, and college faculty. The Reflective Practice Group process involved ten steps could be completed in one and a half to two hours.

While discussing the pedagogical architecture named Collaborative Reflective Practice for the Graduate Certificate Programme in Open and Distance Learning in the University of Southern Queensland, Naidu refers to the Kolb Learning Cycle (1984) which involves four processes necessary for learning to occur. These are:

- ***concrete experiences*** (e.g. laboratories, field work, observations, films);
- ***reflective observation*** (e.g. learning, logs, journals, diaries, brainstorming);
- ***abstract conceptualization*** (e.g. lectures, papers, analogies); and
- ***active experimentation*** (e.g. simulations, case studies, home work);

Basing on the processes suggested in Kolb Learning Cycle, the 'Collaborative Reflective ' Practice' constituted four critical elements, viz. *experiencing, reflecting, conceptualizing,* and *applying.*

Experiencing refers to participation in purposeful learning activity that may be presented as part of a course or prior learning experience. *Reflecting* is conscious and deliberate mulling over one's personal experiences with or without self-evaluation. *Conceptualizing* comprises studying, interacting with peers and also critically reflecting on the subject matter. *Applying* involves reformulating the theoretical concepts and using them in specified meaningful situations for further reflection.

Constructivists Approach to Curriculum Design

Based on the processes involved in the collaborative reflective practice it is possible to conceptualize a teacher development curriculum for an ODL based programme or course. The reading materials, media based materials, resource materials, interactive sessions including face-to-face contact classes and technology based interaction, assignments and projects could play appropriate roles in facilitating the trainee going through the processes under experiencing, reflecting, applying and conceptualizing. The core reading and other media materials would consist of cases, stories, critical incidents, scenarios, simulations and problems derived from the classroom, school and community situations based on the roles the teacher has to play and the competencies he/she has to develop to function in these situations.

The cases, problems etc. will be designed and developed in such a way that the trainee while going through them will at appropriate points have to take a decision, perform an activity, experience in real situations and/or an audio- video episode, recall prior experiences, read a relevant theoretical writing or factual information and/or reflect on the issue either individually or collaboratively in face-to-face or technology mediated human interaction. Such a transactional process is

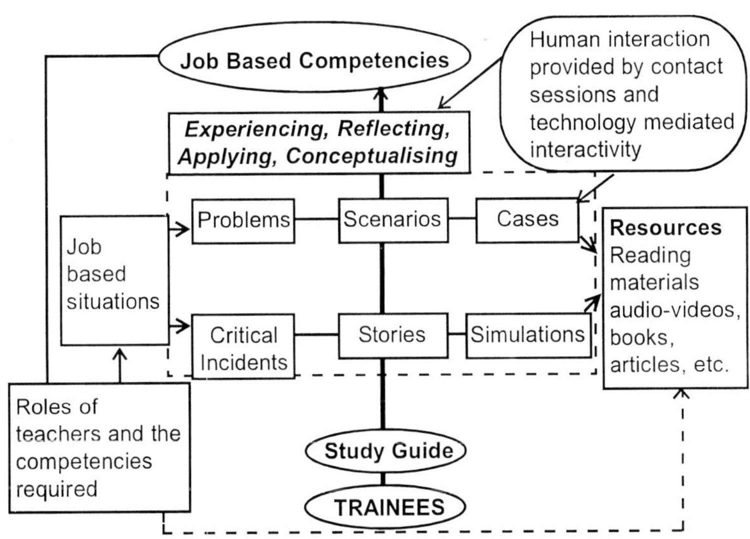

Fig. 2.2: Constructivist Approach to Curriculum Design

expected to develop in the trainees those competencies required for performing the pre-specified roles effectively (Fig. 2.2).

COL Initiatives in TE by ODL involving Constructivist Approach

Commonwealth of Learning (COL) has been partnering with organizations across the Commonwealth countries in order to build adequate capacity in developing and launching ODL based teacher development initiatives mainly to provide better opportunities in this sector. COL gives equal importance to make sure that the courses and programmes offered are of quality. It has been working in cooperation with organizations such a National Accreditation and Assessment Council (NAAC) in India and the National Commission for Colleges of Education in Nigeria in formulating norms and standards of quality in teacher education courses offered by ODL. There are two course development initiatives taken up by COL, one with the Open University of Sri Lanka and the other with the Centre for Environment Education, Ahmedabad, India wherein constructivist curriculum design and transaction is being experimented. *MATE programme* of *OUSL* is a project aimed at developing a MA teacher education programme based on constructivist approach. A mixed approach is being attempted in the curriculum of the *Diploma in Environment Education Course* being developed with CEE.

Conclusion

It is evident that the area of teacher education is surely undergoing fast change both in its content and transactional processes. Education and thereby teacher education probably is gaining a much important role considering the significant responsibility vested on all types of teachers and facilitators involved or expected to be involved in awareness building, education and training of the large number personnel involved in sustainable development. The boundaries between different modes are slowly vanishing and the importance of creating the basic transactional processes in teacher development irrespective of modes is becoming more and more evident. Let us hope that the coming years will see much closer networking among institutions involved in teacher development using variety of modes.

REFERENCES

Barrows, H. S., and Tamblyn, R. (1980). *Problem-based learning: An approach to medical education.* New York, Springer.

Bates, A. (1999), 'Restructuring.the University for Technological Change', in *Whar Kind of University? International Perspectives on Knowledge, Participation and Governance,* eds J. Brennan, J. Fedrowitch Huber and T. Shah, SRHE and OUP, London.

Cady, Joan M. (1998) Reflective Practice Groups in Teacher Induction: Building Professional Community Via Experiential Knowledge, *Education,* Spring.

Jonassen, D. (2000) *Computers as Mindtools for Schools, Engaging in Critiacal Thinking,* Prentice-Hall, New Jersy.

Kolbe, D.A. (1984) *Experential Learning: Experience as the Source of Learning and Development,* Prentice-Hall, New Jersy.

Menon M.B. and Dash, N.K. (2000) 'Professional Development in Higher Education at a Distance', in *Training of Professionals through. Distance Education in South Asia,* eds N.K.Dash and S.B.Menon, IGNOU, New Delhi.

Menon, M.B. and Phalachandra, B. (2001) Transactional processes for professional development and use of ICT, *Staff & Educational Development International,* 5(1), 9-25.

Naidu, S., Oliver, M., & Koronios (1999). Approaching clinical decision-making in nursing practice with interactive multimedia and case-based reasoning. *The Interactive Multimedia Electronic Journal of Computer Enhanced Learning* [On-Line].

Tuli, Mark (2000) India in Slow Motion, New Delhi.

Schank, R., Fano, A,, Jona, M., & Bell, B. (1994). The design of goal-based scenarios. *The Journal of the Learning Sciences,* 3(4), 305-345.

The Cognition and Technology Group at Vanderbilt (1991). Technology and the design of generative learning environments. Educational Technology, May, pp. 34-40

3

Teacher's Role in Co-curricular Activities

K.C. Sahoo, S. Kumar, U.C. Vashishtha and M.S. Sodha

Making primary schools daringly different is to bring the co-curricular and the curricular activities together, bridge the artificial divide between the two and emphasize with conviction that the **co-curricular activities are very curricular.** We strongly believe that such an intervention will significantly contribute towards the **universalisation of primary education** by ***increasing enrolment, regularizing attendance, enhancing retention, reducing drop outs and promoting achievement*** of students in the primary schools.

It is an important exercise for giving primary education a new approach, unlike the earlier experience. It is much more ambitious than the literacy efforts. It is making schooling a ***"social experience rather than formal instruction"***. It is about converting the school to the ***cultural hub of the community,*** full of activities, full of play, full of joy, full of freedom, full of sharing, full of enjoyment; all these are to be meaningfully managed as a vehicle of pleasant learning experiences. It is an attempt towards making students' experience encouraging in facing challenges of life that are present in myriad forms, within the school itself. It amounts to ***foundation of a social revolution!***

The Vision

The vision of the school is to make it a ***community cultural hub*** humming with hundreds of activities around the year. It starts with the immediate face-lifting of the school by a little rearrangement and restructuring of existing infrastructure for optimal use. It requires white washing the school building, putting a mirror and a clock on the wall, hanging a map, arranging a meeting, celebrating a festival over a community feast, organizing games and sports, narrating stories to the children, cleaning the campus and planting saplings. It is about immediate building of low cost toilets, if these are needed. It provides an orientation and training for the teachers to go beyond the four walls of the classroom. It is an open invitation to the community to participate in the activities of the school and develop an intimate relationship, rather than just sending the children to complete the curriculum. It is the opening of the flood gates to seamless possibilities in education. It is a new understanding, an ***adventure in consciousness*** and an ***added commitment*** for all concerned with education and welfare of the child.

It is an earnest attempt for elevating the primary schools to a coveted position by ***overhauling the content, process and pedagogy of learning.*** It is the labour of love for making the primary school an attractive, sought after and valued place, not only for the child, but also for the teachers, the parents and the community. It is like building a second home, which is cozy, caring and concerned about the all-round growth and development of the child.

Co-curricular and Curricular Integration

Integration of the co-curricular activities in the curricrlum is an effective, meaningful and relevant means for a quantum jump in quality. The co-curricular components of a wholesome and complete education, which take into account 80 per cent of the student's time, spent outside the classroom is every bit as important to learning as the formal curricular component. Yet, most institutions of learning focus a disproportionate amount of effort on the small piece of a much larger whole.

Normally, in out-of-classroom experiences, students tend to take greater responsibility for their own learning: they learn from one another as well as their instructors. In addition, the co-curricular activities help in promoting personal growth, physical and mental health, academic achievement, socio-cultural awareness and formulation of short and long range goals by students themselves.

Successful co-curricular programmes promote experiential learning, development of friendship, a sense of belonging, enhanced intellectual awareness, better academic performance, appreciation of different perspectives and plurality of causes, optimum utilization of creative talents in meaningful pursuits and above all development of healthy interpersonal and social relationships.

Making Learning an Enriching Fun

Play is the other name of the child. Until and unless learning is fun, it is hard for a child to be attracted to it: however great is its promise for the future. The Yashpal Committee's concern for ***'learning without burden'*** and ***'reducing the load of school bag'***, virtually necessitates a high priority to the **games and sports** as important and inseparable components of the school programme and to make ***learning a fun.*** Educationists like to avoid the risk of trivializing learning in the name of fun and warn us to constantly remember that learning, and for that matter schooling, demands serious and deliberate planning. Thus, the teachers need to be oriented in the ***play way pedagogy.*** Learning should be as far as possible spontaneous with the invisible guidance of the teacher. This brings the child to the ***centre-stage*** and provides excellent motivation for attending the school and learning.

The NPE-1986 Review Committee's perspective in this regard is:

> *"Although implied in the 'warm, welcoming and encouraging approach' mentioned in NPE, it would be better if the policy would explicitly refer to the elements of joy, fun, exploration and play as integral to learning in the early stages of primary education. This explicit mention is required because the prevailing educational practice in the school system not only excludes these elements, but seems to consciously resist their introduction in the learning process. Similarly, the policy statement should emphasize the role of singing, drawing, clay-modeling, games and particularly all forms of folk art and folklore in enriching the learning process."*

Cultural Context

Unless the school programme is customized and contextualized to its socio-cultural surroundings, it neither attracts the child, nor tends to retain him/her. It is not conducive to making the learning meaningful and relevant. It does not make the parents concerned in the school affairs, particularly in a primarily rural society. The school keeps on demanding without caring for the needs and necessities of the parents and the community. Instead of being an opportunity, the school becomes a burden, initially financial, and ultimately socio-cultural; the final result is a ***culturally alienated and uprooted*** child, in a school without roots in the society.

Since primary education is a fundamental right of the child and is not directly related to employment (at least in the short run), there can be no reason other than cultural considerations , which may induce the society in general and the parents in particular to accept responsibility for the primary education. The school and its entire programme should emerge from, and be designed organically in the cultural context. Or else, the school-community divide will continuously increase.

Besides these, if education does not address and promote culture, who else is going to do it and what for? Sports, dance, drama, song, music, painting, art, architecture, literature, customs and traditions are not merely for entertainment by professionals but earnest attempts towards human excellence by the society at large.

Contextualizing learning and education to one's own culture is extremely important without which there shall always be an identity crisis and a sense of being uprooted. No foreign culture or system, however sound it may appear, can be affordable and sustainable. The Anglicization of Indian culture in general and the colonization of the educational system in particular are potential threats to the mind-set of the people and legacy of India as a proud nation for more than five thousand years of gloriously rich cultural heritage. The very fabric of our nation is systematically and continuously weakened by de-contextualizing education from its culture and tradition which have been its life line over the centuries. In the same spirit the following quote from Mahatma Gandhi reinforces our line of thinking:

> *"Nothing can be further from my thought than that we should become exclusive or erect barriers. But I do respectfully contend that an appreciation of other cultures can fitly follow, never precede, an appreciation and assimilation of our own. It is my opinion that no culture has treasures as rich as ours. We have not known it, we have been made even to deprecate its study and deprecate its value. We have almost ceased to live it. An academic grasp without practice behind it is like an embalmed corpse, perhaps lovely to look at but nothing to inspire or ennoble. My religion forbids me to belittle or disregard other cultures, as it insists under pain of civil suicide upon imbibing and living my own."*

Conflicts of Curriculum and Culture

There is a big gap between an Indian child's life at school and at the home. The statement may be validated by a visit to any one of the nearly one million primary schools in the country. The school's daily activities have no reference to the children's life outside the school. The teacher is, of course, free to make such a reference, and some teachers occasionally do. But the curriculum makes no such demand from the teacher. On the contrary, the curriculum policy permits the teacher to teach all the school subjects without establishing any link between the child's life and the social milieu on the one hand and the knowledge content of the syllabus on the other".

Curriculum and its Transaction

National Policy on Education-1986—A Review states that:

"The prevailing curriculum of elementary education suffers from several lacunae, some of which are:

- *Inflexible and unresponsive to the local needs and environment;*
- *Devoid of component of skill formation;*
- *Lacking in social and cultural in-puts from the community;*
- *Unrelated to the 'world of work' which exercises a strong pull on the life of a large number of children after the age of 10 years;*
- *Transaction mostly in a non-participative mode;*
- *Near-absence of activity based learning; and*
- *Discouraging exploration, inquiry, creativity and initiative on the part of the students."*

Evolving a Culture-specific Pedagogy

The NCTE, in its Curriculum Framework for Quality Teacher Education states that:

> *"Every region and state has its typical cultural identity, and there is a need to utilize the same as a basis for meaningful and relevant pedagogies. Since there is no one universal way in which the children learn, there is a strong need for looking into the cultural context in which a child is placed. A child*

in a tribal society may process information in an altogether different manner as compared to the one from the urban area and high socio-economic stratum. Pedagogy, therefore, should be culture specific. Instead of using one uniform, mechanistic way of student learning, cultural practices, such as story telling, dramatics, puppetry, folk play, community living etc. should become strong basis of pedagogy. Cultural specificity should get embedded in the pedagogical practices which should be evolved for tribal, rural, urban and other ethnic groups and communities."

We will also like to quote from Letter to a Teacher

After delving little deeper into the philosophy and practices of pedagogy "we might discover that it says one thing and one thing only. That each boy is different, each historical moment is different, and so is every moment different for each boy, each country, each environment, and each family. Half a page from the textbook is all that is needed to explain this; the rest we can tear up and throw away."

Life and Education

Education has to be life size. Confining it within the four walls of the school and that to inside the framework of the curriculum and textbooks is like 'adorning the cage but starving and killing the parrot inside'. The idea is alien to Indian ethos for which the 'universalization of elementary education within 10 years from the commencement of the Constitution' has been an illusive goal till date. The mandate of universalization of elementary education makes us aware of the need to broaden the scope of the curriculum to include in it the rich inheritance of different traditions of knowledge, work and crafts. Some of these traditions today face a serious threat from market forces and commodification of knowledge in the context of globalization of economy. The development of self esteem and ethics and the need to cultivate children's creativity must received primacy. In the context of a fast changing and competitive global context, it's imperative that we respect children's native wisdom and imagination. In our attempt to make children educated we must not uproot them from their own cultural heritage.

Critical Concerns

Because of being a fundamental right, the primary education needs to be under strict and continuous scrutiny. Apart from the 'right-responsibility conflict' one should dive deep into the problem and try to trace as to what are the real fundamentals of primary education. The primary education must not be lost in the paraphernalia of secondary details. In the parlance of Tagore's observation of 'adorning the cage but starving the parrot inside', the child must not be lost in the legal and political imbroglio. First things must come first and the primary education must be the prime concern of one and all.

It is instructive to visualize the attitude of conservatives to any change in status quo. The best one can expect from an enlightened conservative is typified by the constraints, imposed on Giju Bhai Badheka, by the education officer in the following words:

> *"Forget it. You won't be able to do it. Teaching children at the primary school level is no joke. It is an uphill task. You are a thinker and writer. It is easy to dash off an article, sitting at a comfortable table and chair; it's quite easy to imagine yourself teaching. But it's extremely difficult to put your ideas into practice and carry out the experiment through.*
>
> *...All right. If you are so keen, by all means try it out for one year. I'll arrange for you to take a class of Standard Four in a primary school. Here's a copy of the syllabus. These are the text-books. Here is a copy of the departmental rules regarding leave and other ancillary matters.*
>
> *Look here! You may conduct whatever experiments you like; but, please bear in mind that there will be examinations at the end of the academic year. Your work will be evaluated by the outcome at these exminations."*

However, the education officer, like his friends today was happy at the outcome of the change and said after a year:

> *"At this stage I should like to inform you that when this gentleman came to me last year, with a request for permission to make an experiment in standard four of the primary school, I considerd him to be an impractical fool.*
> *I had thought that he was just like many others of his kind and would run away at the first opportunity when put to test. So I gave him permission. I had no faith in him. But, I must admit that he has achieved success in his experiment. He has changed my ideas. I am convinced in my heart of hearts that we must put an end to the old routine in primary education. Teachers and officers like me should voluntarily retire and yield place to imaginative educationists of the new generation.*
> *How shall I express my joy? Look at the children of his class. How orderly, healthy, and cheerful they are! I am a witness to their development and growth. Their parents have often expressed their satisfaction to me."*

If the universalisation of primary education, despite constitutional mandate and world-wide efforts, has remained an illusive goal for us till date, it is possibly because of our failure to touch upon the underlying spirit of education and give it the right perspective in due course of time. It is dislocated from its prime position in human life and societal development. One can very well see the hiatus between the world class brand image of IITs/IIMs of the country on one hand and the worn out, odorless, roofless, dull, dreary, dilapidated and unexciting primary schools on the other.

Oral Learning

Gandhiji's views on primary education are still relevant. A close look at the same gives many inputs to the cause. His thought "After a great deal of reflection and experiment I have come to the conclusion that primary education should be given for at least a year without books and even after that the use of books should be restricted to the minimum" deserves serious consideration.

If books are introduced from the very start and the children made to master the alphabet, the development of their various abilities may get arrested and their intelligence stunted. However, this is the time when it should grow rapidly. A child begins to learn immediately after birth, but mostly through the eyes, ears and other senses. As soon as he has learnt to speak i.e. to imitate the sound of words. he begins to rapidly acquire the use of language. Naturally he speaks the same language as that of his parents. If the parents have taste and refinement, he also develops those qualities. He pronounces the words correctly and copies their manners and conduct. This is his real education. And if our culture and tradition had not fallen part, children would still be receiving the best kind of education in their homes.

But if the child has to go to school, we must see that (at least to start with) it should look like a home to him and the teachers should appear to be similar to parents; the education provided should be such as would be provided in a cultured home. This means that most, if not all preliminary teaching should be oral. A child educated in this way would learn in a year many times more than the one taught in the conventional way, i.e., through the alphabet.

This would enable the children to learn with ease the usual rudiments of history and geography much in the same way as they love stories. They will naturally commit to memory a fairly good number of poems and they would learn the counting of numbers automatically without any effort. Because children will not be subjected to the burden of recognizing and learning the alphabet, the growth of their minds would not be unnecessarily hampered.

The children will use their hands in drawing figures and simple pictures. This would be good preliminary training for the hand, as it would develop both coordination and skill and subsequently the handwriting. If we want to provide meaningful education to the crores of children of India, this is the only way in which primary education should be organized.

Conclusion

Education is more than schooling, and schooling is more than curriculum. Such an orientation of the school is essentially required to make learning a joyful experience. It is liberating the child from the stultifying and mind numbing exercises of the school. It is empowering the child with tremendous sense of pride and privilege in his/her own people and culture. It is helping the teacher and the parents to mutually appreciate and benefit from sharing the school and home experiences. It is recognizing the role and resources of the community making them responsible for schooling of the child. It is developing a new pedagogy, full of life and living experiences.

Considering the limitations of the government role in primary education, a sustainable public-private partnership is proposed, not only for universalisation of primary education but also for a drastic change in the content, process, and pedagogy. This would help towards attaining individual well-being and social justice.

REFERENCES

1, 2. *National Policy on Education—1986—A Review* (1992), New Delhi, MHRD, pp. 133, 153.

3. Kumar, Krishna. (1991) *Political Agenda of Education*, New Delhi: Sage Publication, pp. 47-48.
4. *National Policy on Education—1986—A Review.* (1992). New Delhi, MHRD.
5. NCTE (2005) *Curriculum framework for Quality Teacher Education*, New Delhi, pp. 1-15.

4

Revitalizing Teacher Education for a Cohesive Society

SAROJ PANDEY

The world has been witnessing tumultuous changes unfolding new promises, challenges and threats. Global interdependence has now become a reality. Eastern and Western block nations have entered into a new era symbolized by the dismantling of the Berlin wall. The bygone century however has acquired the dubious distinction of being full of paradoxes unparalleled in human experience. The most significant paradox has been the shrinking geographical boundaries due to easy access to most sophisticated type of information and communication technology and as a result of the process of globalization. On the other hand, however, new walls of caste, class, region, ethnic, cultural and gender discriminations, religious fanaticism and fundamentalisms have been erected challenging the basic human values such as peace, tolerance, love and affection, dignity of human being, and respect for each other. Therefore, while the iron curtains are gone, there are many more curtains in the minds of men than ever before giving rise to serious socio-political problems all over the world. Shrinking geographical boundaries have resulted in migrations from one part of the world to another which calls for respect for individual as a human being and living together in peace and harmony. However the harrowing tales of Jews sufferings in the hands of Nazis, ethnic based upheavals in Bosnia and Kosovo, massacre of Albanian minority in the names of 'ethnic cleansing' and the recent attack on U.S. by fundamentalists are blatant slap on the face of humanity, gross violation of basic human rights, manifestation of false pride of race superiority, growing intolerance and religious fanaticism among people. In spite of unparalleled scientific, technological and material advances the finer and delicate bonds of humanity has somehow been forgotten and the world seems to be going back to the primitive age where 'might is right' was the rule of law, and from where it had started its journey to the highways of civilization.

Therefore there is an urgent need to promote a cohesive and peaceful society which has respect for human values and a clear understanding of the socio-cultural, economic and religious diversities that lead to the unity of nation and the interdependence of the world. Education in this context is seen as the vehicle to promote a cohesive society by taking into consideration the diversity of individuals and groups and by ensuring that the education system itself does not contribute to social exclusion.

In the process of education however there is a chain of connecting agents: teacher educators, teachers and students. What and how students learn is affected by the knowledge structure of their teachers, who in turn are largely dependent upon the teacher education programmes for the grooming and legitimizing of these knowledge structures. Preparing teachers for a cohesive society calls for a global perspective in teacher education programmes which takes into account the diversity and multicultural contexts, encourages aesthetic and cultural sensibility, promotes reflective thinking, generates awareness of human rights and fundamental duties among the teachers so that they can prepare their students for world citizenship.

Preparing Teachers for Cultural Diversity

The large-scale migration of population, during recent years, in various parts of the world and the thrust on equal opportunity for education for all resulted in schools inhabited by students with diverse cultural and ethnic backgrounds.

Teachers of today are more likely to encounter students who have different cultures than their own. There is ample research evidence, to suggest that the beliefs of teachers play a major role in how they respond to the diversity of classroom, how they teach (Clark and Peterson, 1986; Nespor 1987, Kogan 1992) and how they understand multiculturalism (Chavez O'Donnel and Gallegos, 1994; Sleeter 1992). Multicultural education, therefore, is currently receiving a great deal of attention from researchers and practitioners interested in addressing social and academic problems associated with increasing linguistic and cultural diversity (Hernandez 1989; Mitchell. 1990: Verma, 1989; Takaki 1991 ; Saravia Shore and Aruizu, 1992) threatening the delicate fabric of a cohesive society. It is being increasingly felt that teacher education programme, both at the pre-service and in-service level, should help teachers to perceive and value cultural diversity inside and outside the country; acquire knowledge about their own cultures, have confidence, disposition and skill to be at ease with other cultural groups and have perceptions of other cultural and national groups based on upto-date evidence, free from any distortions of stereotype, prejudice or bias. The goal of multicultural education is to reduce racism and bigotry through teachers who are rational and unbiased in their attitude towards diverse cultural groups in the classroom.

Various countries have taken a number of initiatives to address the issue of cultural diversity in education through its teacher education programmes. The American Association of Colleges for Teacher Education, for instance, recommended the introduction of multicultural education in pre-service teacher education programme in mid-1970s (Howsam, 1976).

The University of Akron, implemented a new teacher education programme in 1992. Beginning Teacher Competencies (BTCs), interwoven throughout the course, reflect the theme of Teachers as Decision Maker. Students take seven core courses in addition to courses in their programme studies areas. Divided among four phases, each building upon the previous one, the core course 'Diversity in Learners' is in the second phase of the Teacher Education Programme,

Learning about Teaching. It provides students with an overview of the diverse characteristics of students in classrooms throughout the United States. Thus pre-service teachers are acquainted with the effects of race, ethnicity, gender, social class, religion exceptionality of learner behaviours in the classroom and use of effective teaching strategies with diverse students.

The Teacher Education Curriculum Framework (1998) in India also lays emphasis on the need of adopting culture specific pedagogy and cultural context in teacher education programme to deal with the cultural and linguistic diversity of its multicultural and pluralistic society. Efforts are being made to ensure that cultural plurality and diversity gets embedded in the pedagogical practices both at pre-service and in-service teacher education programme.

Equipping Teacher to Resolve Conflicts

The greatest threat to the evolution of a cohesive society is the growing intolerance, aggression and violence among the younger generation, which has permeated up to the school level. There is growing concern that schools today must address multiple levels of conflicts in the lives of children and communities. A survey conducted by the National League of Cities (1996) ranked gang activities, school violence and ethnic conflict among the top ten worsening conditions facing their citizenry. During that same year one out of seven teachers responding to a survey by the National Center for Educational Studies reported being attacked or threatened by a student (Nicklin, 1996).

Widely reported school shootings in Jonesboro, Arkansas, Springfield, Oregon and other locales prompted a special White House Conference on school violence in Oct. 1998. More recently a survey of American children conducted by Kaiser Family Foundation (2001) reported that bullying teasing and discrimination are big problems in American Schools. Nearly 30 per cent of the children surveyed accepted that teasing and bullying occurred at their schools, and about 50 per cent of children in the age group 8 to 11 years conceded that discrimination and violence were 'big problems' for kids of their age. Violence influenced by media portrayals has been on the rise in India during recent years. Ethnic conflicts resulting in school violence among students is becoming one of the most serious concerns of educational authorities world over, be it caste related violence in India, ethnic violence in Britain or most recent catholic and protestant violence in Belfast.

There is increasing need to understand multiple conflicts facing children and youth. But our education system is still strongly influenced by a larger societal urge to enforce norms of behaviour, and in the words of Focault (1977) 'to discipline and punish'. Nevertheless, rather than merely maintaining discipline it is perhaps time for educators to become peacemakers in a diverse society between children and adults with different cultural backgrounds and belief systems. The teacher of today is required to identify the behavioural symptoms indicative of potential violence among students, and deal with it positively.

A teacher desirous to promote a culture of cohesion and harmony among the students needs to adopt a cooperative and holistic approach within the wider framework of school curriculum. Respect for human rights, tolerance for cultural, ethnic, and racial diversities and consciousness for one's own duties may help in developing cooperation and better understanding among students.

It is also essential for the teacher to realize that conflict is an inevitable aspect of human existence, but the students must be prepared in skills and techniques to resolve conflict through positive dialogue rather than by violent means. Growing need, therefore, is being felt that teacher trainees in the pre-service programme must be aware of various conflict resolution and problem solving techniques, provide more opportunities to students to express themselves, their hopes and their images of the future. This may not only provide students an opportunity for catharsis of their feelings but also develop better understanding of others removing their own pre-conceived biases, which is the first step in ladder of promoting a cohesive society. Brain storming, role playing, engaging in individual or group projects on lives and cultures of others may help in better understanding of other, which needs to be incorporated in teacher education programmes both at the pre-service and in-service level.

Promoting Religious Tolerance

Religion has been the most significant factor in the evolution of cultures, providing both meaning and behavioural and social codes to its followers. However, it is also the major cause of contention as it has been the basis of division, intolerance and conflict around the globe. Religious fanaticism has witnessed some of the most serious acts of violence and territorism all over the world, the terrific being the suicidal terrorist attacks on major buildings of United States of America (on 11th Sept 2001). Religious intolerance is one of the major causes of violence in schools which results from the belief of superiority of one's own religion to others. There was never such urgent need as today on the eve of twenty first century to help students realise that the basic tenants of all religion are same and the diversities which are visible are man-made. Religious fanaticism blocks the rational and reflective vision, which may be overcome by a comparative analysis of basic principles of different religions. The UNESCO Department of Intercultural Dialogue and Pluralism for a Culture of Peace (2000) observes that" it is from early childhood that children should be introduced to the discovery of "otherness" and to value of tolerance, respect and confidence in the 'other" that will bring about a change of behaviour and attitude towards others". The Chavan Committee (1999), and the National Curriculum Framework for School Education (2005) in India strongly advocates education about religion as an instrument of social cohesion and social and religious harmony.

However the most crucial question in this context is— Are our teachers prepared with the relevant content and pedagogical knowledge to present an impartial and transparent picture of various religions in the class? Hardly any teacher education programme dares to touch this delicate and controversial issue. There are numerous instances of schools and teachers themselves promoting religious prejudice and intolerance through their behaviour and teaching either directly or in subtle ways. It is high time now that we seriously consider the matter and prepare a curricula in which religion is integrated with the whole teacher education programme in such a way that it helps in developing a rational knowledge about the basics of all religion. The teachers should know and transmit it in their classrooms, that, all the religions teach the same basic values of life and discriminations in the society are only the creation of human mind. However, as indicated in the preceding section teaching of religion as an instrument to promote a cohesive society is an extremely sensitive issue and requires high level skills in planning and integrating such curricula in teacher education programme.

Preparing for Global Citizenship

Effective teachers in the new century are expected to help students to become reflective citizens in pluralistic democratic nation states, where they are well informed of the events taking place in the international arena, conscious of the basic human rights which each individual is expected to enjoy and their own duties as citizens of a particular nation as well as that of the global society. Citizens of global society also need to have the knowledge, attitude and skills required to function in diverse communities beyond their geographical national boundaries and help in developing a national civic culture that embodies democratic ideals and values such as those enshrined in the Universal Declaration of Human Rights. A strong sense of national identity along with a positive global perspective may help in developing a balanced global citizenship among the younger generation.

Teachers in this context are expected to develop reflective culture, and national and global identifications themselves if they are to help students become thoughtful, caring and reflective citizenship in a politically and culturally diverse world society. An ever increasing demand for developing curricula and teaching strategies, which recognizes our interdependence and strengthens the connection among us is being felt all over the world. Teachers are expected to acquire the content knowledge and pedagogical skills to teach from a world centric rather than ethno-specific or nation-state, perspective. A global perspective is, therefore, essential in all teacher education programmes today to help students to consider themselves as 'human beings whose home is planet earth, (who are) citizens of a multicultural society living in an increasingly interdependent world, and who learn, care, think, choose and act to celebrate life on this planet (to meet) the global challenges conforting human kind" (Anderson, 1994).

The Teacher Education Curriculum Framework (1998) of India tries to address this concern by laying emphasis on competency based and commitment oriented teacher education programme with the objective to prepare teachers to function effectively within prevailing social, economic and cultural contexts and foresee new educational needs and challenges likely to arise in the future. Ten competencies identified by the National Council for Teacher Education (NCTE), in this context, have very comprehensively tried to include the cultural and ethnic diversities in education and prepare teachers for a society where there is strong recognition and commitment for basic human values which is a pre-requisite for developing global citizenship.

In spite of all these efforts more focused and sustained attention needs to be paid in teacher education programmes, to prepare teachers for global citizenship. Global education offers teachers opportunities to guide students on their twenty-first century journey to shape a more peaceful and cohesive world. Teacher education programmes intended to prepare students for global citizenship are expected to help pre-service teachers to:

(i) Perceive and value cultural, social and political diversities;

(ii) Be knowledgeable about cultures and political systems other than their own:

(iii) Base their perceptions of other cultures and national groups on up-to-date empirical evidences free from the distortions of personal prejudice or stereo types;

(iv) Be aware of the societal structure of oppression and their actions relative to these structures and groups who live within them;

(v) Be aware of the threats of the environment and strategies to protect and enhance the environment;

(vi) Appreciate and be proud of the distinctiveness of their own culture and national identity from an international perspectives; and

(vii) Realize that they are preparing to enter a professional community which has to. shoulder a serious responsibility of building the future (children) of the nation and the world.

Helping Teachers to become Reflective Practitioners

The goal of education for a cohesive society is to develop the intellectual, moral and social dispositions that predispose individuals "to accept those ways of life that are consistent with sharing the rights and responsibilities of citizenship in a democratic society" (Gatman 1987). To reach this goal teachers need to engage in critical reflection. Such reflection includes considering multiple perspectives or viewpoints and weighing the long term social and moral consequences of decisions. Lately reflective practice has taken a great significance because of its relevance to teachers' involvement in the process of social and educational reforms. A wider perspective of reflection in the, context of teachers role in promoting a cohesive society is essential involving moral, ethical, political and instrumental issues embedded in teachers' every day thinking and practices. It means that teachers exercise their decisions with responsibility and accountability.

Developing reflectivity in teachers acquires all the more significance because of increasing racial, ethnic, cultural and language diversities in the school and in society which demand reflective and broad minded citizens. Teachers need to be unbiased and transparent in their act and behaviour which can be encouraged only when prospective teachers are helped to see the consequences of their own decisions through different perspectives. The teacher education programmes today need to provide orientation to pre service teachers through theory and school experience based knowledge to practice, analyzing one's own teaching and the school context for the purpose of effecting change; viewing a situation from multiple perspectives; seeing alternatives to and consequences of ones' action, and understanding broad social and moral embeddedness of teaching (Valli, 1990). Teachers must be able and ready to modify their actions according to these insights and examine various issues in the light of promoting justice, equality and freedom which in turn may promote the feeling of living together among the younger generation.

Strategic Considerations

We are marching towards a highly complex and volatile global society, which calls for equal opportunity for all while preserving the local, social, cultural and political identities and diversities. The teacher has to play a major balancing role in such society. It suggests that teacher education programmes should impart knowledge of cultural differences, cultural sensitivity, reflective decision-making and personal motivation amongst teachers to promote equity in schools, which may later on permeate to the larger society contributing to the development of a cohesive and, peaceful world order.

Haberman (1991) maintains this is difficult to achieve unless teacher education institutions change from the traditional transmission model to more powerful instructional modes. Because these goals are in both the affective domain with emotionally laden attitudes, and the cognitive domain requiring intellectual comprehension of the various issues, concepts, conflicts and diversities etc. The pedagogy of on-going teacher education programme will decide the success or failure of teachers in promoting a cohesive society. The teacher education curricula and teaching strategies therefore needs to be developed in such a way to recognize and strengthen our interdependence and connections while maintaining our unique identities. Hence a global perspective and human rights education must form essential parts of teacher education programme and efforts must be made to develop an appreciation of global society among teachers. Banks (1995) outlined five primary dimensions, which may be included in teacher education curriculum to prepare teachers as torch bearers in promoting cohesive society.

(a) **Content integration:** Whereby teachers may be prepared to integrate examples and content from a variety of cultures and groups when they teach particular subject: This may be possible only when the teacher education programme integrates content from diverse cultures in the cuniculum.

(b) **The knowledge construction process:** Whereby teachers are made familiar with content and pedagogical inputs to help students in understanding how implicit cultural assumptions, frame of references and bias influence the process of knowledge construction within a particular discipline.

(c) **Prejudice Reduction:** Which highlights the teacher's focus on the characteristics of students' racial attitudes.

(d) **An Equity Pedagogy** as a goal of the teacher whose priorities are the academic achievement of all students;

(e) **An Empowering School Culture:** Which is the attention paid by the entire school to issues of equity and interactions between members of the school community irrespective of caste, class, ethnic or racial divide, for the purpose of developing a school culture of empowerment for all students.

To conclude, the time is ripe enough to pause and reconsider our teacher education programme to map a course of professional education that will develop collegiality, partnership, collaboration, professional commitment, competence, professional ethics, appreciation of equity, justice and equality among teachers and which will serve simultaneously the needs of practioners and more utopian ideal of learning to live together in a cohesive society at large.

REFERENCES

Anderson, C.C., Nicklas, S.K. and Crawford. R.(1994). Global Understandings: A Framework for Teaching and learning. Alexandria. Va: Association for Supenision and Curriculum Development.

Boyer, E.L.(1986). As cited in Tucker, 1L. and Peter J.C. (1991) Global Perspective for Teachers: An Urgent Priority. Journal of Teachher Education, 42(1), 3-10.

Bullough Robert V. Jr. (1989). Teacher Education and Teacher Reflectivity. Journal of Teacher Education, 40(2), 15-21.

Bursteen, M.D. & Cabello, B. (1989): Preparing Teachers to work with Culturally Diverse Students: Another Educational Model. Journal of Teacher Education 540(5), 9-16.

Baker, G. (1973). Multicultural Training for Student Teachers. Journal of Teacher Education, 24, 306-307.

Banks, J.A. (1993). The Canon Debate, Knowledge Construction and Multicultural Education: Educational Researcher, 22(5), 4-14

Banks, James A. (2001). Citizenship Education and Diversity Implications for Teacher Education. Journal of Teacher Education, 52(1), 5-16

Bruce, M.G., Podemsk, RS. and Carrel, M.A. (l991). Developing a Global Perspective: Strategies for Teacher Education Programmes. Journal of Teacher Education, 41 (1), 21-27.

Barry, N.H. and Lechner J.V. (1995). Pre -service Teachers' Attitude about and Awareness of Multicultural Teaching and Learning. Teaching and Teacher Education, 1 1 *(2),* 149-161.

Clark, C.M. and Peterson, P.L. (1986). Teachers' Thought Processes. In Wittrock, M.C. (Ed), Handbook of Research on Teaching, (3rd Ed), New York: Macmillan. 255-296.

Carr, W. & Kemmis, S (1 986). Becoming Critical: Education, Knowledge and Action Research. London: Falmer Press.

Chavez, RC.,O' Donnel, Jand Gallegos, RL. (1994) Pre Service Students' Perspectives to 'Dilemmas' in a Multicultural Education Course. Paper Presented at the Annual Meeting of the American Education Research Association. New Orleans, L.A

Cruickshank D. and Applegate, J. (1981). Reflective Teaching as a Strategy for Teacher Growth. Educational Leadership, 38(7), 553-554.

Day, Christopher (1 999). Developing Teachers. The Challenges of Life Long Learning. London: Falmer Press.

Gillnick, D.M.(1992). Multicultural Education: Policies and Practices in Teacher Education. In C.Grant (Ed), Research and Multicultural Education: From the Margins to the Mainstream. Bristol, P.A: Falmer Press.

Gipe, Joan P. and Richards, J.C.(1992): Reflective Teaching and Growth in Novices' Teaching Abilities. Journal of Educational Research. Vol. 86(1) 52-57.

Gore, Jennifer-M. (200 1). Beyond our Differences: A Reassembling of what matters in Teacher Education. Joumal of Teacher Education, 52(2), 124-135.

Goodwin, AL. (1 994): Making the Transition 5om Self to Other: What Do Pre service Teachers Really Think about Multicultural Education. Journal of Teacher Education, 45(2) 119-131.

Hanvey, R (1976). Developing a Global Perspective. Newyork: Center for Global perspectives in Education

Howsam R.B. (1976): Educating a Profession. Washington, D.C: American Association of Colleges for Teacher Education.

Hall, S.C., MacDonald, S. and Smolen, L. (1995). Preparing Preservice Teachers for Diversity in Learners. Journal of Teacher Education, 46(4), 195.

Hutchinson F.P. (1996) Educating Beyond the Violent Future. New York: Routledge.

Kirkwood, T.F. (2001). Our Global Age Requires Global Education: Clarifying Definitional Ambiguities. Social Studies,92(1), 10- 15.

Kagan, D. (1992). Implications of Research on Teacher Belief. Educational Psychologist, 27(1), 65-90.

Liston, D. and Zeicher, K. (1987). Reflective Teacher Education and Moral Deliberation. Journal of Teacher Education, 38(6), 2-8.

Langrall, C. W. et al. (1996). Enhanced Pedagogical Knowledge and Reflective Analysis in Elementary Mathematics Teacher Education. Journal of Teacher Education, 47(4),271-276.

Labree, D.F. (2000). On the Nature of Teaching and Teacher Education: Difficult Practices that look Easy. Journal of Teacher Education, 57 (3), 228-233.

Noordhoff, K. and Kleinfeld, J. (1993). Preparing Teachers for Multicultural Classrooms. Teaching and Teacher Education, 9, 27-39.

Nespor, J. (1987). The Role of Beliefs in the Practice of Teaching. Journal of Curriculum Studies, 19(4), 317-328.

NCTE (1998). Teacher Education Curriculum Framework. India.

NCERT (2000). National Curriculum Framework for School Education. India.

O.Bidah, J.E.(2000). Mediating Boundaries of Race, Class, and Professional Authorities as a Critical Multiculturalist. Teachers College Record, 102(6) 1035-1060.

Peretz, M.B. (2001). The Impossible Role ofTeacher Educators in a Changing World. Journal of Teacher Education, 52(1), 48-56.

Pandey, Y.S.(1998).Teacher for the Twenty First Century: Redefining Professionalism for Global Perspective. University News, 36(6), 15-19.

Saravia-Shore, M. Arvizu, S.E. (Eds) (1 992). Cross Cultural Literacy: Ethnographies of Communities in Multiethnic Classrooms. New York: Garland.

Susuki, B.H. (1987). Cultural Diversity: Increasing Achievement Through Equity **Los** Angles C.A.

Sleeter, C. and Grant C.(1987). AnAnalysis of Multicultural Education in the United States. Harvard Educational Review, 5 7(4), 421-444.

Sleeter, Christine .E. (2001). Preparing Teachers for Culturally Diverse Schools: Research and the Overwhelming Presence of whiteness. Journal of Teacher Education, 52(2), 94-106.

Smnith, M.C. and Lytle, S.L.(1992); Interrogating Cultural Diversity: Inquiry and; Action. Journal of Teacher Education, 43(2), 104-115.

Sochan, D.A.(1983). The Reflective Practioner. New York: Basic School.

Sochan, D.A.(1987): Educating the Reflective Practioner .San Francisco: Jossey Bass.

Takaki, R(1991). The Content of Curriculwn: Two Views: The Value of Multiculturalism. Liberal Education, 77(3), 9-10.

Tran, M.T.,Young, R.L. and Dilella, J.D.(1994): Multicultural Education Courses and the Student Teacher: Eliminating Stereotypical Attitudes in our Educationally Diverse Classroom.

Tucker, J.L. and Cistone, P.I.(1991). Global Perspectives for Teachers: An Urgent Priority. Journal of Teacher Education, 42(1),3-10.

Verma, G.K. (Ed) (1 989). Educationfor All: A Landmark for Pluralism (ERIC Document Reproduction Service No. E.D. 310210).

Val1i, L. (1 990). Moral Approaches to Reflective Practices. In R.T. Clift W.R. Houston and M. Pugach, eds, Encouraging Reflective Practice in Education: An analysis of issues and programmes (pp. 39-56). New York: Teachers College Press.

Zeichner, K.M. and Liston D.P.(1987). Teaching Student Teachers to Reflect. Harvard Educational Review, 57, 2348.

Zeichner, K.M. (1 993). Connecting Genuine Teacher Development to the Struggle for Social Justice. Journal of Education for Teaching, 19(I), 5-20.

5

Socio-Political Contexts of Teacher Education Curriculum

CHENNA REDDY

Universally, education is seen as central to the future prosperity and wellbeing of society. Further, the new challenges and demands on schools and teachers emerge from new and heightened expectations of schools, advances in research on teaching and learning and the need to manage classrooms that are increasingly diverse in terms of ethnic, linguistic and cultural backgrounds. These challenges and demands require new capacities and knowledge on the part of teachers. The current situation is both dynamic and varied. Schools are being organised in different ways, in terms of both tasks and the responsibilities assigned to teachers, the differentiation of roles among teachers and between teachers and other school staff. In many countries, teachers' work is now more clearly defined with respect to specified objectives set out for schooling and in relation to the policies and measures taken to achieve these objectives. The breadth of challenges and demands and the pace of change make the current situation different from earlier years. Teachers must be able to accommodate continuing change—dramatic in some countries—in the context of what is to be taught and how it can be taught best. (Centre for Educational Research and Innovation, OECD 1994).

In recent decades society has looked more carefully at the achievements of schools; recognizing the need to improve teaching-learning process. There is a shift in the systemic inputs to education—funding levels, student/teacher ratio, curriculum—to a more explicit focus on defining, measuring and reporting on the outcomes achieved by students, schools and systems.

The nations seek to be more productive and economically competitive. Education therefore, becomes an instrument more closely serving the national interest. Concomitant with increasing pressures for education to serve more, instrumental purposes have been emphasized for greater accountability by schools and school systems for the use of public resources. Within decentralized education systems, this demand for greater accountability has manifested itself in calls for open and public reporting of student outcomes on common and standardized tests.

Notwithstanding these external pressures, schools and teachers see benefits for their teaching and the learning of their students in adopting an outcomes approach. There are tensions about whether the reforms will come through the curriculum or changes to teaching-learning practices, or whether they will be assessment driven through national testing and benchmarking. There are also confusing differences in the terminology. Even the term ***outcome*** is ambiguous. It is used at both micro level to describe curriculum statements defining expectations of what students completing a course will know, understand and be able to do; at macro level it is used to describe class, school or system performance indicators.

> *Educators and the public need to understand why society will be better served if schools clarify their purposes, reorganize as necessary to achieve these purposes, and expect students to demonstrate knowledge and skills needed for success in life.*

Educators and the public also need to know how these goals can be achieved with an outcome focus.

Researches have explored informing an outcome approach and traced its origins to the pioneering works during 1980s, which challenged notions about students' capacity to learn and the normative distribution of intelligence across the population (Bloom, 1981). Their research was initially translated into practice as the 'mastery learning movement'.

The views have been expanded about the nature of outcomes and have now identified three categories of outcomes: traditional outcomes, transitional outcomes and transformational outcomes.

- ***traditional outcomes*** specify the subject content, knowledge and skills which learners will acquire.
- ***transitional outcomes*** set out the practical and cognitive competencies and attitudinal qualities which students will display as they exit from school.
- ***transformational outcomes*** relate to the student's ability to perform effectively in a variety of life roles, requiring students to transfer their learning to new situations, integrate their learning and create new applications of it.

In contrast with mastery learning which is primarily an instructional process, the critics comment that the current outcomes-based education model in the United States is principally a goal-driven curriculum reform model with implications for assessment of student learning. The principles underpinning the current form of outcomes-based education and its interpretation in the classroom are:

- *Every student can learn and succeed:* given sufficient time, appropriate methods and materials all students can succeed at a satisfactory level.
- *Success breeds success:* when students experience success at one task, they are more likely to succeed on a task at the next level of difficulty because they now have a foundation of knowledge on which to base their learning and are motivated by their success.
- *Schools control the conditions of success:* schools adopt practices designed to enable students to achieve success in desired outcomes. This requires a restructuring of

> curriculum design and delivery, student grouping and assessment. Above all, though, it requires a change in teachers' expectations of their students.

Nonetheless, communities are increasingly demanding that schools articulate their expectations of students and hence report in clear and concise terms on their achievements and the achievements of teachers. Typical of such community pressures are those illustrated in the following extract from the United States, 1996 National Education Summit Policy Statement:

We believe that efforts to set clear, common, state and/or community-based academic standards for students in a given school district or state are necessary to improve student performance. Academic standards clearly define what students should know and be able to do at certain points in their schooling to be considered proficient in academic areas.

Establishing curriculum standards whereas efforts to establish curriculum outcomes or expectations are about defining the knowledge, skills, understandings and values we want students to develop, curriculum standards are concerned with the question of the progress, students should make in particular areas of learning by particular stages in their schooling.

Outcomes List Approach

These can take the form of unstructured content standards setting out what students are expected to achieve in a particular learning area. Or, they can take the form of performance standards or benchmarks setting out lists of outcomes to be achieved by students by particular chronological ages, school years or stages of schooling. Benchmarks generally define the minimum expectation of all students at a particular stage of schooling.

Achievement Progression Approach

These attempt to set out the typical patterns of student growth in particular areas of learning. The intention here is not simply to develop a relatively unstructured list of outcomes but to produce a map of developing competence within an area.

The notion of an *achievement progression*—expressed across the stages of schooling or within a stage—relies on the assumption that there is an underlying hierarchy of knowledge and skills within a field of study. Acceptance of this assumption is not universal. Many contrast the idea that learning in a field occurs in a particular or fixed sequence and that the achievements we measure are uni-dimensional.

Implications for Classroom Practice

Despite reservations by some academics and others in the education community, those teachers who have adjusted their practice to adopt an outcomes-approach, have reported benefits for their students. The teachers see syllabus outcomes supporting more student-centred approaches to teaching, shifting the emphasis from practices focussing on what is taught to what is learned. The focus on syllabus outcomes allows teachers to concentrate more on the specific of what is expected of students, to judge the success of their teaching and to adjust their practices accordingly.

Students at all stages of school also see benefit in knowing what is expected of them. In many instances this has led to more effective collaboration between students and teachers, with students negotiating their own learning against the expected outcomes. After all, to enable students to take more responsibility for their own learning is an increasing characteristic of education in the 1990s.

The kinds of higher order cognitive and social skills and understandings associated with transitional or transformational outcomes, requiring students to research, analyse, critically appraise and effectively communicate information; to exercise appropriate interpersonal and task-oriented skills in work-teams, to make imaginative and critical leaps in applying their knowledge to new settings and to carry a complex and relatively vague project successfully through to completion, patently require cultural capital which will be unequally distributed amongst school students. Yet it is the transitional and transformational outcomes which are marketed as the more desirable for schools to pursue.

The expectations of educators in relation to the contribution of outcomes-based education to the amelioration of educational inequity, need therefore, to be tempered until more research is completed into these ***complex and enduring issues*** in education.

Implications for Teacher Education Programmes

The adoption of an outcomes approach in the school sector is not isolated from broader trends in education and training. Demands to identify and articulate course outcomes, adopt strategies to measure outcomes and to report on levels of achievement, are now essential features of the education and training sector.

Universities are not exempted from these demands and are under increasing pressures to be more accountable to both governments and the general community. As schools and the training sector continue to adopt an outcomes approach to teaching, learning, assessment and reporting, it would seem inevitable that the university sector will need to review its courses and practices, not necessarily to embrace such an approach but at least to consider it as one way of ensuring the quality of student achievement.

Certainly, education faculties, with their commitment to developing beginning teachers who can adjust more easily to the present demands of teaching and learning in schools, should, without surrendering their right to critique all government policies, examine more systematically the outcomes approach to education. Further, it is important for teacher educators to lead the debate around teaching and assessment practices in universities. Teaching is a complex intellectual task and it needs to be subject to the same rigour to which research is subjected.

REFERENCES

Bloom, B.S. (1981). New Directions in Educational Research and Educational Practice, In B.S. Bloom (ed.) All Our Children Learning, New York: McGraw Hill.

OECD (1994). Centre for Educational Research and Innovation, OECD.

United States (1996). National Education Summit Policy Statement, USA.

6

Curriculum Framework for Teacher Education

P. SAHU

Professional development implies updating, strengthening and sharpening of the professional competencies and development of understanding and insights in different processes of a profession. The International Dictionary of Adult and Continuing Education (1990) defines professional development, "as resulting in a person's being of greater use to the organization for which he works through the acquisition of greater knowledge skills and different attitudes". An individual's personality has many facets like social, emotional, aesthetic, moral etc. He continues to improve or deteriorate in different dimensions of personality, which are interrelated and interdependent as change in any one aspect is likely to impact many other aspects of his personality. Professional dimension of an individual's personality plays an important role in shaping his overall personality. Therefore professional development is essential for the wholesome development of an individual's personality and his functioning at the optimum level.

Most definitions of professional development emphasize its principal purposes as being the acquisition of subject or content knowledge and teaching skills (Hoyle, 1980; Joyce and Showers, 1980). Further, professional development consists of all natural learning experience and those conscious and planned activities which are intended to be of direct or indirect benefit to the individual, group or school and which contribute, through these to the quality of education in the classroom. It is the process by which alone and with others, teachers review, renew and extend their commitment as changed agents to the moral purposes of teaching and thereby they acquire and develop critically the knowledge, skills and emotional intelligence essential to good professional thinking, planning and practice with children, young people and colleagues through each phase of their teaching lives (Day, 1999). This definition reflects the complexity of the process.

The teacher learns naturally over the course of career. However, learning from experience alone will not serve the desired result as it only limits development. Hence, continuing career long professional development is necessary for all teachers in order to keep pace with change and to review and renew their own knowledge, skills and vision for good teaching.

Various dimensions about the professional development of teachers and subsequent school improvement are as follows:

- Professional development is a lifelong process beginning at the pre-service stage, induction and during the service career. Professional development is a vehicle for achieving school improvement and sustainable change.
- Professional development is a continuing and regular process.
- Professional development must include individual development and organizational improvement and development in order to improve the capacity of the school/organization to solve problems and renew itself.
- Professional development must be driven by a clear, coherent strategic plan for the school/district, for each school and for each individual.
- Professional development should have a focus on students' needs and learning outcomes.
- Professional development should have multiple delivery mechanism.

- Professional development should include a combination of generic and content specific skills.

Hence, professional development is the vehicle for improving the education of teachers and thereby the education of children. It is an ongoing systematic growth process for all individuals involved in the school enterprises.

Teachers need to further strengthen and sharpen their professional competencies in view of changing demands of school curricula, emerging concerns of the society, latest development in pedagogy and advancement in technology. In order to achieve this, teachers have to be always fully aware of the latest developments taking place in teaching-learning process. Pre-service and in-service education must be viewed as part of single process, thus reiterating the concept and principles of continuing education for the teaching profession. It does clarify and justify the need for constant updating and development of skills on the part of all professionals. "Until teaching is seen to require professional growth and responsibility, the effect that in-service education has on the behaviour of teachers will be short lived" (Lockhead and Verspoor, 1991). It portrays teachers as persons needing initial and ongoing professional development (Good,1981). Teacher trainees should not be prepared simply to perform certain skills in certain prescribed ways but rather must be given the mental tools needed to meet professional tasks in ways that are adaptive, questioning, critical, inventive, creative and self reviewing (Sahu, 2005).

Professional developments programme should be continuing process instead of being built upon the usual series of one short event. Nonetheless, there are distinctly different strategies or routes for achieving that goal. The problem of teachers' professional development can be addressed through a variety of strategies such as self-study, participation in seminars, workshops, orientations or training programmes, participation in educational debates and competitions, contributions in journals, magazines and newspapers on educational topics.

Over the years, especially in pursuance of the recommendations of the National Policy on Education-1986, a standing network of training institutions has been established in the country. The training network includes institutions like NCERT and NUEPA at the national, SCERT, IASEs, CTEs and DIETS at the state and district levels. These institutions have the mandate to provide in-service education on a continuing basis to all the teachers in position under their jurisdiction. In addition to periodical organization of formal in-service education programmes, these institutions are also expected to provide such professional support to the teachers as will result in their professional growth. But this can happen only when these institutions approach in-service training as rigorous professional activity adopting the adult learning approach based on problem-centered and experimental learning. They shall have to develop the expertise to identify training needs of different target groups and develop training design and training materials accordingly.

Professional development of teachers alone may not yield the desired results, if it is not accompanied by professional development of principals and supervisors on the one hand and that off supporting staff like librarians, counsellors, laboratory staff on the other. Thus professional development programme in the education sector should be a total effort addressed to all kinds of educational personnel.

Amidst the type of work culture prevailing in the country at large, a majority of teachers are not intrinsically motivated for their own professional development. Recognizing the importance of enriched and enlightened human resources for improving the quality of education, suitable measures are necessary to create extrinsic motivation among teachers

In short, teachers' professional development is widely recognized as an essential pre-requisite for improving quality of school education. In-service education of teachers is only one though very important strategy, for their professional growth. A variety of other strategies are needed to sustain and further strengthen gains of both pre-service and in-service teacher education. On the basis of above background a study was undertaken to critically examine the existing curriculum of B.Ed programme and its potential for professional development of teachers.

Objectives and Methodology

1. To analyse the existing one year and two year B.Ed curriculum in the context of emerging challenges.
2. To examine the development of professionalism in one year and two year B. Ed. programmes.
3. To suggest remedial measures for qualitative improvement of teacher education curriculum.

The present study is concerned with pre-service secondary stage teacher education of 5 teachers training institutes of Orissa. Questionnaire for teacher educators and teacher trainees were developed. The existing one-year and two year B. Ed. curriculum was reviewed. Interview with principals was conducted to discuss on the above issue.

Analysis and Interpretation

The content analysis of Secondary Stage Teacher Education Curriculum focuses on ten major variables and some other variables. A teacher of 21st century is expected to function in the context of rapidly changing socio-cultural, political, techno-economic scenario, onset of information revolution, value crisis, increasing complexity in society, classroom etc. in order to design the vision of perspective teacher at secondary level a few paradigm shifts have been visualized. The success of teacher education training programme depends to a considerable extent on proper development of the affective domain of teachers.

The content analysis of ten important variables of curriculum input in two-year B.Ed programme as well as one year B.Ed programme is given below.

1. **Reflection of Indian Heritage in the Curriculum**
   Reflection of Indian Heritage in curriculum is one of the important concerns. It is observed that in the content of two year B.Ed programme there is a proper reflection of Indian history of education and cultural practices, but there is no reflection on the issues of Indian philosophical system, family practices and family systems. It was found that in one year B.Ed curriculum none of the above issues are reflected neither in objectives nor in content of any paper.
2. **Fulfillment of National goals in tune with Societal Expectations**
   The variables like Fulfillment of National Goals in tune with societal expectations were analyzed. It was found that in the content of two year B.Ed syllabus the sub-variables like Education For All (EFA), quality of life improvement, developing life skills, economic progress, social mobility, developing values were properly reflected in the content of both two year B.Ed and one year B.Ed syllabus. But the input on national goals stated in preamble of Indian Constitution was not reflected in content or objective of any paper of either two year B.Ed or one year B.Ed course.
3. **Response to latest Developments in the Field of Education**
   The third variable is "Response to the latest developments in the field of education". The analysis was done both on one year and two years of B.Ed programme. The six sub-variables are not found in either objective or content of any paper of B.Ed one-year course. The first sub-variable "modes of learning" was in both contents and objectives of two papers in two years B.Ed course. The second sub-variable "evaluation procedure" was also present in both content and objective of two years B.Ed course. The third sub-variable "modes of acquisition of knowledge constructivism" was there only in content not in objective of B.Ed two years course. But the rest three

sub-variables i.e.—multiple intelligence, cross-domain construction, learning centered processes/learning orientation were there neither in objective nor in content of any paper of B.Ed two years course.

4. **Establishment of any integration between Theory and Practice : practicum/practitioner**

   The fourth variable was "Establishment of any integration between theory and practice". It was found that there were nine sub-variables and the analysis was done in both one year and two years B.Ed course. In both two years and one-year B.Ed courses the sub-variables: *seminars, group work, evaluation practices* were not there in the practicum. In addition to these *material developments* was also not there in one year B.Ed course, but it was present in two years B.Ed course. The rest sub-variables like, *assignments, projects, simulation, practice lesson* etc were reflected in both objectives and contents of both two year and one-year B.Ed courses.

5. **Provision of Experiences for Multiple roles of Teacher**

   The fifth variable was "Provision of experiences for multiple roles of teacher". It was very much clear that the first three sub-variables like, *facilitator, resource mobiliser and counsellor* were reflected in the contents and objectives of the curriculum of both two year and one-year B.Ed courses. The rest two sub-variables were not found in any of the papers of both the B.Ed courses.

6. **Enough Flexibility to create scope for Teacher educators to innovate**

   The sixth variable was "Enough flexibility to create scope for teacher educator to innovate". There were six sub-variables like, *curriculum content, curriculum transaction, evaluation procedures, teaching practice-internship, information systems, and teacher education appraisal.* In two years B.Ed course the first four sub-variables were present in both objectives and contents and the last two sub-variables were not found in any of the papers. In one year B.Ed course the first two sub-variables and the fifth sub-variable were reflected in both contents and objectives. The rest third, fourth and sixth sub-variables were not reflected in any of the papers of one year B.Ed curriculum.

7. **Promotion of critical thinking for inculcating emerging goals and values in Indian context**
   The seventh variable is "Promotion of critical thinking for inculcating emerging goals and values in the Indian context".

- Under the sub-variable "critical thinking there were four other sub-variables. The three sub-variables such as mention of activities like—seminars, *debate, micro-studies, group discussion, lesson observation, criticism lesson* were not found in any of the papers of two year B.Ed course. Only the second variable, lesson planning was found in both objectives and contents of two year B.Ed curriculum. In case of one year B.Ed curriculum only the sub-variable mention of activities like--*seminars, debate, micro-studies, group discussion* were not found in any of the papers. The rest sub-variables were available in both objectives and contents of one year B.Ed curriculum.
- Under the sub-variable "emerging loads" there were six other sub-variables. In two year B.Ed course only the third sub-variable i.e.—*sensitivity to social issues* was present in both objectives and contents and the rest five sub-variables were not found in any of the papers. In one year B.Ed course only the first sub-variable i.e.—*right to education* was found in both the content and objective and the rest five variables were not reflected in any of the papers.
- Under the sub-variable "values" there were two other sub-variables like,—*tolerance for cultural pluralism, secular, democratic, ecological and the other is techno-ethics.* In both two year and one-year B.Ed courses neither of the sub-variables were found in any of the papers.

8. **Enabling Teacher to act as an agent of Societal Change**
   The eighth variable is "Enabling teacher to act as an agent of societal change". There were five sub-variables

like, *sensitize them to social issues, use of technology, empowerment of women and girls, sensitivity regarding issues related to marginalized section, school community relationships.* In two years B.Ed course the second, third and fifth variables were found in both the contents and objectives and the rest were not found in any of the papers. In case of one year B.Ed course all the five sub-variables were reflected perfectly in both objectives and contents, which were very much, clear from the conent analysis.

9. **Promotion of International Understanding**
   The ninth variable is "Promotion of International understanding". Under this four other sub-variables like, *globalization—global village, universal brotherhood, role of international agencies, internalization of education e.g., GATS.* From the above table, it can be concluded that none of the above were found in any of the papers of both one year and two years B.Ed course.
10. **Promotion of Professionalism among Teachers**
   The tenth variable is "Promotion of professionalism among teachers". Under this there are four sub-variables like—*period and training, accountability, professional code of ethics, professional developments.* It was found that none of the above sub-variables were there in any of the papers of two years B.Ed course. But in one year B.Ed course the last two variables were present in both objectives and contents of the curriculum. The first two sub-variables were not found in any of the papers of one year B.Ed curriculum.

Conclusion

The teacher education curriculum should be made relevant to the personal and social needs of children and schools. The pedagogical theory should reflect our national ideology and the problems and issues that our society is facing today. The content and methods of teaching all the courses need to be made relevant to Indian conditions. Strategies and approaches of teaching the children inside and outside the classroom should confirm to their physical and social environment.

REFERENCES

Day, Christopher (1999). *Developing teachers: The Challenges of life long learning*. London: Flamer Press.

Good, T.L. (1981). Teacher expectation and student perceptions: A decade of research. *Educational Leadership*, 38, 415-421.

Hoyel. E. (1 980). *Professionalisation and de-professionalisation in education, In Hoyel. E and Maggaty, J. (Eds) World Yearbook of Education 1980 : The Professional Development of Teachers,* London; Kogan Page.

Joyce, B.R: and Shower, B. (1980). Improving in-service training : The messages of research; *Educational Leadership*. 37. 5, Feb, pp, 379-85.

Lockheed, M., Verspoor, A. (1991). *Improving Primary Education in Developing countries,* The World Bank Oxford University Press, New York.

MHRD, Government of India, New Delhi, National Policy on Education (1986).

Sahu, P. (2005). *Pre-service Secondary Stage Teacher Education for Emerging Diverse Educational Contexts- Perspectives, Practices, and Prospects;* ERIC Research Project, NCERT, New Delhi.

II

Globalization, Knowledge Economy and ODL Contexts

7

Knowledge Economy and Teacher Education

S.P. Malhotra

Knowledge has been termed as power. Power not only in terms of strength but also in terms of decisive factor controlling economy. Knowledge industry including those in the fields of telecommunication, information technology, electronics and pharmaceutical sector are affecting economies of the countries. Success in these sectors, it is claimed, has been substantially raising the competitiveness of economy. There has been close association between sectors with poor economic performance and those that have very low representation amongst the knowledge sectors. The successful development of Silicon Valley has been due to factors linked with close academic linkage and generous employers, allowing time for formal and informal study leave for employees. Currently a link has been established between economic performance and applicability of ideas generated by universities in the world of work. The knowledge based businesses is now recognized to be key drivers of growth at all levels in proportion to other businesses. Knowledge intensive functions help in getting higher wages and lesser unemployment.

The concept has already entered the teacher education programme and has brought a large number of changes even when the society and a group of the hard teacher educators have been opposing it. Opening of large number of teacher education institutions under the umbrella of self-supporting institutions is on the increase. The persons who have never been in the area of teacher education system are opening these institutions. In some cases totally illiterate people are opening these institutions. The apex body of NCTE has been helpless in this drama. The need is not to stop the ongoing process but to bring a shift in the system to make it more meaningful. The present paper delineates envisioning change so as to make teacher education more need based.

Changing Role of Teacher Education Institutions

The knowledge economy will mean adding entrepreneurship to teacher education system. The role of teacher education institutions will be significant changing process of economy.

(a) Institutions provide nourishment to the economy

The teacher education institutions are desired to provide continuous manpower. Despite the existence of students who will earn the degree of teacher education to serve a school or sit at home, most of the students may come to the teacher education institutions to explore entrepreneurial market. They have to be trained for the purpose. Deep insight in to the problems of education and market needs will provide infrastructure link to act as incubators for new firms. These areas provide things such as shared secretarial support, legal advice, financial accounting, consulting and export marketing.

(b) Institutions provide supportive environment

Three basic elements of the environment are to be provided by the teacher education system. These include basic infrastructure, social climate for knowledge workers and a permissive commercial system. The basic infrastructure for training and exploring the market needs is, what are the basic needs of the school system or the needs of the stakeholders or the students. The social climate of knowledge workers is built up in the system. The teacher who has become knowledge worker has to be helped in gaining knowledge of social functioning.

(c) Institutions show the way for interdependence

These provide horizontal linkage among various departments. Specialization works best if it can relate to other aspects of any system. Hardware and software aspects of any system can work in the teacher education system. Similarly vertical connections with different organizations in the teacher education institutions have to exist together. If the Learning Material Development Department in the teacher education institution develops software module for the students of a particular class, other department e.g., Psychology department in the teacher education institution can develop data resources with the models, and the Philosophy department can develop rationale to go through the said module. Then there is linkage among individuals. These networks are essential for collective knowledge creation and diffusion. It has been observed that informal training and links are actually more important and common than formal links.

(d) Institutions provide skills for working as knowledge workers

The academic training provided by the teacher education institutions orients an individual socially as well as professionally. High grade and low production activities carried out by different manpower have to be reoriented for socially approved functioning. It can be well carried out by the teacher education institutions.

(e) Institutions provide training support to knowledge workers

The training provided by the teacher education institutions has to be flexible and transferable. They should help in increasing general skill level of the workers.

(f) Institutions to be well associated with research and development process

Most of the academic researches are carried out through the teacher education structure. They need to identify the major problems of the schools, colleges and other teaching learning organizations and provide a good research base for the same. The functionaries in the knowledge market have to be helped in this direction with good research base.

Changing the Aims of Teacher Education

In the era of globalization the need is to change the very aims of teacher education programme. The aim should not be to train the teachers to work in the schools but the aim should be to train specialized personnel who can serve the society as per the needs of stakeholders and the student consumers. All parents or the guardians' desire these days that their wards should go to reputed institutions of higher learning and this factor needs to be taken care of during training programme.

Making Teacher Education Totally Professional Programme

Knowledge economy does not require raw material, land or cheap labour but knowledge, skill and creativity. Therefore, the teacher education programme has to be totally professional. Meaning thereby that the teacher education courses must have specialized knowledge, specialized skills and inherent code of ethics. For this purpose the teacher education programme must have:

(a) Strong Knowledge Base

The economic approach to teacher education programme does not simply require to adapt to changes in the practical world but also needs roots in the ideas and ideologies. Ideas stressing new theories across a wide range of ar.eas help in growth of symbiotic relationship between growth and investment in people and infrastructure. Therefore the theoretical base is must for any discipline to grow and make dent in the market. People with specialized knowledge are given greater credence in the social system. The basic disciplines of philosophy, psychology and other such aspects have not to exist in isolation but to be taken in to view in a global manner so that various phenomena in the teacher education programme could be fully explained. Different theories that guide the functioning of the teacher and the environment have to be grounded for explaining different phenomena. Indifference to theory will take out professionalism from the teacher education programmes.

(b) Specialized Skill Training

A professional requires specialized skills to convince the consumers that his/her profession is not every body's cup of tea. Moreover specialized skills add quality to the professional functioning. Specialized skills mean having hard, technical expertise along with softer interpersonal capabilities. All these have to be conceived as personal characteristics or attributes rather than a skill in traditional sense. The teaching skills, organizational skills and the guidance skills have to be developed in the teacher trainees in such a manner that these become a part of their life. However, a trainee may be asked to specialize at the micro level in any of the following skills:

(i) Skills of Quality Teaching

Quality teaching is a process that makes the consumer student feels that he/she has understood the teacher and his/her teaching. In quality teaching process there has to be a good conflict between the teacher and the students. The conflict has to achieve good learning situation. Both the teacher and students will bring out a problem and work hard to find good solution to the problem. May be sometimes students find better solution to a problem. Only difference between the teacher and the taught is that former is maturer than the later. The processes of making students work hard and become independent learner is a matter of quality teaching. Posing problems, before the students and helping them find solution to these problems is a skill and such skills have to be developed in the teacher trainees.

(ii) Skills of Quality Assessment

The teacher trainees have to be trained in quality assessment procedures. The student has to be assessed with respect to his/her abilities, thinking process and learning style. The process of testing abilities of students may be ordered along a continuum in terms of specificity of experiential background. At one extreme may be the course oriented achievement tests covering narrowly defined technical skills or factual information. Next in the continuum may come the broadly oriented achievement tests commonly used to assess the attainment of major long-term educational goals. Still broader in orientation are tests of intellectual skills that affect the individual's performance in a wide variety of activities like reading comprehension, arithmetic computation etc. Another aspect that has to be tested is students' cognition and their learning or achievement. The idea is that teaching or instruction affects achievement through students thought process. In brief, learning from instructions is not automatic. It occurs primarily through active and effortful information processing by students. It has to be tested and interpreted. To accurately assess it is a skill and needs developing a testing procedure that suits an individual student. The way in which the learner selects, acquires, organizes or integrates new knowledge is the learning style of the learner. This may involve activities like : coaching, imaging, notes-taking etc. If these activities are evaluated, the students can be helped to develop effective ways to handle the barrage of information coming from the environment as well as their own thinking process.

(iii) Skills of Quality Guidance

The function of the teacher is to continuously guide and counsel the student in the process of teaching learning. Specialized skills are needed for the purpose. The process of teacher training has to be so organized that these skills are developed among trainees.

Many aspects can be added to the list of skill training of the teacher. However, it will mean more specific training in some areas and general training in other fields. This has been pointed out by Bootle (1994) that it is easier to mouth the magic words 'education and training' than devising a practical strategy, which actually pay dividends. Therefore the training strategies have to be devised to train the professionals called "Teachers'.

(c) Developing Strong Research Base

The colleges of education or university departments of teacher education work as catalyst agent in the process of Knowledge Economy. They provide ideas to work upon. The basic research done in the colleges/universities helps in organizing innovations in the field. Examples can be found in the training equipments developed in the colleges/university system that have been used by these industries. Therefore there is a need to develop strong research base in the education system. Every action of the teacher trainee should be supported by research. There has to be strong link between training laboratories and field functioning.

(d) Developing Entrepreneurial Culture

The teacher education institutions will have to develop entrepreneurial culture amongst the students so that they do not simply wait for jobs in the schools rather they explore the market to find their own place. Entrepreneurship is social marketing where the individual sells the ideas to the needed persons and bases his economic exercises accordingly. Only those persons can be enterprising who have deep insight of their subject matter. Entrepreneurship has following characteristics:

(i) Creating ideas: Entrepreneurship is an economic activity and involves creation and operation of an enterprise. It is basically concerned with satisfying needs of the customer with production and distribution of goods and services.

(ii) Entrepreneurship shows professionalism: Entrepreneurship shows that the task being performed is totally professional. Specialized field of knowledge and special skills are required for performing the relevant functions and need based specialized training.

(iii) Organizing function: Entrepreneurship means bringing together various factors of production for economic use. It is a process of coordination and controlling the factors of productions in a novice manner.

(iv) Innovation: Entrepreneurship is an automatic, spontaneous and creative response to changes in the environment. It involves innovation of something new to the cause of dynamic change and spectacular success in economy and creates conditions for growth of economy.

(v) Risk bearing capacity: Risk is an inherent and inseparable element of entrepreneurship. It is assuming the uncertainty of future.

(vi) Managerial and leadership function: Entrepreneurship means having such managerial and leadership skills. These qualities predominate orientation in the direction of productivity, working relations and creative integration along with desire to make profit. Entrepreneurship demands tactful handling of risk and uncertainties because new commodity and its acceptability are uncertain.

(vii) Gap filling: The gap filling between human needs and available products and services leads to entrepreneurship. It identifies the gaps to achieve action-oriented motive in the enterprise with the help of entrepreneurship process. The process of entrepreneurship will indicate quality of the teacher education programme.

Quality Inputs in Teacher Education Entrepreneurship

The students in teacher education programme are trained in large number of skills as well as in theoretical framework. The theory consists of learning philosophical schools of thought, some learning theories, personality development programmes, intelligence and reasoning process in the children and some management theories. On the practical side the syllabi consist of acquaintance with training process, skills of communication, writing lessons in learner friendly ways etc. All the exercise revolves round teaching children at the elementary level or secondary level. In the entrepreneurship process they have to be trained in finding out market needs and utilizing the acquired skills for the requirements of the market. It will consist of the following:

- Knowing one's capacities i.e. introspecting what type of skills have been achieved by the student teacher.
- Surveying the market i.e. exploring the market requirements in the shape of what the stakeholders are looking for improving the capabilities of their wards.
- Designing creative solutions for the problems of the stakeholders that are, helping their wards to come out of the problems of learning and personality development.
- Giving consultancy services to the managers of education systems so that they run their institutions in an organized manner.
- Developing evaluation systems for the objective evaluation of capabilities of the wards of the stakeholders.
- The entrepreneurial culture will mean to shift the focus of quality assessment from the institution to learner. Only indicator of quality will be the entrepreneurship.

The teacher education system thus may have to seek participation both of the government as well society at large. In the context of existing social and economic fabric of the country, it appears almost certain to go in for private funding of education at least for making up the deficit caused by inadequate State funding. This makes the beginning of partial privatization of the existing teacher education institutions in the country. If it is done, the money earned by the teacher education institutions will have to be ploughed back to the educational sector for its own improvement. This in other words is business trend in education where money is earned and the same is put back in to the system to sustain it and make it stronger.

Teacher education institutions currently represent a collection of individuals trained to a high level. Most of these academics have specialist knowledge in order that they might become experts in that part of their subject as it is possible to be neither they to broaden their knowledge to deal with vagaries of business, nor they get incentives to change topics due to the disinterest of the public at large. This means that teacher education institutions contain a repository of knowledge and expertise different from those of business houses. Any change to the requirement of academics with respect to work that they carry out may change the nature of this repository of knowledge. It is uncertain whether teacher education institutions provide better support by being more like business or by providing a wide-ranging collection of knowledge and expertise.

Conclusion

It will be unfair to project education as a marketable commodity because it is not the result of a mechanical manufacturing process. In production process quality of output can be expected. But in education it is not possible to measure the returns in the form of input-output process. Reason being that education is a process involving minds. All the students brought to an educational system cannot achieve same level of skills, efficiencies, dexterity etc. Expecting uniform quality is a remote possibility. After all teaching and learning is not a fabrication process. Business economy in education is business neutral and above the concept of quality.

REFERENCES

Felsteed et al. (1997), 'Getting the Measure of Training' Leeds Centre of Industrial Policy and Performance.

Finegold, D. (1999), 'Creating Self-sustaining and High Skill Ecosystem' Oxford Review of Economic Policy, 13(2), p. 68.

Ivan, T. (1993), 'Loose Connections? Foreign Investment and Local Linkages in Silicon Glen' Strathclyde, University of Strathclyde, p. 4.

Williams, P. (1995), 'Universities Waste Science Funds' Nature.

Bootle, R. (1994), 'Our Competitive Future: Building the Knowledge Driven Economy', Oxford Review of Economic Policy, 33(12), p. 32.

8

Research Issues in DE Based Teacher Education

P.K. Sahoo

Of late Distance Education has emerged as one of the significant modes of imparting education. Development of knowledge concerning distance education (DE) and searches for solving various problems concerning DE system constitute a significant component of educational research in the knowledge based society. It involves multidisciplinary approach in the sense that the problems of DE system will have to be visualised with holistic perspective and its solutions will have to be drawn from knowledge and experiences related to education and relevant disciplines. Hence, philosophical, sociological, historical, behavioural, scientific, economic and technological perspectives of educational research will play a major role in strengthening the base of research in DE.

The major scope of research in DE focuses on understanding DE system with broader perspectives, understanding its internal structure and functioning, making interventions in development and functioning of the system, more specifically in the context of development of curriculum, instructional strategies and programme evaluations at macro and micro level. While researches in different brances of education can strengthen the base of development of knowledge on DE, empirica! studies, specially focussing on different problems of DE system occupy greater significance.

Areas of Research in DE

In the above context the areas of research in DE can be suitably classified on five headings:

- Perspectives of DE
- Understanding Internal Structure and Functions of DE System
- Planning and Management of DE System
- Curriculum Development, Instructional Strategies, Media and Implementation
- Programme Evaluation

Perspectives of Distance Education

Several questions related to philosophical bases of DE can be raised regarding the concept of DE vis-à-vis open learning system; openness in formal system of education, the nature of knowledge, the process of acquiring knowledge vis-à-vis the role of technology, the nature of learner, the nature of teachers and academic supporters/facilitators, the nature of evaluation and learners development etc. Moreover, analysis of the role of DE as one of the components of education system and study of the relationship of DE with other components of education system in achieving the goals of education will lead to rationalise the base of DE at different stages.

DE draws its meaning from developments taking place in the area of learning such as learning as a process and product; experiential learning, constructivism, learning environment and self study, learning style, learning in independent study situations, interpersonal communications and self study, the role of academic counselling and different kinds of feedback mechanism in promotion of self learning etc. Studies on these dimensions can throw light on identifying suitable strategies for distance learning. The role of DE in democratising educational system is also to be analysed with a social-anthropological perspective. The goals of DE in providing open access to education as well as giving opportunities for success of learners are to be linked with the existing structure and functions of DE system. Adopting sociological approach to understand the relationship of DE with national goals of education; social value system, cultural ethos, development of attitude, social mobility, the process of socialisation, global linkage, group relations, professionalism etc., can contribute a lot towards knowledge base on DE system. Moreover, forecasting the role of communication technologies and its utility in open learning society draw special attention of sociologists of education in the context of achievement of democratic goals of education. The changing role of DE in the knowledge based society is to be analysed in the context of knowledge system, multidisciplinarity, changing job patterns, globalisation, privatisation, transparency in communication and open sharing of knowledge in various fields. Such dimensions may be subject to cross-cultural enquiries in DE.

Understanding Structure and Functions of DE System

Scientific investigations on the status of different inputs adopted in different models of DE and its relationship with different modes of operation of the system can broaden the understanding of the system. Different input variables subject to such analysis can be identified as : learners background, their needs and aspirations, organisational structure, academic and professional experiences of academic/semi academic personnel, physical resources, financial support, organisation of activities, involvement of subcomponents of DE system as well as collaboration with other system, nature of programmes, course requirement enrolment system etc.

The study of process dimensions can incorporate areas like procedures adopted in course design and development, delivery of media and materials, academic support activities, inputs and processes of learner evaluation, monitoring of academic and administrative functions of institutions. Moreover, the status of different structural components will have to be understood in the context of various functional dimensions of DE.

Planning and Management of DE

The scope of studies of this area can be categorised under programme level studies, institutional level studies, studies of DE system at state level, regional level, national level etc. Research inputs can strengthen the base of perspective planning of DE system. The long term and short term planning incorporates futuristic approach to research. Moreover, studies related to management of DE can incorporate the inquiries on evolving alternative models of management, its theoritical and operational dimensions, the strength and limitations of different management system, information technology based management in DE, management of media and technology, management of human resource system, intra-unit and inter-unit co-ordination in programme production, delivery and evaluation activities, organisational behaviour, linkage with outside agencies concerning policy making, planning, execution and accreditation of DE system etc. Networking of institutions and its modes of operation is an emerging area of research in management of DE system.

Curriculum Development, Instructional Strategies, Media and Implementation

Research inputs must be integrated with different stages of design of different curricula, design of mix-media strategies for instruction, development of materials to be used for different media, development of alternative packages of evaluation etc. Moreover empirical support is essential for designing various strategies for interactivity, development of specific competencies, field activities, workshop and laboratory based learning experiences etc. Suitable strategies need to be evolved for operationalising networking based instruction, feedback mechanisms to learners, resource persons, course designers, experts involved in material development, media production and delivery evaluators etc. Formative research has to play a key role in this area.

Programme Evaluation

Policy research draws major strength from programme evaluation studies. The scope of programme evaluation is so wide that it encompasses all the structural and functional dimensions of DE system. The context variables, inputs variables, process variables and product variables of DE system can be incorporated for evaluation studies. The qualitative process based studies give major emphasis on analysis of different factors operating in context specific situations. Thus qualitative descriptions and context specific interpretations on operational dimensions of DE system is to be given major priorities. The quantitative approaches lay emphasis on identification of relevant criteria for evaluation of context, input, process and product of DE system. Moreover, cost benefit studies and technology assessment studies will have to be encouraged in the field of DE system.

Distance Education for Professional Development of Teachers

The action plan on New Policy on Education (1992) emphasised on use of DE and distance media for continuous professional development of teachers. DE institutions like IGNOU, State Open Universities and Institutes of DE offer a number of preparatory teacher education programmes for in-service school teachers mainly working at secondary and primary stages. The National Open School's proposal for preparation of elementary teachers through DE mode is yet to materialise.

Use of distance media based teacher education packages have been encouraged either in isolation or as a component of any mix-media based teacher education programme. Distance Media based teacher education programmes are mostly confined to ETV programmes. Such programmes are produced by different institutions like IGNOU, CIET, NOS, AVRCs, EMRCs, SIETs and DECU (ISRO). As a component of DPEP the IGNOU DEP project has taken special initiative in integrating DE programmes as an integral component of in-service elementary teacher education programmes. The programme delivery includes use of recorded video programmes during training sessions, direct telecast of ETV through terrestrial system, *Gyan Darshan* operating through satellite mode and teleconferencing mode operating through satellite channel on special occasions. Besides the coverage of target of school teachers and teacher educators, the DE media is also used for training of resource persons involved in academic activities of DE institutions like IGNOU, State Open Universities and NOS. However, looking at the coverage of target of around 50 lakhs teachers and personnel working as para teachers at different stages of education DE media will have to expand its scope very fast. There is an urgency in focussing on quantitative expansion and quality improvement of DE system for professional development of in-service teachers. In this context research will have to play a vital role in policy formulation, curriculum design, production of media, delivery system and programme evaluation of teacher education system operating through DE mode.

Perspectives of Teacher Education Through DE Mode

Several issues concerning education for professional development of teachers are to be addressed in totality through research studies. For instance identification of various external and internal factors affecting present and future roles of teachers in school system, the role of teacher education in the context of universalisation of elementary education, various roles of teachers in development and functioning of education system, participatory role of teachers in various programmes of professional development, policies and priorities in encouragement of in-service education and promoting DE based teacher education etc. are some of the problem areas which need to be tackled through research studies. Answers to several questions concerning the role and future perspectives of teacher education in the country will form the ground for integrating DE as one of the major inputs of professional development of teachers. This effort will lead to reviewing researches on different perspectives of teacher education and undertaking analytical studies on the role of DE in total development of teacher education system.

Curriculum Studies on Teacher Education

As stated above DE based teacher education forms one of the major components of teacher education especially in the context of in-service education of teachers. While analysis of philosophical, social, psychological and pedagogical perspectives of curriculum for teacher education is very much essential empirical, studies on needs, expectations and motivation of teachers, job analysis of teachers, identification of essential competencies of teachers, reforms in school curriculum etc. form sound bases for development of alternative curricula for teachers. Since the target of teacher education is very wide exploring training (pre-service and in-service) needs of different target groups like formal school teachers, teachers of NFE, teachers of alternative schools, teachers of DE institutions, para teachers etc. will pave the ways for framing group specific need based curriculum. While macro level studies will focus on exploring core needs of teacher education micro level studies will focus on context specific needs of different kinds of teachers. In this context, forecasting future needs for teacher education in the context of future of education system will make curriculum more relevant and development prone.

Preparation of teacher educators acts as a major input for successful implementation of teacher education programme. More specifically in the context of DE based teacher education programmes there will be distinct role of teacher educators and resource persons to carry out various activities involved in it. Exploring various alternative curriculum frameworks for teacher educators will draw the major attention of curriculum research in teacher education.

From methodological perspective it is worthwhile to encourage participatory approach in exploring training needs where in-service teachers, teacher educators, school level administrative functionaries, learners, parents and community members act as stakeholders of school system. Their participation is also very much significant in identifying the aims and objectives of teacher education programmes and expected outcomes of different short-term and long-term programmes, organising course content, and designing alternative strategies for implementation of different modules for teachers. Identification of suitable methods and media for different kinds of DE based training programme form a significant component of curriculum design. Various criteria will have to be kept into consideration for identification and selection of appropriate strategies for implementation of DE programmes. This will involve empirical data based studies with systems perspective. While previous experiences on effectiveness of various methods and media will smoothen the process of strategy building, empirical evidences on context specific DE situations will make decision making about methods and media more relevant.

Media Studies in Teacher Education

Media forms a significant component of curriculum design of DE system. There are two major aspects in placement of media in DE system. One aspect is linked with development and production of DE based media and another aspect is linked with the process of delivery of media. Since teacher education programme gives major emphasis on development of different competencies of teachers there is need for identifying alternative mix-media strategies whereby suitable media and materials will have to be integrated at course design stage for development of specific competencies. It is also worthwhile to ensure quality control at production stage as well as at delivery stage. Media research studies which are of formative type need to be integrated with programme development activities. Besides, media management studies need to be encouraged since delivery of media incorporates involvement and coordination of various functionaries and agencies at different stages. Process oriented media studies need to be integrated with decision making and execution of different DE media in teacher education programmes.

Programme Evaluation Studies on Teacher Education

Programme evaluation studies on professional development of teachers serve two major purposes. One is to judge effectiveness of any programme or any component of a programme and another is to facilitate decision making in organisation of DE based teacher education programme. Effectiveness of a programme can be linked with external as well as internal criteria. Such criteria may be linked with the inputs of a programme, its processes and products. The evaluation of inputs include learner, teacher educators, curricular objectives etc. The process evaluation is concerned with development of curriculum, identification of strategies for curriculum transaction, the procedures adopted for development of materials and media, quality of course materials and media, the process of adoption of curricular strategies, delivery mechanism of various methods, media and materials, monitoring and evaluation mechanism etc. The outputs of the programme are also included as major criteria of evaluation. Programme evaluation studies can be of varied nature. For instance one study may focus on studying effectiveness of a video programme on any topic, another study may focus on effective use of a teleconferencing programme, the third study may focus on effectiveness of a multi-media based training package of in-service education and so on. While micro level studies of such categories are conducted in isolation, the macro level studies may focus on evaluation of DE system in totality. It may focus on evaluation of an institution offering DE based teacher education programme at state level or at national level or impact of DE based teacher education programmes in the context of Universalisation of Elementary Education (UEE) etc. There can be process based institutional studies integrated with the programme evaluation starting from its policy framing and planning upto its execution and evaluation stage. Such studies aim at providing empirical support to decision making at different stages of programme development and implementation. Programme evaluation studies can be of short term as well as of long term nature. Each category of studies has its significance. The short term studies like content analysis of a video programme or analyzing participants' reaction to a teleconferencing package can give on the spot feedback for improvement of the programme where as long term integrated studies lead towards decision making on major issues and policy framing of the system in totality.

Studies on DE based Teacher Education in India

Review of different studies conducted in the area of teacher education through DE mode in India indicates a wide gap between the needs and priorities of research and attempts made so far in this direction. The area wise classification of studies reveal that only one attempt has been made by Indradevi (1985) to analyse philosophical perspective of DE vis-à-vis teacher education. Two more works have been carried out by Sabhanval (1999) and Singh and Singh (1999) doing conceptual analysis of teacher education programme, its relevance and scope inside DE system, implications of formal teacher education programme on DE based teacher education etc.

Empirical studies on curriculum of teacher education through DE mode have been mainly restricted to analysis of social, academic and psychological background of the beneficiary learners undergoing various programmes and the expected learners. The studies also aim at exploring needs of in-service teachers for teacher education, their motivation to pursue teacher education programmes through DE mode, job analysis of teachers, analysis of teacher competencies to be incorporated in in-service curriculum etc. Exploring training needs of in-service elementary teachers for professional development has been attempted by independent studies of Arora and Singh (1999), Kapoor (1998), Sahoo (1999), Senapaty (1999), and Shastri (1999). Aiholi (1996) and Benekanal (1996) conducted studies on exploring in-service education needs of secondary and college level teachers respectively. Curriculum areas identified by these studies bears a lot of implications for designing DE programmes for teacher education. Besides these studies a number of studies have aimed at identifying background of learners of various kinds of DE based teacher education programmes. Such attempts have been made by Sahoo (1985), Kamar et al. (1985), Upreti (1988), Khan (1991), Pugazenthi (1992), Patil (1996), Patri (1996) and Khan (1999). Of course these evidences have been utilised for understanding the coverage of DE programme and exploring scope for modification of existing curricula for in-service teachers.

Scanty efforts have been made to integrate research with designing curricula for various kinds of teacher education programmes through DE mode. Mukhopadhyay (1999) has attempted to design different models for imparting teacher education through DE mode. Researches encouraging participation of stake holders of in-service curriculum must be encouraged at institutional level.

Media studies conducted on in-service teacher-education are mostly of evaluation type. A number of studies have been conducted to explore the nature of media and its utilisation in various kinds of teacher education programmes. Such attempts have been made by Nagaraju (1982), Sahoo (1985), Rathore (1991), Pugazenthi (1992), Phutela (1996), SRRI (1994) etc.

So far, one can came across a systematic attempt which has been made by DPEP, Karnataka (1999) to develop film based teacher training module. The study was conducted in different phases. The first phase of the study incorporated soliciting reactions of participant teachers on various aspects of training module through written feedbacks, brainstorming activities and workshops The second phase of study aimed at designing activity based participatory training modules through a number of workshops. The third phase of the study incorporated development of a series of films as a component of training package. The films were produced involving participatory mode. The workshops spread over a year with children, teachers and VEC members. The last phase was linked with operationalising DE based teacher education programme where face-to-face training at district level teacher education institutes was integrated with programmes transmitted through satellite from a studio set-up in Bangalore. The experiences suggest that such kind of institutional formative studies must be encouraged with a view to integrate distance media within a holistic framework of teacher education curricula.

Major emphasis of researches on DE have remained on evaluation of different components of the system in terms of different criteria. Different components which have been subject to evaluation are : learner inputs, coverage of the system, relevance of curriculum and course content, usefulness of course materials and electronic media, usefulness of student support services, flexibility in organisation of various kinds of student support activities, suitability of delivery mechanism, usefulness and flexibility in learner evaluation system, learner output in terms of examination results, development of teaching competencies, and long term impact, the quality of resource persons, cost effectiveness, effective co-ordination between different agencies of DE programme etc. The studies which focus on evaluation of teacher education programmes as one of the components of DE read as Sahoo (1985), Kumar et al. (1986), Upreti (1988), Khan (1991), Patil (1996), Patri (1996), Bhusan and Bhusan (1999), Khan (1999), Sahoo and Khan (1999), Singh and Rana (1999) and Sahoo et al. (1999). These evaluations either focus on any one or more than one aspects of teacher education programmes.

It will also be worthwhile to highlight programme evaluation studies exclusively conducted on distance media. Mainly the quality of television programmes and its utilisation strategies have been subjects for evaluations. Moreover, teleconferencing based teacher education programmes have also been evaluated through a few studies. For instance attempts were made by Mohanty and Behera (1 984) and Behera (1991), Patra et al. (1985) and Sahoo (1999) to conduct content analysis of national telecast programmes of CWCR and Tarang. The expert opinion and reaction of in-service teachers were used as the basis content evaluation. The studies undertaken by SRRI (1994) and UNICEF (1995) highlighted on utilization of school ETV programmes having relevance for teachers' professional development in the states of Andhra Pradesh, Uttar Pradesh and Orissa. The Development of Education Communication Units of ISRO has been conducting the assessment studies on Accelerated Literacy through TV. The Jhabua project where teacher preparation through TV lessons and face-to-face mode is one of the components of evaluation. Pal and Passi (1999) conducted a study on utilisation of educational media programmes for teacher educators. Besides these studies some of the teleconferencing based teacher education programmes have also been evaluated. They read as study on teleconferencing based ECC programme for PGDHE programme of IGNOU (Sahoo 1994). Studies related to utilisation of interactive video technology in the orientation programme of primary school teachers were conducted by Phutela (1996) and Das (1997). As a unique dimension of educational media research Dharam Prakash (1998) attempts to evolve criteria for effective ETV programmes for children adopting qualitative approaches to research. The study bears significant implications for orientation of teachers in development of ETV programmes and its utilization in formal and in-formal situations.

Future Directions

The review of studies conducted in the area of DE and media based teacher education reveals that so far limited efforts have been made to integrate research activities with development of teachers' professional development programmes. These studies have gained ground, during past one and half decades. The IGNOU UNESCO chair explored a number of micro level studies. The futures of education system will lead towards adopting integrated modes of teacher education having alternative strategies. In this context the role of DE and information technology inputs in teacher education will play a significant role. Moreover, the scope of teacher education will expand in multifacet forms for catering to the professional development of teachers at different stages of education. Hence, researches in the area of DE need not be visualised in isolation. As stated in foregoing sections researches in various components of teacher education must be visualised in totality having direct bearing for curriculum studies, media studies, studies on management of teacher education through DE mode etc.

From methodological perspective the studies conducted so far adopt different approaches like status surveys, reaction studies, comparative studies and expost-facto experimental studies. Accommodating philosophical, historical and socio-anthropological approaches to education will have the ways for identifying perspectives for teacher education and making DE based teacher education learner relevant and context specific. Formative and developmental researches will have to be integrated with curriculum design, course development and media production activities. Participatory approach in research must be encouraged with a view to develop need based and learner specific curriculum. Since the process of teacher education will be dynamic in nature, continuity will have to be maintained in adopting such approaches to research. Studies on technology forecasting and assessment will have to be linked with a broad perspective and futures of teacher education. Such studies will throw light on use of media and technology based professional development programmes in formal, non-formal and informal situation. Moreover, systems management studies on teacher education will have to be given priorities since DE based teacher education programmes operate in multifarious situations involving networking of different agencies of teacher education institutions, expertise, media and technology system etc. Discussions on these dimensions of research will lead towards pin pointing various dimensions of research with a holistic perspective of development of teacher education in the country.

REFERENCES

Aiholi, V.D., Forecasting Needs and Resource Potentials for In-service Education for Secondary School Teachers of Karnataka State towards 2005, Unpublished Ph.D. Education Thesis, DAVV, Indore, 1996.

Association of Indian Universities., Hand Book of Distance Education, 1996, AIU House, Delhi, 1997.

Behera, S.C., An Investigation into the Impact of ETV Programmes on the Competency of the Teachcrs of Elementary Schools, Paper presented in AIAET Annual Conference, Dec. 1991, Bhubaneswar.

Benekanal, V. A,, Forecasting Needs and Resource Potentials for In-Service Education for College Teachers of Karnataka State towards 2005, Unpublished Ph.D. Education Thesis, DAVV, Indore, 1996.

Bhushan, **A,,** and Bhushan M.A., A Critique for Instructional Material for Distance Teacher Education, IGNOU UNESCO Chair Project, 1999.

Das, N., Reactions of Primary School Teachers Towards Training Through Interactive Television, Indian Journal of Open Learning, Vo1. 6, Nos. 1 and 2, 1997.

DECUIISRO, Ahmedabad, Pursuit—The Jhabua Development Communications Project, Dec. 1998.

Dharam Prakash, Evolving Criteria for Effective School ETV Programmes, Ph.D. Education Work in Progress, Kota Open University, Kota, 1998. DPEP Karnataka, Satellite Based Interactive Training Programme for Teachers : A Training Design, 1999.

Government of India, Ministry of Human Resource Development, National Policy on Education, New Delhi, 1986

Gautam, R., A Study of success in distance learning system in relation to some key learner and institutional variables, unpublished Ph.D. Thesis, Kurukshetra University, Kurukshetra. 1990.

Ghosh, A,, Role of Media in Education for All, Project on Year 2000 Assessment Education for All, NIEPA, New Delhi, 2000.

Indradevi, V., Philosophical Analysis of the Concept of DE and its implication on the Teacher Education, Unpublished Ph.D. Thesis, Ostnania University, Hyderabad, 1985.

Kapoor B.K., Development and Validation of In-Service Education, Curriculum for Primary School Head Masters of Delhi, Ph.D. Education Work in Progress, Kota Open University, Kota, 1997.

Khan, M.: A Study of In-Service Teacher Education Programmes through Distance Education in M.P., Unpublished Ph.D. Thesis, DAVV, Indore, 1999.

Khan, N.: Effectiveness of DE programme with reference to the teachers training course, unpublished Ph.D. Thesis, University of Kashmir, Srinagar, 1991.

Koul, L., Open and Distance Education in Fifth Survey of Research in Education (1988-92), NCERT, New Delhi, 1997.

Kumar, K. et al., Motivation of B.Ed correspondence-cum contact programme students NCERT Project, New Delhi, 1986.

Mohanty, J. and Behera, S.C., Teacher Education Programme under INSAT, EPA Bulletin, Vo1.8, Nos. 1 and 2, 1985

Mukhopadhyay, M., Alternative Strategies in Teacher Education paper presented in National Seminar on Teacher Education organised by DEP-DPEP, IGNOU, March 22-24, 1999.

Nagaraju, C.S.: Evaluation of Radio Correspondence cum Contact Programme in Kerala, ISEC Bangalore, Project Report, 1982.

Pal, R. and Passi B.K., Utilisation of educational media programmes for teacher educators, IGNOU UNESCO chair project report, New Delhi, 1999.

Passi B.K., Research in Open Education, Mimiograph, IGNOU UNESCO chair, New Delhi, 1999.

Patil, S.S., Management of different forms of Distance Education at Higher Education Stage in Karnataka, Unpublished Ph.D. Thesis, DAVV, Indore, 1996.

Patra, S.N. et al., Teacher Training Programmes : A Feedback in Mohanty, J. (Ed.) Studies in Educational Broadcasting, New Delhi: Deep and Deep, 1998.

Patri, K.L., A Study of Future Expansion and Instructional System of DE at Higher Education in Orissa (By 2005) unpublished Ph.D. Thesis, DAVV, Indore 1996.

Phutela, R.L., A Pilot Project on Utilisation of Interactive Video Technology in the Orientation Programme of Primary School Teachers in the State of Karnataka. Project, CIET, NCERT, New Delhi, 1996.

Pugazenthi, G., A Study of Teacher Education Programme Through Correspondence System in M.K. University, Unpublished Ph.D. Thesis, M.S. University, Baroda,.1992.

Rathore H. C.S., A critical evaluation of systems adopted for management of teaching and learning in the existing correspondence institutes in India, NIEPA, New Delhi, Project 1991.

Sabhanval, V.K., Innovative Face-to-Face Teacher Education Programmes and their Implications for Distance Mode Teacher Education, IGNOU UNESCO chair project 1999.

Sahoo, N., Content Analysis of CIET ETV Programmes for School Teachers, Paper presented in 35th Annual Conference of AIAET, Bangalore, 27-29 Dec. 1998.

Sahoo, P.K., A Study of Correspondence Education in an Indian University, Unpublished Ph.D. Thesis, M.S. University, Baroda, 1985.

Sahoo, P.K., Open Learning System, New Delhi : Uppal, 1994.

Sahoo, P.K. and Bhat, V.D., A Study of Students Attitude towards Correspondence Education, Journal of Indian Education, 1985.

Sahoo, P.K. and Patri, K L., Open Learning Facilities in Distance Education, Paper presented in AAOU International Conference, Hong Kong OU, Hong Kong, November 2 to 6, 1997.

Sahoo, P.K. and Khan, M., In-Service Primary Teacher Training through DE in M.P., In Quest of *Bharateeya Shikshan,* Vol. 1, Nos. 6-7, 1998.

Sahoo, P.K. and Khan, M., Madhya Pradesh Main *Patrachar Sevakalin Shikshak Prashikshan Pathyakram Ki Prasangikta Ka Adhyayan, Bhartiya Adhunik Shiksha,* Vol. 16, No. 3, Jan., 1999.

Sahoo, P.K. et al., Caste Study of B.Ed Programme of Kota Open University, IGNOU UNESCO chair project, 1999.

Sahoo, S.N., Exploring Needs for In-Service Education for Primary School Teachers of Tribal Districts of Orissa, Ph.D. Education Work in Progress, Kota Open University, Kota. 1999.

Sarma S.C. et al., Distance In-Service Teacher Education, CIEFL, IGNOU UNESCO Chair Project, 1999.

Senapaty, H.K., Professional Needs of Elementary School Teachers : A Case Study, IGNOU UNESCO chair project, 1999.

Shastry, V.B., Preparing a Plan for a Block in Orissa for .the Development of Teachers, Supervisory Staff and Community Members, IGNOU UNESCO chair project, 1999.

Singh, L.C. and Singh, A., Paradigm for Teacher Development through Distance Education, IGNOU UNESCO chair project, 1999.

Singh, R.P. and Rana, G., An Inquiry into the B.Ed Programme of Indian Universities—Face to Face vis-à-vis distant modes, IGNOU UNESCO chair project, 1999.

Social and Rural Research Institute, New Delhi, Impact of Educational Telecasts—A Study among Rural Primary Schools in Andhra Pradesh, Uttar Pradesh and Orissa, CIET Project, 1994.

University grants Commission, Report of the Delegation to Study Correspondence Education in the USSR, New Delhi, 1967.

UNESCO, Bangkok : In-service Training and Tomorrow's Primary Education, Report, 1987.

UNICEF, New Delhi : Attitudes Study on Elementary Education in India Project, 1995.

Upreti, D.C. : Impact of Teacher Training through Correspondence Courses (B.Ed, SSCCC) on upward occupational mobility of the elementary teachers in the western region, RCE, Bhopal Project, 1988.

9

Professional Development of Teachers At a Distance

N.K. Dash

Teacher education constitutes an important sector which contributes to the process of national development. Therefore, professional development of teachers has always been an important concern for the various commissions and committees set up from time to time while recommending various measures for educational development of our country. According to Selected Educational Statistics, out of total teaching workforce in our country about 10 per cent are either untrained or undertrained. Moreover, India's initiatives to universalize education at elementary and secondary stages and making education a fundamental right have brought in new pressures on the school systems in terms of student enrolment, infrastructure development and demand for trained teachers. Added to this, unprecedent growth in knowledge technology has compelled the government to introduce Information Technology (IT) as part of the school and tertiary level curricula, which demands preparation of a cadre of teachers who could stand up to such technology induced changes in teaching-learning process.

Although efforts are being made by several face-to-face teacher education institutions, such efforts are very minimal at the requirement of large number of teachers. The Open and Distance Learning System (ODLS) has undertaken the challenge of providing professional development programmes to a large number of trained and untrained teachers. Indira Gandhi National Open University, State Open Universities and Correspondence Course Institutes (CCIs) have initiated a number of teacher education programmes at different levels to meet such demands. However, there is hardly any effort to consolidate and appropriate such initiatives to avoid duplication of efforts, wastage of financial and other resources through evolving collaborative and networking mechanisms. This paper discusses professional development programmes for teachers at various levels of education being offered by the ODLS with a brief historical background and suggests collaborative and networking measures that could be adopted by these institutions to consolidate teacher education in India.

Professional Development of Teachers through Distance Mode

The need for training teachers through distance mode was felt in 1960s when there were large number of untrained teachers in schools and inadequate teachcr training facilities in the country. Realising that about 45 per cent of the teachers in schools were untrained in 1965, the All India Association of Teacher Educators adopted a resolution at their annual conference recommending that the untrained school teachers having at least five years continuous teaching experience be trained through two consecutive summer school programmes with some correspondence lessons in between (NCTE, 1995). This programme called the summer-school-cum correspondence course (SSCC) was started by Central Institute of Education (C.I.E.) in 1966 and by the Regional Colleges of Education in 1970 (NCTE, 1995). However, the C.I.E. stopped this programme in 1971 and a decade after the Regional Colleges of Education also stopped this programme in 1985. The efforts of C.I.E. and the RCEs gave rise to a new model of correspondence-cum-contact programme for B.Ed degree which was started in several universities. The enrolment in these courses varied from 3000 to 30,000. The NCTE (1995) looked into the deficiencies in various aspects of the correspondence-cum-contact B.Ed Programme offered by the Universities and recommended that correspondence/distance education mode should not be used for pre-service teacher education. However, it suggested that distance education can be effectively utilised for up-dating in-service teachers' knowledge in any special subject of teaching.

Present Scenario

Many distance education (DE) institutions started offering B.Ed and M.Ed programmes as per the NCTE guidelines. By 2001, four open universities including the Indira Gandhi National Open University offered either B.Ed or both B.Ed and M.Ed programmes (vide Table 9.1). Of Late, M.P. Bhoj Open University also launched a B.Ed programme for special education teachers. Afterwards initiatives made by the Open Universitieis got an impetus by as many as 12 Correspondence Course Institutes (CCIs) offering either B.Ed/M.Ed (vide Table 9.2) or both B.Ed and M.Ed programmes. All these teacher education programmes are meant for in-service teachers only. No programme was offered for fresh graduates. The delivery system opted by both Open Universities and Correspondence Course Institutes varied from institution to institution.

The delivery mechanisms include self-instructional material, audio/video programmes, interactive radio counseling, assignments, tele-conferencing, face-to-face workshop, academic counseling, practicals, broadcast/telecast, personal contact programme, multimedia, online education, internet, etc. Apart from these two teacher education programmes, namely B.Ed and M.Ed, Indira Gandhi National Open University also offers Post Graduate Diploma in Higher Education (PGDHE) for college and university teachers, Diploma in Primary Education (DPE) and Certificate in Primary Education (CPE) for in-service primary school teachers. It also offers Certificate in Teaching of Primary Mathematics (CTPM) and Certificate in Teaching of English as a second language. Added to the list of Open Universities, Tamil Nadu Open University is also contemplating to launch teacher education

Tabe 9.1: Teacher Education through Distance Mode—Open Universities, 2000-01

S. No.	*Name of Institution*	*Name of Prog.*	*Target Group*	*Delivery System*
1.	Indira Gandhi National Open University, New Delhi	B.Ed.	In-service teachers only	• SIM, Audio-Video • Face-to-face programme • Interactive Radeo Counselling • Assignments • Practicals
2.	Kota Open University Kota	B.Ed.	In-service teachers	• Print material • Audio-Video • Face-to-face • Phone-in-Radio
3.	Karnataka State Open University, Bangalore	B.Ed.	Graduate	• Print material, Audio/Video • Face-to-face counselling
		M.Ed.	B.Ed. Teachers	• Interactive Radio Counselling • Multimedia
4.	YCMOU, Nashik	B.Ed.	In-service teachers	• Print material • Multimedia • Face to face counselling • Audio-Video
		M.Ed.	B.Ed. Teachers	• Radio/TV Broadcasting, • Online Education • Internet

programmes. From the above discussions, it is evident that distance teacher education in our country has expanded significantly and is also in the process of further expansion. Although, the growth in distance teacher education institutions and programmes are encouraging, there have been duplicity of efforts, under utilisation of resources, increase in cost, variation of standard and quality, etc. with these institutions. Hence, there is an urgent need for collaboration amongst these institutions to optimise the uses of resources available with them in view of achieving the objective of providing quality teacher education programmes.

Tabe 9.2: Teacher Education through Distance Mode—Correspondence Course Institutes

S. No.	*Name of Institution*	*Name of Prog.*	*Target Group*	*Delivery System*
1.	S.V. University, Tirupati	B.Ed.	In-service teachers	• Print material • Telephone counselling
2.	Andhra University, Vishakhapatnam	M.Ed.	In-service teachers	• Print material • Contact Programmes
3.	University of Jammu, Jammu	B.Ed. M.Ed.	In-service teachers B.Ed. Teachers	• SIM • Audio • SIM and Audio
4.	Gujarat Vidyapeeth Ahmedabad	M.Ed.	B.Ed. Teachers	• Print materials
5.	M.D. University, Rohtak	B.Ed.	In-Service Teachers	• SIM • On line interaction • Tutorials • Assignment
6.	Himachal Pradesh University, Shimla	B.Ed. M.Ed.	In-Service Teachers B.Ed. teachers	• Print materials • Print materials
7.	Mother Teresa Women University, Kodiakanal	M.Ed.	B.Ed. Teachers	• Print materials
8.	Tripura University, Agartala	B.Ed.	In-service teachers	• Print materials • Seminars • Project Assignments
9.	Punjabi University, Patiala	B.Ed. M.Ed.	In-service teachers B.Ed. Teachers	• Print material • Radio talks • PCP and Assignments • —do—
10.	University of Kashmir, Kashmir	B.Ed.	In-service teachers	• Print materials
11.	Berhampur University Orissa	M.Ed.	B.Ed. Teachers	• Print Material • Contact Programme

Source: Data Base of Distance Education Council, IGNOU, New Delhi, 2001.

What is Collaboration?

Collaboration refers to sharing of any kind of resources between or amongst collaborating institutions optimally in order to achieve mutually arrived at predetermined objectives. Collaboration, according to Moran and Mysinger (1999) "has become an almost ubiquitous element of distance education over the last decade, but mostly as relatively discrete projects." Braimoh (2002) visualises that collaboration in distance education could become a sine-qua-non to achieving wider accessibility, democratization, equity and globalization of education within and beyond the national territorial boundaries. Collaboration can take place between two institutions or amongst more than two institutions. It can happen at local, regional, national and international levels. Collaboration may not warrant for the partner institutions to have resources at par with each other. An institution deficient in certain resources may collaborate with another institution sufficient with those resources. The primary principle of collaboration is that partner institutions must have a sound and reasonable basis for collaboration. This paper delineates collaboration among distance teacher education institutions in India.

Collaboration among Distance Teacher Education Institutions

In India, there exist three major genres of institutions which offer distance teacher education programmes. These are National Open University, namely, IGNOU, State Open Universities and Correspondence Course Institutes. The following options are possible for collaboration among these institutions.

1. Collaboration between National Open University and another State Open University.
2. Collaboration among National Open University and many State Open Universities.

3. Collaboration between one State Open University with one or many State Open Universities.
4. Collaboration between one State Open University with one or more than one CCI(s).
5. Collaboration between National Open University with one or more than one CCI(s).
6. Collaboration among National Open University, State Open Universities and CCIs.

The following diagram represents the possible options of collaboration among these institutions.

Areas of Collaboration

Collaboration among distance teacher education institutions can be initiated in several areas. These areas may broadly be categorized under the following:

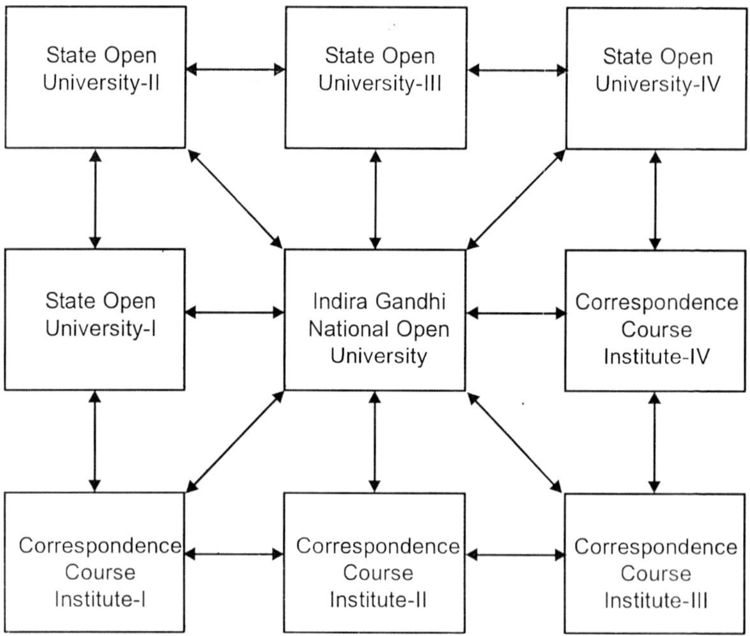

Fig. 9.1: A Model for Possible Collaboration Options

- Sharing of human resources
- Sharing of infrastructure resources
- Sharing of financial resources
- Sharing of cultural resources
- Sharing of network resources
- Sharing of online resources
- Sharing of material resources

Sharing of Human Resources

When we talk of sharing human resources among DE teacher education institutions, we broadly come across three major types of human resources. These are: academic, administrative and technical human resources.

Academic Resources

Academic resources constitute distance counsellors and experts. They are the backbone of a DE institution. In collaboration, their expertise in planning, designing, development, delivery and evaluation of courses or programmes can be shared by the partner institutions. Exchange of faculty can take place between the collaborating institutions for the professioiial development of teachers. Joint R and D (research and development) activities can be undertaken to generate and disseminate new knowledge. The expertise of the faculty to plan, design, produce and choose education media like print, audio/video, computer and internet can be shared.

Administrative Resources

Administrative resources constitute the second most important component and is responsible for the smooth running of programmes and activities in DE institutions. The personnel in administration take part in a number of activities like advertisement, admission, course development and delivery, monitoring and supervision, management of assignment and counseling, conduct of examination, student assessment, credit transfer, student certification, etc. Hence, sharing of their expertise will certainly be a boon for the partner institutions.

Technical Resources

Technical personnel constitutes those people who are involved in production of audio-video programmes or production of print materials. The partner institutions can make use of media experts like producers, cameramen, graphic artists, engineers in production of audio-video programmes, in organization of teleconference programmes and phone-in counseling programmes. Similarly, they can share the expertise of copy editor, production officer and proof readers in the production of print materials.

Financial Resources

When we talk of sharing of financial resources we generally talk of sharing of cost associated with operations of DE teacher education programmes. There are different types of cost involved in DE programmes. These are cost of development, production and delivery of courses/programmes, cost of maintenance, monitoring and supervision of courses, programmes, cost of admission, implementation, examination, assessment and certification, cost of developing and offering online resources, etc. All these costs can be shared by the partner institutions. Cost are generally permanent and recurring in nature. Suitable mechanisms can be evolved to share these costs.

Infrastructure Resources

Infrastructure resources are mainly physical and technological in nature. Physical infrastructure like office premises, conference facilities, audiotorium, warehouse, studio, guest house, etc can be made use of by the partner institutions whenever they are required. Similarly, technological infrastructure like electronic gadgets, production equipments, in-house shooting facilities, tele-conferencing facilities can also be shared.

Cultural Resources

Cultural resources are those which reflect the cultural settings of DE teacher education institutions. These include institutional philosophy, policy perspectives, vision and mission, belief and value systems, leadership and management styles, institutional traditions and conventions. All these cultural resources can be shared by the partner institutions for their mutual growth.

Network Resources

All distance teacher education institutions have a well developed network of regional centers, study centers, programme study centers and distance education facilitators. These are field level institutions which are mainly responsible for the implementation of academic programmes. Hence, the potential of these network institutions can be optimally used by the partner institutions.

Online Resources

Very shortly, online teacher education programmes are going to be initiated by distance teacher education institutions. As a result, online resources like software for development of online programmes, multimedia software, instructional and web designers, webware, network facilities, sewer, etc., can be made use of by the partner institutions.

Sharing of Material Resources

Very often, the partner institutions may not go for any of the above resources. They may be interested in sharing only material resources like print material, audio and video programmes, CD-ROM, etc. Therefore, collaborating institutions may also be encouraged to share material resources.

How to Collaborate?

It is not only important to know the areas of collaboration, but also essential to evolve the mechanism for collaboration. There may be different ways for collaboration.

Mechanism of Collaboration

The following steps may be followed to undertake collaboration.

Analyse Needs

The partner institutions must analyse their needs for initiating collaboration. If there are genuine needs, then only they should go for collaboration.

Identify Goals and Objectives

The partner institutions must spell out in clear terms long term goals and short term objectives to be achieved through collaboration.

Operationalise Modalities

Detailed modalities have to be formulated in operational terms. These may include the areas of collaboration, the nature of collaboration, the role and responsibilities of collaboration etc.

Draft and Sign MOU

Once detailed modalities are finalized, Memorandum of Understanding (MOU) incorporating the goals and objectives and the modalities has to be drafted and signed.

Implement Collaboration

Collaboration initiative is to be implemented by the partners in accordance with the MOU signed.

Conduct Formative Assessment and Corrective Measures

During the course of collaboration, formative assessment may be undertaken to find out any difficulties and based on such assessments corrective measures may be incorporated.

Conduct Summative Evaluation

At the end of target period, a summative evaluation may be carried out to know the effectiveness of collaboration and successful achievement of target goal.

Review Collaboration

The feedback obtained from summative evaluation may be used to review collaboration in order to decide whether to carry on collaboration, improve upon the existing collaboration or close the collaborative initiative.

Roles of Distance Education Council (DEC), National Council for Teacher Education (NCTE) and University Grants Commission (UGC)

Three major national apex bodies like DEC, NCTE and UGC can come together and form a consortium which would act as the nodal agency to look after all kinds of collaborative initiatives by any DE teacher education institutions.

The major functions of the consortium would be:

- To promote and support all networking and collaborative activities undertaken by DE teacher education institutions.
- To formulate and implement enabling supportive policies to bring about effective networking and collaboration in the area of teacher education.
- To suggest and undertake quality measures for consolidating the activities undertaken by these institutions.

- To create a national fund out of the contribution of national apex bodies, responsible for DE teacher education programmes activated by National Open University (IGNOU), State Open Universities and CCIs.
- To provide financial, technical and expertise support to all these institutions in activities like organization of seminars, workshops, research and development, faculty improvement and capacity building, etc.

Benefits of Collaboration

When we talk of benefits accrued out of collaboration, we find two major beneficiaries. They are students and the collaborating institutions.

To Students

- Wider accessibility to courses/programmes
- Good quality instructional materials
- Efficient administration
- Competitive Course fees
- Quick and smart support services
- Inputs from best brains
- Credit transfer
- Wider acceptability and recognition' of the programmes and degrees
- Exposure to emerging technologies

To Collaborating Institutions

- Avoidance of duplicity of efforts
- Quality maintenance
- Competitive standard in materials and services
- Reduced cost
- Shared vision and mission
- Optimum use of resources
- Increased financial strength

- Improved institutional culture
- Marketability of Products
- Widening of accessibility
- Provision of equity
- Expansion of network facilities
- Creation and expansion of knowledge base
- Promotion of R and D activities
- Opportunity for professional growth

Constraints in Collaboration

The following constraints may generally crop up in collaborative activities among DE teacher education institutions. These are:

- Differences in institutional goals and objectives
- Differences in institutional philosophy and culture
- Clash in leadership and management styles
- Incompatibility in institutional requirements and strengths
- Profit sharing
- Breach of contract/agreement
- Copyright problem
- Intellectual property right
- Institutional dynamics
- Lack of enabling policies
- Administrative and logistics problems
- Lack of intent and fund

Conclusion

Increasing demand for teacher education at all levels, rapid development of internet technology, reshaping the discourses in education, impact of globalisation on education and training have made collaboration among the institutions a necessity. Just like collaboration among business enterprises help them to be the market leaders, collaboration among DE teacher education institutions will certainly make them efficient and effective education providers. Hence,

"Collaborate and Be the Market Leader"

REFERENCES

Braimoh, Dele (2002) Assuring quality through institution collaboration on study materials development for distance learners, in Dikshit, H. P, et a1. (2002) (ed.) *Access and Equity : Challenges for Open and Distance Learning,* New Delhi: Kogan Page India Limited, 243-251.

Government of India (1999), Selected Educational Statistics, New Delhi: MHRD.

Moran, L. and Mysinger, B. (1999). Flexible learning and university change, in Harry Keith (Ed.) Higher Education through Open and Distance Learning, London and New York: Routledge and COL, 57-71.

NCTE (1995) Different Modes of Education used for Teacher Preparation in India—a Study, New Delhi: National Council of Teacher Education.

10

Teacher Education in Post Modernity

M.T.V. NAGARAJU

Society always wants teachers to change. Rarely has this been truer than in recent years. These times of global competitiveness, like all moments of economic crisis are producing immense demands about how we are preparing the generations of the future in our society. At moments like these, education generally and schools in particular become a somewhat politically receptacle into which society's unsolved and insoluble problems are deposited. Everyone including politicians, the media and the public alike—seems to be anxious to do something about education.

Along with economic regeneration (more emphasis on mathematics, science and technology, improving performance in basic skills, restoring traditional academic standards) teachers in many places are also being expected to help rebuild national cultures and identities. In response to global economic integration and multicultural migration, schools are therefore being expected to carry much of the burden of national "reconstruction", as a way to prevent the lost of cultural and political identities and distinctiveness, as well as environmental awareness. To meet all these needs, school curricula are being packed with new content that stresses historical, geographical and cultural unity and identity, along with cultural diversity and environmental consciousness, contents which teachers are supposed to master and cover.

This paper points out how the definition of new trends in education, namely the need to develop students' attitudes, values and skills, more adapted to a complex and uncertain world, meets new challenges and demands in respect to teacher education models and practices. Our main statement is that teachers can no longer contribute to change students' attitudes and values, unless teacher education programmes deal with complex reality approximately. These include social, multicultural and environmental awareness, sustainable development and solidarity, among other more personal skills such as autonomy, initiative, communication, critical reasoning, and the ability to select different kinds of information from various sources.

All these educational features are present in education for citizenship and should also be perceptible in teacher education models. It means to avoid the reproduction of traditional forms of knowledge, now described as ineffective, and to change the still frequent theoretical and transmissive model of teaching teachers, replacing it for a reflective one. To give a brief account of our thoughts regarding the relationship between education for citizenship and teacher education in the context of post modernity is the main focus of this paper.

The Context of Post Modernity in Teacher Education

The crisis of "Welfare-State" and students' movements are phenomena that since the sixties characterise the change and the historical transformation of civic, political and social citizenship, based on the paradigm of technological rationality. Since then, innovation and social change are due to the engagement of new social actors, that working outside the official institutions pursues new interests and concerns. Ecological, feminist, pacifist and anti-racist movements, among others are examples of new social groups whose interests and motivations came to light at a local scale but proved to be strong enough to play a world-wide role. Only giving rights to the minorities can no longer solve oppression and social exclusion. It is also necessary to change socialization processes, cultural inculcation and development strategies. Participation and solidarity can contribute to create a new political culture and a new quality of life based on self-government and autonomy. Citizenship is seen as independent from bureaucracy, giving a special importance to individual and collective skills and pay attention to social exclusion, in the same manner that a citizen should not to be considered as a simple unity but as a complex articulation of individual discourses. Given this context, the liberal concept of Education for Citizenship and the role of Schools are contested. According to the new paradigm, School should be able to give opportunities to reflect and exercise practices of citizenship that contribute to youth participation as *social agents.* Therefore, the aims of Education for Citizenship are to develop autonomy, initiative, respect for others, capacity of innovation and to find answers for new social and cultural challenges.

The discourses and practices of modernity are characterised by an emphasis on progress and a faith in rationality and science as the means of its realisation. Modernist discourse provides ways of talking and knowing which we cannot readily dispense with. But although post-modernism cannot yet provide an alternative, the post-modern attitude does at least enable us to recognise this. Postmodernism enables a questioning of scientific attitude and scientific method, of the universal efficacy of technical-instrumental reason, and of the stance of objectivity and value-neutrality in the making of knowledge claims.

To recognise the significance of language, discourse, socio-cultural locatedness and power in any knowledge claim, is therefore also to question the modernist notion of universal and transcendental foundations and thus of canonical forms of knowledge. There is, instead, a decentring of knowledge where modernist certainty is undermined, with consequent uncertainty pervading throughout action and identity. This is another aspect of fixed references and traditional anchoring points disappearing.

The difficulties in the process of changing schools and teaching are to be found in the wider social context in which schools operate and of which they are a part. The fundamental problem is to be found in a confrontation between two powerful forces. On the one hand is an increasingly post-industrial, post-modern world, characterised by accelerating change, intense compression of time and space, cultural diversity, technological diversity, national insecurity and scientific uncertainty. Against these stands a modernistic, monolithic school system that continues to pursue deeply anachronistic purposes within opaque and inflexible structures. Sometimes school systems actively try to resist the social pressures and changes of post modernity.

First, as the pressures of post modernity are felt, the teacher's role expands to take on new problems and mandates—though little of the role is cast aside to make room for these changes. Second, innovations multiply as change accelerates, creating senses of overload among teachers responsible for implementing them. More and more changes are imposed and the timelines for their implementation are truncated. Third, with the collapse of moral certainties, old missions and purposes begin to crumble, but there are few obvious substitutes to take their place. Fourth, the methods and strategies teachers use, along with the knowledge base that justifies them, are constantly criticized—even among teacher educators themselves—as scientific certainties lose their credibility.

Education for Citizenship

Civic education, moral and civic learning, education for citizenship, education for democracy are concepts that change according to different times and authors, at the same time that each of them covers different approaches to education for citizenship. From historical point of view, the process of transforming civic learning in education for citizenship meant the enlargement of the subject field. Although for some educators the option between instruction and education marks a difference in the way we define the role of school, we think that is in fact an irrelevant issue, as "instruction", "education" and "socialization" are and always will be the three goals associated with school's social role, since its origin and development along the last two centuries. Nevertheless, some of those expressions are used in many official and government texts with different meanings. For that reason, we will adopt the concept of Education for Citizenship to appoint the whole domain, thus reducing the term civic learning to the subject that can be found in many countries' curricula.

No matter which concept we use the implementation of education for citizenship in our schools is linked with the development of the modern Democratic State and its function is mainly political. From this point of view, the skills we expect to notice in any citizen's behaviour are the same that concern the knowledge and conduct we hope to find in any democratic society as a whole. To protect democracy it is important that citizens not only engage in different political activities but also be aware of its rules, in the sense that taking part in social initiatives does not mean to pass over the limits of legality. It also means a certain kind of awareness regarding a wide range of social problems that can put in jeopardy that same democracy: discrimination, racism, and social exclusion, among others.

The topics of education for citizenship can be defined at three levels:

(i) the knowledge about today's societies as well as about their past, as this knowledge enables us to understand the social conditions in which we live today and allows each one of us to participate and debate our common problems and choose our political representatives;

(ii) the knowledge about the rules that are supposed to guide our life in society and the ways through which we can solve our conflicts, thus turning explicit the values and the principles underlined, principles that we usually associate with civic rights;

(iii) the knowledge about the political frame in which we live and act, its Institutions, the way these operate, assuming this knowledge is just enough for us to join democracy and than have access to political power.

According to the context of post modernity presented earlier, we believe that these three levels are insufficient to define all the potentiality of education for citizenship. The questions we raise can be stated as follows:

- Is democracy guaranteed, on the one hand, by the capability of individuals to create non-governmental organisations, or by their willingness to put into action their freedom and initiatives, allowing the political establishment to assure that social rules are respected, or on the other hand, should democracy be reduced to the capability of individuals to control that same political power in the community where they live by exercising the right to vote?
- Is school the place where young people simply acquire knowledge about mankind's intellectual and scientific creations and civic learning, or should it also be the place where they get acquainted with their cultural identity as well as others?
- Does education for citizenship concern the whole educational community (students, teachers, parents, local authorities), then risking to disappear in a complex net of contradictions and interests, or should it be regarded as a domain to be taught and structured the same way all the other curriculum subjects are?
- If we agree that education for citizenship refers to models of social behaviour, as it concerns the education of individuals we hope will act and behave in society in accordance to principles and values of "good citizenship", should that same education emphasize individual experiences and social relationships, then organising the teaching and learning processes accordingly, or should it mainly stress the teaching of positivist knowledge, the development of skills that lead students to adopt behaviours socially accepted and defined as "good"?

Viable Approaches

Where can we find education for citizenship? The topics we recognise as necessary for students learn how people "live together" in any democratic society, can be found in all school systems and in various curricula's subjects, although under different names. Another way of presenting it refers to well known cross curricular approaches such as "education for peace", "multicultural education", or even "environmental education".

Therefore, the contents of education for citizenship can change between meanings that are more or less confined. But whatever those meanings might be, the practical purpose seems always to be the same: to change peoples' behaviour and the way they relate to each other and to promote new kinds of social engagement. In this context we think it is important to discuss the relations between "personal experiences" and "knowledge". When we talk about changing peoples' behaviour, we mean to develop a sort of conduct grounded on critical reasoning and individual rationality; a kind of critical freedom one can only achieve as a result of open and responsible social relationships. On the other hand, the emphasis on "knowledge" does not forcely mean that teaching and learning ought to be organised around abstract notions and concepts, frequently senseless to students, but on the contrary that they should highlight students' social representations, in order to develop decision-making skills and the desire to be socially active.

It is between these two approaches that it is possible to find most of the curricular designs regarding education for citizenship. For those who put an accent on "experience", results show that neither formal and abstract teaching nor reflexive practices, concerning the study of civic rights, or about the principles of democracy and of it institutions, are enough to change students' daily attitudes, values and behaviours.. For those who proclaim "knowledge" is the key factor, it seems fair to say that teaching must at least show some affinities to the ethics students are supposed to accept and understand. In any case, to accept the role of knowledge does not mean to put aside action, as well as to stand for "experience" does not suggest we keep out reasoning and reflexibility. Knowledge is also experience, as much as experience is knowledge that was transposed to action.

When trying to synthesise education for citizenship, some essential remarks have to be made. The most important of all is the one that concerns the relations between experience and knowledge and the attributes in which they must lay the foundation:

(1) to promote people's engagement, particularly the contribution of teachers and of any other adults;
(2) to listen to students and to take their words seriously;
(3) to give priority to different teaching methods, specially those that favour students' participation either in school activities or elsewhere;
(4) to support the development of all new sorts of relations between schools and other institutions;
(5) to pass over the mere study of both the official political institutions (local, national or international) and of peoples' civic rights and duties, in order to deal with more actual social problems and students' interests. School must become a place where collective projects are created, where young people's expectations can be fulfilled.

The purpose of education for citizenship is to develop students' social skills, attitudes and values, as well as to reveal concepts that once being used by students as an intellectual tool, might encourage them to reflect critically upon those same skills, attitudes and values.

Education for Citizenship and Teacher Training

As we tried to make clear, education for citizenship and its disciplinary counterpart—civic education—covers a wide range of school procedures and processes. Openness to others, social engagement, project approaches, debates and critical reasoning, rejection of positivist knowledge, conceptualisation and reflexibility, institutional partnerships, merging of curriculum subjects, and so on, are some of the elements that distinguish the new educational paradigm from the more traditional ones. Such paradigm is a coherent and enduring construction, in which are combined a comprehensive set of skills, learning theories, teaching methods, knowledge assessment and evaluation instruments.

That new paradigm marks the emergence of post modernity in school systems, just as the impact of the post-modern mood of scepticism about modernity has helped to render teacher education centred in the university problematic and has contributed to the state of crisis which many teacher educators feel. Mainly because the role of teacher education lies in shaping a self with certain kinds of work-oriented vocational skills rather than a self with certain qualities and attitudes, with a certain kind of subjectivity. Teacher education, particularly for its emphasis on "serious" academical based study, did not provide "learning for its own sake", but training for a certain kind of citizenship. It still is an important instrument in the formation of the "liberal" citizen, individualistic, rationalistic, with a faith in benevolent progress through science and "truth".

Teacher education in the university is still based on the notion that theory and practice can be separated because each is located in its own separate domain, although we can now see that disciplinary knowledge (theory) is not a disembodied form but is itself inseparable from particular practices and personal educational philosophies. The latest have been found to be associated with teachers' conceptions of learning and teaching as well as with their conceptions of what they are learning. If we want to improve teacher education and to reinforce its role in changing teaching practices in the school, it is also indispensable to know the content and the structure of those conceptions.

Knowledge about Education

Knowledge about education can be described as an "outsider" view, usually university-based, expressed in prepositions, and positivist or ethnographic in its epistemology or assumptions about the nature of knowledge and how it is acquired. It is knowledge that comes from research on education, usually as a range of examples and illustrations.

Educational Knowledge

Firstly we think it is important to categorise educational knowledge pointing out our belief that it is a form of knowledge that is distinct from "scientific" prepositional knowledge in many ways, but it is no less systematic or rational. It is appropriate for teachers because they generate it from their practice and through dialogue with other reflective professionals, in a process we can say that it puts teachers at the heart of it. Therefore, it is possible to make a distinction between Educational Knowledge and Knowledge about education. This distinction brings about the separation of theories about education, which are rooted in an atomised "disciplines" approach and are theoretical-based, with a questionable direct relevance to practice, from educational theories which we can see as practical-based and holistically appreciated.

Challenges for Teacher Education

In our society, knowledge is considered to be a source of power and that is perhaps why professionals in other fields acquire power through their ownership of specialist knowledge. Teachers, however, apart the scientific knowledge they teach, are detached from the location of knowledge-as-power, since they are being told what to teach and what constitutes competent teaching. Therefore, they sometimes are viewed as low status executors, mainly because they are put apart from research and its findings by a division of labour between the "researchers" and the "researched", then loosing the opportunities to learn and develop...through research into (their own) practice a premise we see as being essential to change teachers' practices and to adapt teaching to new educational and social contexts.

Conclusion

The emergence of postmodernism in education, particularly in what concerns the relations between education for citizenship and teacher education centred in the university, gave rise to some paradoxical educational consequences. Firstly, it has contributed to the erosion of the "liberal" curriculum and an emphasis on learning opportunities that optimise the efficiency of the economic and social system. Secondly, the decentring of knowledge has resulted in a valuing of different sources and forms of knowledge and a corresponding devaluing of specialist discipline-based knowledge. The emphasis on experiential learning, both for students and teachers, is one example, although its apparent break with modernity is attenuated by its modernist self-understandings. What these consequences have in common is that they both reflect and give rise to greater uncertainty and conflict over the power and purpose of education, namely in the university.

The apparently non-instrumental nature of the liberal tradition in teacher education is being contested. It is actually possible to argue that liberal teacher education is in fact instrumental, not perhaps in a narrow sense, but in the sense of being directed towards the fulfilment of the project of modernity. Teacher trainers have therefore participated in fulfilling that goal and in particular the task of forming and shaping a certain kind of subjectivity and identity. University-based teacher education has played a vital role here too. Its goals, definition of needs, curriculum, pedagogy and organisational forms have been implicitly structured by the social engineering of the project of modernity. As a matter of fact, it has indeed functioned as one of the carriers of the message of modernity.

A new perspective regarding the place of disciplines in teacher education is required, as the practice of teacher education and training evolves into a variety of forms and is located in a multiplicity of sites under a diversity of programmes. However, it is also necessary to stress that it does not necessarily follow from this that disciplines can be forgotten or removed from scene. Instead, what need to be done are a reconsideration of their role and a reconfiguring of their place in the contemporary post-modern agenda. In relation to teacher education, therefore, the question is not so much whether disciplines have or should have a place, because that question has already been answered once teacher education understood itself as a field of study and once its regulatory potential becomes apparent. As teacher education moves to a mass system of higher education, with increased emphasis on adult students as one of the vehicles of school change, the worthwhileness of the knowledge-centred curriculum, the curriculum based on the study and mastery of disciplines, is increasingly brought into question and gradually downgraded.

11

ICT Venture and Re-Engineering of ODL System

B.C. MAHAPATRA and KAUSHAL SHARMA

The term *open distance learning* and its definition is relatively new in the field of education, having gained prominence only in the recent decades. The language and terms used to describe distance-learning activities can still be confusing, and geographical differences in usage. *Correspondence education, home study, independent study, external studies, continuing education, distance teaching, self-instruction, adult education, technology-based or mediated education, learner-centred education, open learning, open access, flexible learning and distributed learning* are the most commonly used terms for open distance learning.

In addition, Open Distance Learning (ODL) may also have different prior learning experiences, and have different learning styles, preferences, and coping strategies. These differences are important and must be addressed to meet the learners' diverse needs, and to improve the educational experience of distance learning. Although these differences are sometimes treated as marginal or remedial, they are central to Distance Education. Learners who are actively engaged in the learning process and sufficiently supported will be more likely to achieve success. On the other hand, the opposite will be true for learners who do not have the 'right' skills, mindset, and perspectives on distance learning, and whose problems may be worsened by lack of support from their respective distance teachers and institutions.

Today, Distance Education (DE) calls upon an impressive range of technologies to enable distance teachers and Distance Learning (DL) system, which are separated by distance to communicate with each other in real time (synchronous) and delayed time (asynchronous). This means that Distance Learners can access education and learning opportunities at a time, place, and pace to suit their individual lifestyles, learning preferences and personal development plans. Such separations according to Idrus and Lateh (2000) give rise to "an impressive and innovative array of media mix resulting in the application of technology in education". Such development offers a radical new direction for DE enthusiasts, teachers and learners alike, incorporating flexible and open learning methods as well as modified and specially created learning resources.

The main task of any ODL provider is to design and offer distance educational experience that encourages learning. As such, DE providers need to understand that its educational products and services are to facilitate DL process and provide an encouraging educational experience to distance learners. In doing so, many factors need to be considered in developing and delivering DE courses to achieve their effective and efficient implementation.

In the western countries more Information and Communication Technology ICT practices are going on due to Information Technology IT explosion its wider accessibility to the learners residing in rural areas. In India too, some innovative practices have been implemented to facilitate distance education. Some of them are:

- Developing IT hub at the universities or institutes,
- Launching of EDUSAT, i.e Educational Satellite,
- Spread of computer literacy programme for the teachers,
- Publishing e-books, developing e-learning materials, and
- Online programmes for capacity building of in-service teachers.

Beyond the print materials, traditional classrooms, teaching practices/strategies and the relationship, distance education leads the more innovative practices through ICT in fostering learning and fulfill the other needs of the learner.

Learning support is particularly important in DE because many Distance Learners, perhaps for the first time, are now "faced with a new learning environment and the expectation that they will have independent learning skills and the capacity to engage in activities that require self direction and self management of learning" (Mc. Loughlin and Marshall,2000:1). The development of educational technology and the use of media in ODE may add on the 'complexity' of becoming a distance learner. In the present generation of ODE, Distance Learners are required to engage in 'new' patterns of learning. To some students this new way of learning is accepted and does not impede learning. But to others, distance learning is 'not just a plea for knowledge', but a plea for continuous 'presence' of the teacher for learning to take place.

Recent technological developments have increased the overall amount of information available and improved accessibility to that information, while at the same time the costs of publishing information have decreased. These general shifts throughout society are true in education and have caused students to be more demanding and more knowledgeable about alternatives for their education. Combined with demographic trends, political forces, economic factors, the need for lifelong learning, and the changing emphasis in teaching and learning, there is a resurgence of interest in distance education both at traditional institutions of higher education and in organizations whose sole mission is distance education (Dede, 1990; Knott, 1992; Lewis and Romiszowski, 1996).

In the present era of human computer interaction, the educationally under privileged and the rural communities of India are being deprived of technologies that pervade the growing interconnected web of computers and communications. One good solution for this problem would be computers talking to the common man in the languages/he is comfortable to communicate in. A significant percentage of Indian population are educationally under-privileged. There are still quite a large number of areas where people do not have the capabilities of 3R's. The digital divide under such circumstances is constantly on a rise, where on one hand we claim that India is leading in IT sector and on the other hand, the advancement we make are great extent inaccessible by a large number of countrymen. Under such circumstances, we cannot expect rural/educationally under-privileged countrymen to use computers and IT products unless we remove the need of being literate, which exists as a barrier between them and computers.

Major World wide Issues in Education and Learning Process

In this information age, storage and retrieval of information in a convenient manner has gained importance. Because of the near-universal adoption of World Wide Web as a repository of information for unconstrained and wide dissemination, information is now broadly available on the Internet and is accessible from remote sites. However, the interaction between the computer and the user is largely through keyboard and screen-oriented systems. In Indian context, this restricts the usage to a miniscule fraction of the population, who are both computer-literate and conversant with written English. In order to enable wider proportion of population to benefit from information technology, there is a dire need for an interface other than keyboard and screen-interface that is widely in use at present. Speech, being a natural means of communication among human beings, can also provide a consummate platform for man-machine interaction. It is also desirable that human-machine interface permits one's native language of communication. In the context of a multi-lingual country like India, this can be of immense value to our country where literacy rate is considerably low. Certain efforts are currently been undertaken to develop DL and applications, which support the local languages. Localization efforts have been undertaken by most of the leading OS vendors and promoters, which include Microsoft (Windows), Red Hat (Linux), NCST (Indix), IIT Madras (IndLinux) etc. They have extended support some of the leading Indian languages by using international coding standards (Unicode). Speech technologies promise to be the next generation user interface. Software application having speech and voice recognition abilities have a better chance to communicate with a large percentage of population which include educationally under-privileged, visually challenged and computer illiterates, if these applications can speak and understand the native language. Hence we put forward the API (Application Programming Interface) Model based on Unicode for Text to Speech Synthesis and Automatic Speech Recognition in Indian languages.

The use of computer-mediated communication in distance learning to create online classrooms has become a popular means of distance learning, both in mixed mode with face-to-face instruction or as a sole channel of education at a distance. Online teaching or online instructions are limited to primary delivery by computer-mediated online instruction, as opposed to delivery systems such as audio or video/TV. The extension of quality education to remote and rural regions is a Herculean task for a country like India with multi-lingual and multi-cultural populations, separated by vast distances. Satellites can establish the connectivity between urban educational institutions, imparting quality education to the large number of rural and semi-urban educational institutes that lack the necessary infrastructure. One-way and two-way communication will be provided to rural sites via C-Band and high power Ku-Band spot beam coverage that has been implemented on EDUSAT by Indian Space Research Organisation (ISRO). EDUSAT is meant primarily for providing connectivity to school, college and higher levels of education and also to support non-formal education, including developmental communication. The five Ku-Band spot beams covering the country provide higher signal strength than previous INSAT satellites and allow the size of the receiving dish to be reduced.

The EDUSAT will provide a fillip to distance education in the entire country. It has specially been configured for the audio-visual medium, employing digital interactive classroom and multi-media, multi-centric system.

Institute of Communication and Technology, Bangalore is developing software and working on various projects in view of making of learners to overcome their burden of language limitations. *Vaartalaap* is one of the project aims to develop a solution that will cater to the communication needs of people speaking different languages. This has two core features namely MCC (Multilingual Communication Channel) and VC (Virtual Classroom). These features will enable people to communicate in their native language and participate in a virtual classroom and will also support multimedia collaboration along with logging and flexible replay of the session proceedings. The MCC (Multilingual Communication Channel) is a facility using which users will be able to communicate employing various media such as text, picture and voice. The VC (Virtual Classroom) is a simulation of a real-world classroom and provides teaching and learning environment within a computer-mediated communication system.

The most innovative venture of ICT in distance education is to produce any text material (online or offline) in a speech pattern. Most of the learners who have visual problems are withdrawing due to inability to read text may be benefited with this software. Another venture *Matrubhasha* is an Automatic Text-to-Speech and Speech Recognition software project enabling to convert English text into Indian Languages with speech output.

Bharateeya Open Office is the project aims at enabling the support of Indian Languages within the openoffice.org office suite on the main software platforms, so as to facilitate the digital representation, collection and distribution of information by ensuring access to information technology seamless over natural language barriers. Indian language support in the suite will be through localization of the complete user interface and help, in Hindi, Tamil, Kannada, Punjabi, Gujarati, Telugu, Bengali and Malayalam. Internationalization support will also be developed featuring editing and complex text layout processing in Indian scripts, Indian language currency, calendar and spell checking.

Facing the crisis in the era of technology in one of eight strategic business units of the Computer Society of India (CSI), it represents the organization's core activity in the domain of information, communications and space technology. The aim of the unit is to pilot and demonstrate the potential of these technologies for the benefit of India in different regions. This includes implementing relevant and sustainable applications to serve development needs, contributing to 'thought leadership' relating ICT to the India context, and performing custom solution development and consulting, especially to address the more complex ICT-related needs in the market.

Mobile educational systems have started to emerge as potential educational environments supporting life-long learning. However, these environments still suffer from various technological and access related problems in many parts of the world. While adaptivity in desktop based environments has attracted much attention and sophistication in e-learning environments, mobile learning is still struggling with basic technological and pedagogical problems. But there is much evidence that suggests that mobile technology is going to provide a natural extension for e-learning in the long run. With greater restrictions posed on mobile learners due to time, space and varied technical solutions available in different circumstances, adaptivity is expected to play even greater role.

Cross Lingual Information Retrieval

Most of the search engines do not allow querying in Indian languages. Even though a few offer screen layout and static text in Hindi, the querying and results retrieved are still in English. So a person literate in Indian languages but not well versed in English is deprived of access to a vast store of information. To bridge this Digital Language Divide, one of the key technologies required is Cross Lingual Information Retrieval (CLIR). The proposed CLIR system aims at enabling a person to query the web for documents related to health issues and obtain the results, in Hindi. Language problems are the barriers for integration of different region based people in India and as a whole for global market. Geographical cross border differences with cultural gaps among the people for making them to appear at a common platform there is need of avoiding communication gaps between them. Distance Learning System with the intervention of IT minimizes the barriers with any prospects.

Open Distance Learning and Multimedia Learning in India

Open and distance learning in India dates back to the 1960s. By the 1980s there were 34 universities offering correspondence education through departments designed for that purpose. The first single mode Open University was established in Andhra Pradesh in 1982, followed by the Indira Gandhi National Open University (IGNOU), and subsequently in Bihar, Rajasthan and Maharashtra, Madhya Pradesh, Gujarat, Karnataka, West Bengal, and Uttar Pradesh (established throughout the 1980s and 1990s). The establishment of these single mode distance education universities was stimulated by the government's intention to democratize education and make it lifelong. The initiative did not discourage the expansion at the same time of correspondence programmes in dual mode universities. The year 1995 witnessed the enrollment of 200,000 students in open and distance learning, accounting for 3 per cent of total higher education enrollment.

The Potential of Open and Distance Learning

As in every other walk of modern life, the answer to the challenge of education for development will include the use of information and communication technologies, provided the necessary organizational and policy changes can be implemented to make the technologies effective. A range of technological devices is now widely available and relatively cheap (e.g. CD-ROM, various Internet services). They are accepted and often available for domestic use as well as in the workplace. Governments are concerned that educational institutions become connected to the emerging networks, that curricula include the knowledge of and acquaintance with new technologies, and that teachers are prepared and trained to use these new resources. Among the benefits expected from new information and communication technologies, besides that of outreach, are efficiencies derived from economies of scale and qualitative improvements such as greater individualization of learning, easier access to information, and more use of simulation techniques. In addition, the use of new forms of technology will have an impact on the cognitive functions of children and youth.

In efforts to meet the new and changing demands for education and training, open and distance learning may be seen as an approach that is at least complementary and under certain circumstances an appropriate substitute for the face-to-face methods that still dominate most educational systems. While its benefits can be evaluated by technical, social and economic criteria, distance learning methods also have their own pedagogical merit, leading to different ways of conceiving knowledge generation and acquisition. To the learner, open and distance learning means more freedom of access, and thereby a wider range of opportunities for learning and qualification. The barriers that may be overcome by distance learning include not only geographical distance, but also other confining circumstances, such as personal constraints, cultural and social barriers and lack of educational infrastructure. For the student it is often a cheaper alternative to pursuing a course through conventional methods. Since many people cannot afford to leave their work in order to study, it is important that distance education and training may be combined with work. Distance and open learning may also mean a more learner-centred approach, allowing greater flexibility and choice of content as well as more personal organization of the learning programme.

For employers, open and distance learning offers the possibility of organizing learning and professional development in the workplace itself, which is often more flexible and saves costs of travel, subsistence etc. The use of distance learning often puts both the firm and employees in a position of coin vestment (of money and time) in the pursuit of common goals, based on shared values and culture. It increases productivity and supports the development of communication and other work-related skills. With sufficient numbers of employees being trained, open and distance learning is usually cost-effective. Other advantages for the employer include the increased availability of the employee during the course of the training programme, and the portability of training programmes and processes.

The emergence of the Internet and related networks such as the World Wide Web has had and will increasingly have radical effect on the transformation of education and training in all sectors. ICTs (Information and Communication Technologies) are effectively showing new dimensions to old ODLS setups. There is a reinforced thrust for an informed and participatory citizenry for efficient e-governance.

Web based e-Governance is the application of Information and Communication Technology (ICT) for delivering Government Services, exchange of information, communication transactions, integration of various stand-alone systems and services between University and Student (U2S), University and Other University (U2U) as well as Student and Student (S2S). Through the e-Governance, the Student services will be made available to the Student in a convenient, efficient and transparent manner.

The Distance Education Council (DEC), established under statute 28 of the IGNOU Act, 1985, is responsible for the promotion and coordination of the Open and Distance Learning(ODL) system in the country. The DEC has been taking various initiatives to maintain the standards of Distance Education in India. Of late, it has been seen that there is indiscriminate proliferation of Open and Distance Learning (ODL) Institutions in India.

Conclusion

It is a great opportunity that ODL system in world venture captures more than twenty per cent of higher education learners whereas only six per cent of university are working for facilitating the system of learning. There is need of re-engineering the system with Information Communication System (ICS) innovation by which interference requirement of learners can be fulfilled. Considering to Indian Higher Education System, Distance Education Council (DEC) with the understanding between the UGC, AICTE, RCI, NCTE, NCERT and NUEPA came to platform for overcoming educational barriers at any cost for achieving national goal. Indira Gandhi National Open University (IGNOU) and all other state Open Universities are leading the ODLS for promoting higher education. Madhya Pradesh Bhoj Open University(MPBOU) is the example becoming the Global Mega University as a state University by promoting some of the national programmes. It is also challenging task for providing teacher training programme i.e. B.Ed (Special Education) in four disability areas by MPBOU through distance mode. Considering the requirement of the society and facilities by ODL system Govt. should think for promoting the ODL system more and more.

REFERENCES

Dede, C.J. (1990). The evolution of distance learning: Technology-mediated Interactive learning. Journal of Research on Computing in Education. 22(3): 247-64

ICT, Research and Training Centre, India, 2002.

Knott, T.D., (1992). Determining societal needs for distance education in tomorrow's global village. Educational Media International. 29(3): 162-64

Lewis, J.H. and Romiszowski, A. (1996). Networking and the Learning Organization: Networking issues and scenarios for the 21st century. Journal of Instructional Science and Technology. 1(4) [Online.]

Mahapatra, B.C. Computer Aided Instruction: Psychological based learning, Dibrugarh University, Yearly Journal, Assam, 1999.

Mahapatra, B.C., *"Information Technology and Education"*, Sarup and Sons, Dariya Ganj, New Delhi, 2005.

McLoughlin, C. and Marshall, L. (2000). Scaffolding: A Model for Learner Support in an online teaching environment. In A. Herrmann and M.M. Kulski (Ed.). Flexible Futures in Tertiary Teaching: Proceedings of the IXth Annual Teaching Learning Forum, 2-4 Feb. 2000, Peerth: Curtain University of Technology.

Sharma K (2005), "Training for sustainable development", Swaroop and Sons, New-Delhi

12

Professionalism among Teachers in the Context of Globalisation

S.N. Sahoo

Teacher education has two components viz. theory of education and practice of education. The theory of education comprises learning of fundamental principles as derived from psychological, sociological and philosophical basis of education as well as teaching learning pedagogy etc. The purpose of theoretical knowledge is to orient the student teacher about major concepts of teaching, principles of learning, classroom, management, principles of evaluation and fundamental knowledge of communication process. After an acquaintance with the theoretical knowledge, the student teacher is thrown into the areas of teaching itself. But student teaching is not confined only to classroom teaching. Student teaching is very wide term that includes all those activities, which a teacher is expected to do in the school situation. The curricular, co-curricular and administrative duties that a teacher is called upon to discharge when he is employed in a school are to be learnt during his/her professional preparation. All these experiences are to be included in his preparation for the task.

Present Concerns in Teacher Education

Teacher Education programme in India is still not systematic. Teachers are adjusted in the certain system of Education at different levels like Primary, Secondary and Higher Secondary.

Present large scale recruitment of Para-teachers has diluted the identity of teachers as a professional. Present teacher training programmes neither accommodate the emerging ideas in context and pedagogy nor address the issue of linkages between school and society. There is less opportunity in teacher education programme for engagement of teachers with innovative educational experiment.

Teachers are required for different levels of schooling. Each level of schooling has students of different age groups studying various subjects and that necessitates different conceptual input and pedagogical treatment. Teachers training for such a situation needs clear vision and implementing strategies to attain the targets. The teacher-training course and the teacher educators courses recognized by the NCTE are expected to meet the objectives and attainment of goals.

Vision for Teacher Education

There are many determinants of quality of learning of which one is the quality of teachers. The quality of teachers lies in the quality of teachers training. It motivates and updates the knowledge of a teacher. The teacher education must become more sensitive to the emerging demands from the school system. Teacher should prepare themselves to face the following challenges in their field.

- Optimum utilization of human potentiality of a teacher being a responsible citizen in global context.
- Consistent efforts are needed for curricular renewal taking the consideration of societal needs and learners' interest.
- Professional and administrative contexts of the teacher education programme should be moulded with relevant aspects.
- Technical knowledge, skills, proficiency in language should be included in teacher training programme for learners' necessary point of view.

- Necessary learning needs should be indented in teacher training programme for children including those who are marginalized and disabled.
- In the context of respective change it is imperative to pursue an integrated model of teacher education for profesionalisation of teacher preparation.

Professional Aspects of Teacher Education

Teaching is the largest profession among all professions. Still it is not given a status of a profession. It has resulted in poor quality of teachers, which has led to development of the poor quality of human resource. It is a huge loss of nation. Therefore, to neglect quality of teachers is not affordable. For improving quality of teachers' training, recruitment, selection and retention are the important variables in professional context of education system. Manpower planning is an effective tool to achieve this objectives. Assessing the supply and demand of teachers involves an analysis of complicated relationship between different variables to gain insight in to the expected number of teachers employed throughout a period and the number of teacher required in the future. Various types of techniques are used to assess the supply and demand of teachers.

In Teacher Education Programme, student teachers are concerned with the classroom teaching only. They do not find time to acquaint themselves with the broader functioning of the school. They are also deprived of the opportunity of under gaining any experience of co-curricular or administrative nature. The student teachers are deprived of developing teacher like qualities. The isolated student teaching programme therefore does not remain conductive to the development of professionalism among the student teachers. Keeping this in view the NCTE has advocated internship programme for student teaching. The NCERT has even goal for experimenting with the ideas of internship by extending the duration of the existing one-year teacher education programme to two years. The basic idea behind the internship programme is that the:

responsibility of training a teacher should not lie only with the training institution, but should be shared by school system also. In this way teachers are expected not to limit themselves to theory only rather practical activities at school level (internship) will make rigorous teacher education system more professional.

Global Reality in Teacher Education

In a learning society the teacher must be the role model for value education and life long learning. They too must acquire knowledge and pedagogical skills necessary to prepare students in a highly technological and global society. The recent years have witnessed the sources and distribution of information have developed in a spectacular fashion almost everywhere. Increasingly, children come to school earning the imprint of a world far beyond the boundaries of family or the community. The teacher will be expected to use a wide reportoire of teaching styles in order to teach, motivate and reach each of these young people. Learning and teaching well integrated, uses of technology and school restructuring will be interwoven. In the coming decade the knowledge will be the power. The teacher being the resource hub of knowledge will assure the leadership to the community. Like other professional group now they must face the fact that their initial training will not see them through the rest of their life. They will need to update and improve their own knowledge and techniques through out their lifetime.

In coming years, partnership building will be crucial for teaching profession. There will be an increasing emphasis on the importance of home-school and community-school links and community participation will be given due emphasis. Teacher as the social workers and instructors will play the role of catalysts for strengthening the linkages. No system of Education, no syllabus, no methodology and no textbook can rise above the level of the teachers. If a nation wants quality education it must have teachers of high quality. It is the high time to think and rethink how to build the future with vision blended with action.

REFERENCES

MHRD, DOE (1986), National policy on Education 1986, Govt. of India, New Delhi.

MHRD, DOE (1992), Programme of Action—National Policy on Education 1986, Govt. of India. New Delhi.

NCFSE (2000), National Curriculum Framework for School Education, NCERT. New Delhi.

NCF (2005), National Curriculum Frame Work NCERT, New Delhi.

Reynold, A. (1992), What is competent beginning teaching: a review of literature. Review of Educational Research, 62, I, 1-35.

Teacher Education Curriculum, A Frame work NCERT, New Delhi.

13

Making Teacher Preparation Responsive

DHANANJAI YADAV

Globalization and knowledge economy are the facts leading to changes in the way we see our social, educational and business needs. These changes create a growing focus on the importance of lifelong learning. The key to lead success is to have quality education. The mind is not an empty vessel to be filled in but a fire to be ignited. The smoke from the teachers continuously nurtures their students until the fire in students' mind gets ignited. It is the job of the welfare state to provide its citizens best education in the world. Every citizen must know his/her potentials and skills to succeed in knowledge economy of 21st century.

According to New Growth Economics a country's capacity to take advantage of the knowledge economy depends on how quickly it can become a "learning economy'. Learning means not only using new technologies to access global knowledge, it also means using them to communicate with other people about innovation. In the "learning economy" individuals, firms, and countries will be able to create wealth in proportion to their capacity to learn and share innovation (Foray and Lundvall, 1996; Lundvall and Johnson, 1994). Formal education, too, needs to become less about passing on information and focus more on teaching people how to learn. At the level of the organization learning must be continuous.

Organizational learning is the process by which organizations acquire tactit knowledge and experience. Such knowledge is unlikely to be available in codified form, so it cannot be acquired by formal education and training. Instead it requires a continuous cycle of discovery, dissemination, and the emergence of shared understandings. Successful firms are giving priority to the need to build a "learning capacity" within the organization.

Lifelong Professional Development

Lifelong learning is learning at all stages of life. It encompasses the complete range of human experience, a human potential development model for the future, not an education or training model for the present. The importance of lifelong learning has led to an explosion of innovative ideas and programmes. It changes the education paradigm in favour of more courses, better teaching and learning and poses new challenges to the policies and strategies that promote access to education. Distance learning, whether in the form of e-learning/online learning or other mode of delivery, is a remarkable contribution and promotion of lifelong learning. Teacher education should be so designed that it not only promotes lifelong learning but also knowledge sharing, participation and the building of e-learning communities for life long professional development.

Recognition to Autonomy of Learner

The teacher's role would be more subtle and challenging than that of an artist or a sculptor, because a teacher, unlike an artist or a sculptor works with an infinitely subtle. Therefore, teacher education if it has to respond to the challenges of Future's India, its curriculum and process of transaction may have to undergo a paradigm shift. The new teacher will recognize the autonomy of the learner, follow the principles of true teaching and use the concept of integral education for raising the consciousness level of the child.

Value Orientation

Teacher education programmes are expected to provide 'training' not only in pedagogy but also in behavioural attributes including attitudes. motivation, perceptions, preferences, appreciation and value orientation. The courses of study generated for the purpose have, over the years, been broadened in scope from their original emphasis on pedagogic considerations within classrooms, to include several understandings and practices useful for teachers. This continues to be a challenge even today and is likely to persist in the years to come.

Global Perspective

The complexity of teacher education in our country and the challenge of providing quality school education to the children have been the concerns of educationists since long. India is the second most populous nation in the world. The challenge is to provide them proper education so that they will be able to enhance their quality of life. Recent advancements in communication and information technologies have changed the world in to a global village. In principle, each person can contact in real time to any other person in the world through the Internet. Through satellite communication important events that are taking place at any corner of earth are reaching our homes at once. Therefore, education has to be contextualized and at the same time has to have a global perspective since the children are going to become citizens of a global society. This has been rightly emphasized by some thinkers as globalization with localized frame of reference.

Updating Learning

In the age of information technology due to rapid changes in science and technology the nature of future world has become unpredictable. The children, those who are going to enter the school now, will remain a part of the school system at least for the next 12 years, i.e. till the year 2017 and as adults may have to contribute to the world of work for another 35 years. As changes in science and technology are frequent and unpredictable it is not possible to envisage what the nature of occupations will be in the next twenty or fifty years. We, therefore, cannot anticipate today, the skills and abilities that children would need for living effectively for their full span of adulthood. Therefore, the vocational situation that prevailed during most of the 20th century will not hold now. It would now be necessary that the young persons be prepared right from the beginning as life long learners.

Shifting Focus to Learners

Children of today when they grow up will have to continually update themselves with the new technologies and the changing nature of occupations. It is in such a context, the emphasis of learning at the school level will require a shift from teacher-centered to being learner-centered. The principal task of teachers will be to enable children with the ability of learning how to learn. For learning how to learn, it would be necessary that teachers recognize the autonomy of learners and reorganize teaching learning around using human brain for developing thinking skills rather than using the brain for storing information.

Since the children of today have to live in the information age, autonomy of learner has to be valued first. Each learner has the capacity to learn on his own and can construct own knowledge. Therefore teacher education has to be remoulded for preparing such teachers who can help the system to prepare life long learners. Since each person has to adjust to the changing nature of the world of work, which would take place because of new developments in science and technology.

Relook to Pedagogical Analysis

Context-based, stage-specific objectives and transaction strategies have been suggested which have tremendous scope for refinement. It introduces the concept of pedagogical analysis in a focused perspective and highlights its significance in preparation of teachers with analytical competencies. This would be highly needed for future teachers who will have to bring new ideas and concepts in the curricula regularly and at the same time learn to discard what becomes redundant.

Reflecting Constitutional Values

Teacher preparation programmes must be designed with due prominence and strategies critical to the awareness of fundamental rights and commitment to fundamental duties, particularly the aspects of national development, secularism, national integration, social cohesion and value inculcation. The perceived characteristics of the envisaged curriculum framework would suggest that it reflects the Indian heritage, acts as an instrument in the realization of national goals.

Thrust on Thinking Skills

The availability of inexpensive devices for storing information has made the use of human brain as a memory device redundant. Though computers can store and analyze a large amount of information but they lack the ability to think that a human brain has. So the thrust of learning will have to be now on developing in children the ability to think and for making them problem solvers and creative thinkers.

The teacher's role will also shift from that of a person who controls learning in children by pouring information in their brains to that of a person who facilitates their learning by nurturing their thinking skills. Each child is endowed with the capacity to construct his/her knowledge. Therefore, pedagogy, which recognizes the diverse learning styles of children and that the children have the capacity to construct their knowledge, may have to be learnt by student-teachers in their pre-service courses.

Teacher as Learning Facilitator

Nothing can be taught. The teacher is not an instructor or taskmaster rather a helper and a guide. His/her business is to suggest and not to impose. S/he does not actually train the pupil's mind; S/he does not impart knowledge; s/he just shows how to acquire knowledge. S/he does not call forth the knowledge that is within; s/he only shows where it lies and how it can be habituated to rise to the surface. The mind has to be consulted in its own growth. The idea of hammering the child into the shape designed by the parents and teachers is barbarous and ignorant superstition. It is the child who must be induced to expand in accordance to his/her own nature.

Making Teacher Education Curriculum Relevant

The changed scenario of teaching learning can impart radical changes in teacher education. The teacher education programmes that are followed throughout the length and breadth of the country have remained static both in form and content for over 100 years. The pedagogy which was introduced in the later part of the 19th century, relevant to the society then, has continued in its unchanged form not only throughout the 20th century but even today teacher educators follow the same nineteenth century teacher education curriculum, which obviously is no longer relevant.

Preparing for Holistic School Education

An examination of the curriculum framework reveals that the curriculum framework focuses on affective and conative domains, by highlighting commitment and performance, it also apportions adequate weightage to the cognitive aspects through the development of scientific and technological literacy, use of information technology and emerging communication system. New thrust of schooling process will have to be on helping each child to raise its level of consciousness and for use of mental faculties for both intellectual and emotional growth. So the challenge of teacher education will be to prepare such teachers as can take care of the holistic education of children. This would require a total shift of the teacher education curriculum from its present rigid structure of theoretical foundation courses to courses for learning of pedagogy of teaching various school subjects. It has to be now on preparing teachers who can have a comprehensive view of their role as true gurus who can nurture child's holistic development.

Conclusion

Effective and creative mechanisms to upgrade teacher education from its low academic status have yet to be generated. There is still a need for providing better-qualified and interested persons who desire to be associated with elementary education and teacher education. This requires a structural flexibility with an appropriate incentive system.

REFERENCES

Barro, Robert J. and Xavier Sala-i-Martin. (1995) Economic Growth, McGraw-Hill. New York.

Foray. D. and B. D. Lundvall, (1996) The Knowledge-Based Economy: From the Economics of Knowledge to the: OECD, pp. 11-32. Learning Economy, in Employment and Growth in the Knowledge-based Economy, Paris

Gardner. R. 'On-Service Teacher Education', in Second International Encyclopedia of Education. Pergamon Press, Vol. X, 1994. p. 5978.

Ministry of Human Resource Development. Government of India. National Policy on Education, 1986, Pt. 9.6.

Ministry of Human Resource Development, Government of India, Communication No. F 7-10/87-TE. L dated 13th July 1988 cited by B.N. Koul and M.B. Menon, in 'Teacher Education through Distance Mode', Indian Journal of Open Learning, Vol. 1, No. 2 July 1992, pp. 1-9.

MHRD, Government of India, 'Towards Enlightened and Human Society', Report of the Committee for Review of National Policy on Education, 1986, Part I. 1990, p. 309.

NCTE (Department of Teacher Education, NCERT) National Curriculum for Teacher Education, 1988.p. 11.27, p. IV.2, p. IV.3, p. V.8 and p. V.8

NCTE (Department of Teacher Education, NCERT). Committee Report, 1991.

Peter Druker, The Age of Discontinuity; Guidelines to our Changing Society, Harper and Row, New York. 1969. ISBN 046508944.

UGC, Resolution on Correspondence Courses for Teacher Education, 1991.

UGC, Report of the Curriculum Development Centre in Education (CDCE), 1990, pp. 12-13.

III

Professional Ethics and Values

14

Constructivist Approach to Teacher Preparation on Value Education

P.K. Sahoo

Values occupy significant role in shaping individual and social life. Basically values are concerned with guiding forces for determining directions of life and choosing desirable behaviour in society. Abstract qualities like truthfulness, beauty, goodness, peace, respect for co-existence of living and non-living being, justice, freedom and dutifulness are some of the examples of human values. Values qualify with its worthiness to be chosen. John Dewey had perceived values as the act of cherishing something, holding it dear and also the act of passing judgement upon the nature and amount of its value as compared with something else. It is an object of interest as well as the basis of making judgement on any object. Kluckhohn (1957) defined value as "a conception, explicit or implicit, distinctive of an individual or characteristics of a group of these desirable which influences the selection from available modes, and ends of action." He further commented that value is a "conception of the desirable" and not something "merely desired." Values are also associated with the principles and standard of life. It may be contextual as well as universal. It may be enduring as well as changing. What is more significant in value is that it forms—an integral component of personality. Development of personality not taking cognizance of value development indicates handicap in development process. Values are not merely expression of feelings. They must involve rational content and reflective thinking (Seetharm, 2004). Moreover, they are expressed in the forms of human activities. Values are of comprehensive nature, having affective. cognitive and action components of personality. Human and social values are not to be perceived in isolation, since they are interlinked with total value system in holistic form. The major concern of us is to identify such values in the context of well being of total system incorporating existence of animate and inanimate objects on the earth. Even though certain values have universal charater its contextuality occupy significance in a given socio-cultural environment. The socio-cultural milieu play a major role in shaping value system of associated groups. Hence, variations occur in value system of one group from another. 'Strong socio-psychological factors influence value system of human being. Hence value development process must take care of such contextual factors into consideration.

Among different kinds of values morality occupies a significant position from the point of its humanistic appeal. To Peters (1981) morality is concerned with "what there are reasons for doing or not doing, for bringing into or removing from existence." A moral person is not only a person who does the right thing but also one who does the right thing for the right reason. In the process of making right choices the individual adopt moral values. It justifies its role as a mode of conduct or end state of existence. Morality is not concerned so much with 'what is' as with 'what ought to be' and 'what ought to be done.' It is associated with the 'ends' as well as with 'means'. There are some thinkers who link moral values with spirituality. The concept of self realisation is very much linked high order moral and spiritual values. To Bhyrappa (1968) "a moral notion that refuses to recognise its own roots remains vapoury." Moreover "unless morality matures into spiritual perfection it cannot get its fullest justification." Spiritual values are reflected in pursuit of inner source of life and seeing one self in others self. The seers like Sathya Sai Baba elaborates spiritual values as very nature of human being. The value as focused by Sri Sathya Sai Institute of Higher Learning read as Turth, Right Conduct, Love, Non-violence, and Peace. Unless these values are practiced, man is not treated as man. Every human being, by human values, prove himself to be man, in both *'akara'* (in form) and *'achara'* (in conduct). To Sathya Sai Baba, human values are inherent in human being. The major role of education is to bring out such values inherent inside him. Values can not be imposed from outside environment rather they need to be manifested through education. Moreover, manifestation is associated with human conduct which takes place in the form of interaction with external and internal environment. The process of value development programme has been shaped as 'Educare' (Sri Sathya Sai Education Institute, 2000).

Changing Scenario of Values

As presented above contextuality in terms of time and place have strong effect of human and social values. Social development phased in terms of technological interventions as characterised by different waves indicate different value patterns for society passing through different waves. Maynard and Mehrtens (1993) viewed the value discrepancies in the industrial society, post industrial society and the knowledge based society of 4th wave in following ways. The Industrial Society's values were rooted in materialism and the supremacy of man. Moral and ethical values like honesty and integrity were treated subservient to ensuring the means of self-preservation and competitive success. The post industrial society got identified with the values for balance and sustainability. It tended to be more sensitive to the sanctity of life, to the limits on natural resources and to spiritual development of people. Considerations like reducing environmental risk, providing service to others and creation of opportunities for personal growth and self fulfilment have been rated with prime importance in the third wave society. It also witnessed the emerging concern for values like dignity, integrity and inner peace.

There has been a tendency of searching things as meaning, purpose, inner authority and peace, truth, love, compassion, self worth, dignity, wisdom, a higher power, and a sense of unity with others. The value of combining intuitive knowledge and traditional analytical skills have been well accorded in the knowledge society. Major value shifts have been witnessed in the form of 'from competition to co-operation', 'from independence to interdependence', 'from exploitation to caring', 'from materialism to spirituality', and 'from consumerism to a concern for social and economic justice'. There is a growing concern for moving away from materialism towards intangibles like honesty, truth, courage, conviction, the quality of relationships and self realisation. The trend of moving towards wholeness and integration of experiential intuitive knowledge have a lot of implications for a learning society. In this context, educational system must be cautious of such developments and review its role in value development.

Constructivism

Development in the field of learning has witnessed a gradual paradigm shift from behaviourism to constructivism. Behaviourism focused on learning environment where the learners role was response oriented followed by feedback. Cognitivism emphasized on learners placing new information in long term memory. Creating environment for learners exposure to large amounts of information through text-books, lectures and computer-based multimedia programmes served the purpose of cognitivism. Information used to be transmitted from one end (teacher) to the other (learner) through alternative means. Constructivism focusses on learners active participation in the process of construction of knowledge representation in working memory. According to this view, the learner is a sense maker while the teacher acts as a cognitive guide providing guidance and modeling on authentic academic tasks. Constructivism is perceived as a philosophy of learning having a premise that, by reflecting on our experiences we construct our own understanding of the world we live in.

- Constructivism has the following principles (UNESCO, 2002).
- Learners build personal interpretation of the world based on experiences and interactions.
- Knowledge is embedded in the context in which it is used (authentic tasks in meaningful realistic settings).
- Create novel and situation-specific understandings by "assembling" knowledge from diverse sources appropriate to the problem at hand (flexible use of knowledge).

Learners participation in constructing knowledge focuses on searching for meaning by understanding the problems at hand in a holistic framework and not in isolation. The teacher must understand the mental models that students use to perceive the world and the assumptions they make to support those models. There is little scope for imitations, memorisation, passive reception of information and reproduction of current answers to a question. In place of these, instruction consists of experiences that facilitate knowledge construction.

Constructivist Approach to Value Development

Constructivist standpoint of learning can contribute a lot towards value development activities in teacher education programmes. It ensures that the learners must identify value laden issues in real life situations.Accordingly the Problems in hand must be analysed with the help of various interpretative and intellectual support systems surrounding it. Different kinds of cognitive and collaborative tools can be used to manipulate information, find meaning in it and co-construct meaning for the same.

The major drawbacks of value education programme as witnessed with regard to instructional system treat values in isolated form and transmit knowledge/facts related to values not focussing on experiencing the values in contextual and holistic framework. Value education needs reviewing the existing theoretical paradigm of teaching learning system and refocussing on making it experiential, context specific, interdisciplinary and holistic. The learners' involvement in teaching learning situations need to be facilitated with a view to empowering them to think right, to feel the right kind of emotions and to act in the desirable manner. Hence, value education must focus on learners' participation in cognitive, affective and action components of personality development and making it meaningful and relevant to their life.

The role of the teacher educator is of utmost importance in assisting learners to build constructivist environment. Such environment is built by the students with a view to identification of issues and questions, identification of appropriate sources of learning, gathering important information, promotion of collaborative experiences of learners in decision making about how to manipulate the environment, making articulation of learners' ideas and their reflection on the processes they used. The teacher education system must act as intellectual support system in this regard.

Curricular Issues in Value Education

Theoretically, every education system is value oriented. The school curriculum aims at development of proper attitudes, values and skills for holistic development of learners. However, special emphasis of value education remains on development of awareness, sensitivity, appreciation and reflective thinking about social/moral values among children, facilitating opportunity to make judgements about what is good and appropriate, choose among the competing values and internilisation of values. Value education curriculum is both explicit as well as hidden. The hidden curriculum of value education is reflected in subject curriculum, curricular practices, evaluation processes and provision of suitable opportunities for value education programme.

For instance, every component of subject curriculum has value orientation. Science education enables learners to be committed towards free inquiry, rationality, open mindedness, objectivity etc. Social Science focusses on development of values like universal brotherhood, environment friendliness, unity in diversity, civic sense and interdependence. Language and literature contribute towards development of aesthetic sense of life, sensitivity, creative expression and appreciation. An institution sensitive towards hidden curriculum of value education reflects on value education embedded in subject driven teaching learning situations. Enabling teachers to identify value components in every aspect of school curriculum and to empower learners to participate in different kinds of value oriented activities need to be focussed in such programmes. Organisation of teaching learning activities with humanistic touch and promoting experience based learning might be encouraged by teachers.

Explicit curriculum on value education incorporating moral and spiritual values need careful treatment at curriculum development stage as well as curricular transaction stage. Gradation of moral development curriculum must have sound psychological and human base with context specific considerations.

Such curriculum follows significant principles. Some of them read as (Gulati, 2004).

- Conviction that values can be fostered through deliberately planned experiences in schools.
- Value education promotes unconditional striving for goodness.
- Value education is concerned with the total personality i.e. cognitive, affective and conative (knowing, feeling and doing)
- Education in values follows a process—awareness, appreciation, willingness, conviction and action.
- Education in values involves the process of exploration, thinking, reflection and not imposition.
- Education for values to be integrated with the entire school system.
- There is no one prescriptive way to provide education for vlues—Different models can be worked out for this purpose.

- Pedagogy for value inculcation involves commitment, conscious planning and implementation strategies.

As presented above value education must focus on experiential learning activities carried out by learners in liberal environment. Teachers' role is very much significant in helping learners to create conducive environment for experiential learning so that learners make use of learning resources for exploration, articulation and reflection on different value based experiences.

Teacher Education in Promoting Value Education

Teacher Education plays a vital role in sensitising teachers about value education programme. It also, aims at enabling teachers to initiate value education programmes with commitment, to guide the direction of student inquiry, to promote learners' participation in exploring values, preferring values in solving complex problems, imbibing them and reflection of values in day to day life. The teacher's involvement in designing constructivist learning environment is encouraged with a view to help learners in independent thinking, reflection of ideas on crucial issues, exploring values, collaborative efforts in solving problems and interpretation of experiences which may contribute to development of values.

The objectives of teacher education programme need to be articulated with a view to enable teachers in:

(i) understanding the concept, principle and relevance of value education;
(ii) identifying and promoting value education components hidden in subject curriculum;
(iii) designing constructivist environment for learners' participation in development of social, moral and spiritual values;
(iv) transacting value education curriculum by means of helping learners in planning and organisation of different activities;

(v) conducting continuous assessment and evaluation of learners' progress in value development by means of learner initiated assessment through self analysis of thinking, feeling and action.

Proposed Course Content of Teacher Preparation on Value Education

Unit 1: Meaning, Nature and definition of values, Types of Values, Theories of Values, Relationship between Values and Education.

Unit 2: Nature and Concept of Value Education. Sociological, Psychological, Religious and Philosophical Dimensions of Value Education, Need and Significance of Value Education at School Stage with Special emphasis on Moral Education.

Unit 3: Moral Development of the Learner; Stages of Moral Development: Piagetian theory; Kohlberg theory; R.F. Peck and R.J. Havinghurst's theory of Character Development; J. Loevinger's Model of ego development; Maslow's theory of Need Hierarchy and Moral Development and N.J. Bull's theory of Moral Development.

Unit 4: Value Education Curriculum; Value Development as a component of hidden curriculum; Development of values associated with subject curriculum; Value education curriculum as a special component of school education; Objectives and Organisation of Curriculum of Social, Moral and Spiritual values at elementary and secondary stage.

Unit 5: Value Development Strategies vis-a-vis Constructivism; Different Methods and Approaches to Value Development; Self Study: Yoga and Meditation, Review of Texts on Social and Moral Values, Value Analysis Model, Community Intervention Model, Role play, Simulation and Gaming Solution of problems in Virtual Environment, Workshop, Project Method, Parents and Community participation in value education, Visits to Value Education Institutions and Social Service organizations.

Unit 6: Assessment and Evaluation of Value Development of Learners, Continuous and Comprehensive Evaluation of Value Education in the context of total curriculum, Monitoring of Value Education Activities, Self evaluation exercises, Peer evaluation, Teacher assessment and feedback, Internal Evaluation of Projects, group activities, community intervention services, Evaluation of cognitive, Affective and Action Components, Rating and Gradation of value development, Individual and Group performance.

Learning Resources in Value Education of Teachers

Different kinds of learning resources can be made available while accommodating contextual factors. Some of them read as: biographies, scriptures, proverbs, hymns, thoughts of great personalities on socio-political system, stories, moral dilemmas, institutional experiences on implementation of value education programmes, project reports on value education submitted by school children, teachers and teacher trainees, recorded personal experiences group experiences in dealing with contextual problems, intervention strategies on conducting social services, environment conservation, protection of human rights etc. Such resources need to be explored by trainees through self initiatives at local level, institutional level as well as at a wider level. The role of Information and Communication Technology (ICT) play a significant role in this context.

Learning Activities

Various kinds of learning activities can be explored and organized in promoting of values with emphasis on cognitive, affective and action dimensions. Some such activities which may be organized with involvement of trainees are:

- Yoga, meditation, prayer, Self study of scriptures, classical stories like Jataka Kathas, Pancha Tantra and Self reflection exercises
- Problem solving exercises

- Value Discussion/Clarification of conflicting;
- Preparation of value dilemma for creating and resolving conflicts in values;
- Simulated activities in solving problems;
- Role play, Drama, Poetic recitals dealing with value conflicts in virtual environment;
- Group projects; Group discussion on moral and ethical issues; Workshops. Community services, participation in corporate life, Hospital services, *Shram* Dan, Blood donations, Serving needy group, Literacy activities. cleaning the campus, Gardening, Visits to places of worship of different faiths;
- Personality Development Retreats organised with focus on community living, self control, sharing and caring respect for other faiths, co-operation, tolerance, sacrifice etc.;
- Visits to Missionary Organisations, Value Education Institutions and Interaction with eminent Personalities.

Methods and Strategies

Learner Centred Methods and strategies must be highlighted in the context of organization of different kinds of learning activities on value education. The teacher trainees need to be made competent in application of following methods and strategies:

- Group Work Strategy
- Co-operative Learning
- Workshop
- Value Development Models of Teaching like Value Analysis Model and Jurisprudential Inquiry Model
- Project Method
- Interdisciplinary Lesson
- Yoga and Meditation
- Fostering Creativity through Synectics
- Monitoring and evaluation strategies for value judgement and development.

Framework of Evaluation

Self assessment exercises, Peer Evaluation sessions, continuous monitoring of learning activities, feedback mechanism, peer/ teacher evaluation and internal evaluation may focus on continuous progress of learners; Evaluation of Group projects, Yoga practicals, and Tests can be applied for continuous monitoring and evaluation of value education. Practicals/ Projects need to be given 60 per cent credit weightage while the remaining 40 per cent weightage may be given on theory components of curriculum.

Conclusion

It is high time to strengthen value education component in teacher education which can serve two purposes. First is to orient teachers on humanism, moral and spiritual values and second is to empower them on development and implementation of value education curriculum at school level. The above presentation on the constructivist framework of value education programme in teacher education may act as a source for reflection of curricular issues and problems on value education. Emphasis on participatory and experiential learning can serve the purpose of value education. Preparing teachers to build constructivist environment for moral and spiritual values poses a challenge for teacher education. Collaborative efforts need to be made to share fruitful experiences of teachers and teacher educators in this direction.

REFERENCES

Bhyrappa, S.L. (1968) Values in Modern Indian Educational Thought, New Delhi: NCERT (Memeo).

Gulati, S. (2004) Teaching Techniques on Value Education, New Delhi: NCERT (Memeo).

Kluckhohn, C. (1957) "Values and Value Education in the theory of Action". In T. Parsons and E.A. Shills (Eds) Towards a General Theory of Social Action. Cambridge: Harvard University Press.

Maynard, H.B. and Mehrtens, S.E. (1993). The Fourth Wave, Business in the 21st Century. San Francisco: Berrett Koehler Publishers.

Peters, RS. (1981). "Moral Development and Moral Education, London: George Allen and Unwin Co.

Seetharam, A.R (2004). Concept and Objectives of Value Education, Mysore: Ramakrishna Institute of Moral and Spiritual Education (Memeo).

Senapaty, H.K. (2003) Package for Orientation of Teacher Educators of lASEs and CTEs on Training Strategies, Bhubaneswar: RIE (Memeo).

Sri Sathya Sai Education Institute, Mumbai (2000), 'Sri Sathya Sai Educare'.

UGC, New Delhi (2001) UG Model Currkulum, Education.

UNESCO, Paris (2002) Information and Communication Technology for Teacher Education.

15

Professional Development through Interpersonal Relations

MOHD. MIYAN and PRIYA KHANNA

A performance oriented and competency based teacher education programme has been emphasized time and again by various commissions and committees to improve the process and product of education system. This emphasis is all the more relevant in today's scenario as the role of a teacher has become much more complex, challenging and multifarious demanding a variety of skills, abilities and traits. This change is driven by the explosion of knowledge, advancement in technology and inclusion of new techniques in pedagogy and has also affected the relationships of persons working in the organization called school. The rate of change will continue to accelerate requiring a sound teacher education programme to prepare professionally competent teachers to face these new challenges and to work as efficient human resources strengthening the performance of the organization they are working for and to enable the organization transform its vision and mission into desired actions and results.

School, like any other organization may be defined as a consciously coordinated social unit of interdependent individuals working together or separately with a common purpose of providing products and services *(education)* to individuals, communities, and societies. There are four denominators common to all organizations (Bhalla, 2004):

Purpose, products/services, and processes define why the organization exists, what products and services it provides or intends to provide and the activities required for providing those products and services.

Roles and responsibilities explain the roles individuals play and their accountabilities in achieving the organizational purpose.

Integration of resources involve partnerships, alliances, and human and non-human resources required for achieving the organizational purpose.

Competencies define the skills, knowledge, and behaviours, which are required to perform the allotted role for achieving the aims and objectives of an organization. These can be categorized as technical and enabling competencies.

Technical Competencies

These are related to teacher's knowledge of subject matter to be taught and understanding of the basic principles of pedagogy for transacting that knowledge effectively across the learners by creating appropriate learning environment. Technical competencies, though necessary but are not sufficient to work effectively in an organization. Hence teachers need to develop enabling competencies as well.

Enabling Competencies

These involve abilities and skills (generally termed as Human skills/People Skills/Interpersonal skills) which enables a teacher to work with, understand and motivate the other members of the organization called school. These skills are necessary for the development of professional interpersonal relationships and productive working partnerships. (Robbins, 1991; Khanna, et al., 1998).

While it is much easier to buy technology and access resources, both financial and material, it is impossible to buy human processes and skills (such as effective negotiation, leadership development etc).

Studies have reported that primary deficiency in today's business school graduates is not their inability to perform analytical tasks and decision making but it is their people or interpersonal skills (Robbins, 1991). The lack of interpersonal skills and positive behaviour was found to be one of the reasons for teacher *burnout*, a well documented and well-known phenomenon which received considerable attention in past few years (Glasgow and Cathy, 2003).

However, the main thrust of the theory and practicum of the present teacher education curriculum is to equip teachers with technical competencies including understanding and application of various techniques to modify their classroom behaviour (primarily through microteaching, simulation and interaction analysis). Developing enabling competencies and interpersonal skills in teachers to understand the variables affecting their 'out of classroom' behaviour and their influence on the interpersonal relationships and performance of the organization still remains a neglected area in the teacher education programme.

Understanding of the various aspects of human behaviour relevant for organizational performance comes under the domain of *Organizational Behaviour* which is an *interdisciplinary behavioural science* studying the structure and dynamics of organizations and their various human units namely, individuals, dyads, teams, interteams and organizations. Dynamics of organization can be studied both at individual level and at the interactive level. Individual level is concerned with the concept of perception, development of personality, attitudes, motivation of members of organization and stress dynamics whereas interactive dimension of organizational behaviour involves the study of interpersonal relationships, group dynamics, leadership, power and politics, communication, and organizational conflicts. Certain concepts in development of interpersonal behaviour which are generally neglected in teacher education programme are discussed below:

Dynamics of Interpersonal Relationships

Organizations, by definition, require people to work together and communicate with one another. Such interpersonal relationships, if productive, cooperative and satisfying, enhance the performance of the employee as well as that of organization.

A conceptual framework to study the dynamics of human behaviour and interpersonal relationships in an organization is called *Transactional Analysis* (TA). Transactions are the exchanges of verbal and non-verbal signals between people that consist of no less than one stimulus and one response. The objective of transactional analysis is to provide a comprehensive understanding of how people relate to one another in an organization so that they can develop improved communication and healthy and productive human relationships. Transactional analysis mainly involves: *Structural analysis,* proposing people interact with each other from one of the three psychological positions, known as *ego states; Life-positions,* suggesting the four positions individuals adopt in their transaction with outside world and *Game analysis* which discusses the transactions involving covert messages (a hidden one) as opposed to overt messages(open and expressed). Furthermore, mutual understanding between individuals within a group can also be studied by a graphical model of self awareness called as *Johari Window* model which divides personal awareness into four different types, as represented by its four quadrants: open, blind, hidden, and unknown.

These theoretical frameworks are briefly discussed below.

Ego states

Eric Berne, during 1950s revised the Freud's concept of human psyche as composed of Id, Ego and the Superego and proposed that behaviour patterns in people are evoked from three *ego states—Parent, Adult and Child.*

The Parent

People operating from parent ego state tend to be protective, controlling, instructive, nurturing (understanding and caring) and critical (attacking people's personality as well as behaviour). This state is the result of conditioning people received from their authority figures (parents, elder siblings, teachers etc.) in their early childhood. This state is the evaluative part of personality that evokes value laden behaviour.

The Adult

Behaviour evoked from this state could be described as logical, reasonable, rational and unemotional. While a person operates from Adult ego state, he/she is directed towards an objective appraisal of reality.

The Child

This state is associated with emotional response of behaviour. It can be *Happy Child* state where people do things they want to without disrupting others. However, behaviour of people in their *Disruptive Child* state is destructive to themselves or to their surroundings. Other than these states, the child ego state may also be compliant (they do what others want), natural, adaptive or rebellious.

All people behave from these three ego states at different times. A healthy person has a personality that maintains a balance among all three (Hersey and Blanchard, 1994).

Transactions between People

A transaction is said to occur when a stimulus (verbal or non-verbal) from one person is being responded by another person. The transaction is generally routed through ego states and depending upon the ego state involved, it may be of three types—complementary, crossed and ulterior.

- *Complementary Transactions (Open)*—In these transactions stimulus and response from one ego state to another are parallel. Thus, the message by a person gets the predicted response from another person. Both the persons are satisfied.

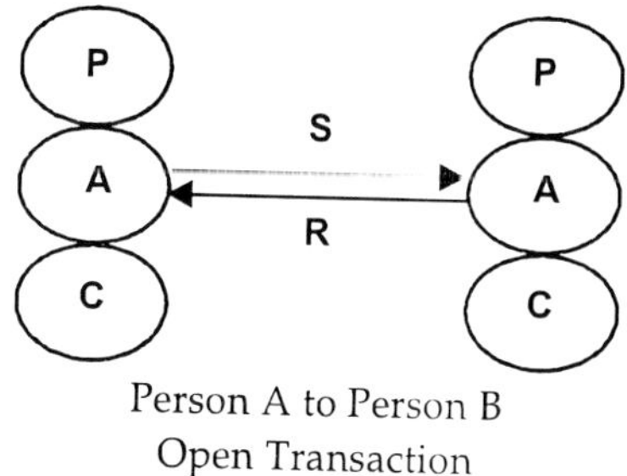

Person A to Person B
Open Transaction

Fig. 15.1:

Note: P : Parent ego state, A : Adult ego state, C : Child ego state, S : Stimulus, R : Response

- *Blocked Transactions (Closed)*—In such transactions, response is either inappropriate or unexpected as well as being of context with what sender of stimulus had originally expected.

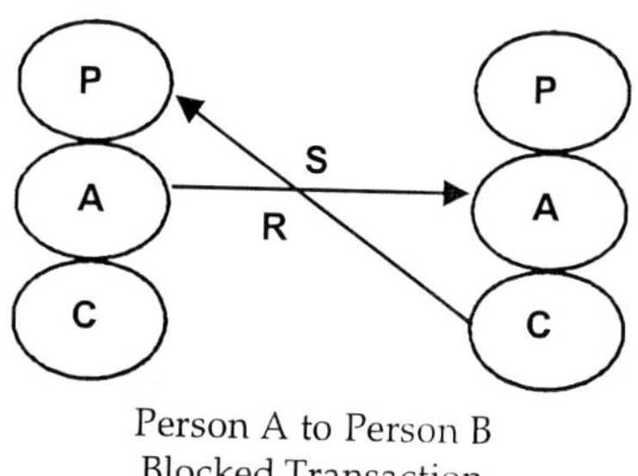

Person A to Person B
Blocked Transaction

Fig. 15.2:

Note: P : Parent ego state, A : Adult ego state, C : Child ego state, S : Stimulus, R : Response

- *Ulterior Transactions*—These are the transactions in which the sender appears to be sending one kind of message but is secretly sending another. An overt message (open and expressed) may contain a covert (hidden) message.

In general, the transaction that is found to be most effective at work is Adult to Adult open transaction. This transaction encourages problem solving and reduces the probability of interpersonal conflicts (Newstrom J.W and Davis, 1998).

Life Positions

In the process of growing up, people develop deeply ingrained assumptions about their self worth and worth of others. Thomas Harris (1967) calls such combination of assumptions as *Life* Positions. They are learned throughout life by way of reinforcements for, and responses to expressed needs. These assumptions are described in terms of "okayness". Four possible relationships results from these life positions:

①	I am OK. You are OK	I am not OK. You are OK	③
②	I am OK. You are not OK.	I am not OK You are not OK.	④

Psychological (Life) Positions

Fig. 15.3

1. *I am OK. You are OK (I* + You +): People with this life position express worth in themselves as well as worth and trust in others. This is a healthy life position.
2. *I am OK, You are not OK (I* + You -): This type of life position is held by those who have critical parent ego state as dominant state. They tend to criticize others and rarely develop trustful relations.
3. *I am not OK, You are OK (I-* You +): People having this type of life position feel inferior to others. These people have generally low self esteem and tend to be depressive and melancholic.

4. *I am not OK, You are not OK (I- You -)*: People with this life position neither trust anyone nor do they have confidence in themselves. They feel life is worthless. In extreme cases they may go into severe depression.

The desirable of these positions is the one that provides open transaction, that is, 'I am OK, You are OK,' which reflects acceptance of self as well as of others (Prasad, 1993).

This can be illustrated from following example (*Example* I).

> Principal/Head to a teacher, "While going through the notebooks of students of your class, I found that you have put a 'right' mark on a wrong answer. I think 'we' need to be careful as students may end up learning the wrong response".
> *Teacher:* "I didn't notice the mistake but I'll be careful next time."

In the above transaction, the principal communicated from a nurturing ego state and teacher operated from compliant child state. The message is communicated appropriately and both feel 'OK' about themselves at the end of transaction. On the other hand the same transaction can be 'crossed' like this (*Example* II)

> *Principal to a teacher,* "How can you be so careless? Inspite of having good experience you still don't know how to check copies? Nothing can be expected from a poor teacher like you." The teacher meekly responds, "I am sorry".

In this illustration, principal's response came from a critical parent state which made teacher feel deeply insulted and did not feel OK .The transaction as a result gets blocked as next time the teacher may not feel comfortable sharing his/her views with the principal. Hence interpersonal transactions should be as far as possible 'open' so that the persons involved feel OK about themselves.

Stroking

It is an act of recognition to another person. The stroke that makes a person feel OK about himself/herself is *positive stroke* which can be in the form of words of recognition, affection, and a pat on back etc. On the other hand, *negative stroke* hurt physically and emotionally and make the recipient feel less OK about himself/herself. Criticism, hating and scolding are negative strokes.

Psychological Games

People who do not get positive strokes often play psychological games which set of transactions having following characteristics (Hersey and Blanchard, 1994).

- Transactions tend to be repeated;
- Transactions make sense on a superficial or social level;
- One or more of transactions are ulterior;
- A set of transactions ends with a negative feeling a feeling of non-okayness.

An understanding of transaction attributes/transactional analysis can help in directing changing and controlling interpersonal behaviour. It can be applied to enhance positive thinking, trust and credibility among members of the school organization and hence contributes to the process of organizational development.

Model for Self Awareness—Johari Window

Self is the core of personality which causes interaction. A model that facilitates awareness of self between individuals and teams was devised by American psychologists Joseph Luft and Harrington lngham in 1950s, hence its name is so. This model is widely used to understand and train self awareness, to improve interpersonal relationships, group dynamics and team development.

Johari Window is a four quadrant figure based on two main dimensions of understanding self—those aspects of a person's behaviour, style and feelings known to him or her (self) and those aspects of behaviour that are known to those with whom the person interacts (others). A combination of these two dimensions reveal four areas of knowledge about self (Pareek, 2004).

	Known to self	Unknown to Self
Known to Others	**OPEN**	**BLIND**
Unknown to Others	**HIDDEN**	**UNKNOWN**

Fig. 15.4: The Johari Window

- *The Open/Public Window:* This quadrant refers to behaviours, style, feelings and other information about the individual which s/he is aware of and is also known to those with whom s/he interacts.
- *The Blind Window:* This area contains those aspects of person's behaviour which are known to others but not to him. Such blind behaviour is often copied by the individual from significant people unconsciously.
- *The Hidden/Closed Window:* This window pertains to information which is known to the person but not revealed to others.
- *The Unknown Window:* The fourth quadrant is also called dark area as it refers to behaviours that neither the individual nor others know about. This information, however resides unconsciously in us.

A person who is aware about his/her behaviour, feelings, attitudes and motivation level has a large open or public self area as compared to other areas. The enlargement of this area can be done by self disclosure and feedback of others.

The model of Johari Window helps to analyse one's own 'behaviour *vs.* reaction' and hence is a tool for self development and also for the development of team and organization as a whole.

Improvement of interpersonal relationships is an essential aspect of *Performance Management*, a process which involves supporting, improving and monitoring teacher's performance both as individuals and as member of team. It promotes professional growth among teachers by encouraging them to be fully engaged in school planning and to control the effectiveness of their own work.

An understanding of these theoretical models of interpersonal relationships also helps in managing *organizational conflicts* which are inevitable part of any organization and hence enhances positive attitude of teacher's towards his/her job i.e. *job satisfaction* which is an important factor governing performance of teacher as well as that of the organization. Hence, teacher education curriculum must incorporate different kinds of activity based exercises for developing enabling competencies among teacher educators as well as teacher trainees.

REFERENCES

Glasgow, N.A. and Cathy, D.H. (2003). *What Successful Teachers Do.* California: Corwin Press Inc.

Hersey, P. and Blanchard, K.H. (1994). *Management of Organizational Behaviour*, New Delhi: Prentice-Hall of India Private Limited.

Khanna, S.D., Lamba, Saxena T.P, V.K and Murthi, (1998). *Teacher Education: Theory and Practice.* New Delhi:Doaba House.

Newstrom, J.W. and Davis, K. (1998). Organizational Behaviour-*Human Behaviour at Work.* New Delhi: Tata McGraw-Hill Publishing Company Limited.

Owens, R. G. (1991).Organizational Behaviour in Education. USA (MA): Allyn&Bacon.

Prasad, L.M. (1996). Organizational Behaviour.New Delhi: Sultan Chand & Sons.

Pareek, U. (2004). Understanding Organizational Behaviour. New Delhi: Oxford University Press.

Robbins, S.P. (1991). Organizational Behaviour—*Concepts, Controversies and Applications.* New Jersey: Prentice-Hall International Inc.

16

Professional Ethics among Teachers

GIRIJESH KUMAR AND GAURAV SINGH

Teaching Profession comprises of teacher's competencies, obligations, devotions towards teaching and leadership in the field of education. It has been pointed out by Dave (2003) that: teachers can act as trail blazers in the lives of learners and in the process of education for development. If teachers acquire professional competencies and commitment, and if they are enabled and empowered to perform their multiple tasks in classroom, school and community in a genuinely professional manner, then a chain reaction can begin starting with a sound teacher performance and culminating into high quality learning among increasingly more students in cognitive, affective and psychomotor areas of human development. The statement is itself recognizing the role of a professional and competent teacher in social development. Any occupation attains the status of a profession if it requires specific qualifications, skills and abilities for its performance and has a procedure for certifying its practitioners. Due to its traditional pattern, teaching does not yet qualify all the criteria of being a profession because it is always treated as a noble service of humanity. Swami Vivekanand had stated *"The teacher must not teach with any ulterior selfish motive for money, name or fame. His work must be simply out of pure love for mankind."*

The situation has changed now. Majority of teachers now a days enter the teaching profession not necessarily out of love for it, but due to other several factors. Gandhi ji remarked that *"the unfortunate position is that educated Indians take the teaching not for the love for it, but because they have nothing better and nothing else for giving them a livelihood."* Being an important profession, there is urgent need to develop teaching as a profession by developing professional ethics and responsibility towards professional obligations among teachers. Teachers like other professionals, have the similar responsibility, not only to their students but also to the society in which they are treated as a conscious and learned members.

Teachers must view teaching as a profession, this would require professional attitude on their part (Singhal, 2003). The professionalism has its own compulsions and pressures. It needs change in attitudes and value systems of the teachers. Teachers have to earn social sanctions from the community by improving the quality of wok. Teachers have to perform many additional roles in society. Apart from teaching, they have to act as the agents of change and modernization, cultural reconstruction and social development to earn recognition as professional from society by acquiring new competencies and commitments. They have to become effective and result oriented by enhancing their knowledge and developing skills for better communication (CFQTE, 1998). For this, it is necessary to develop professional ethics and obligations among teachers and the scope of teacher education has thus been enlarged. The task of sensitizing teachers about their commitment to the learner, society, profession, institute, and values is a great challenge before teacher education (Walia, 2003). There is need to develop mechanisms for content enrichment, augmentation and renewal. Steps also have to be taken for their professional growth and development on a continuous basis to enable them to keep abreast with the changes and developments in their respective fields besides developments in pedagogy and related disciplines.

Professional Ethics among Teachers

Every profession is expected to evolve a set of ethical principles to guide the conduct and behaviour of its professional members. The spirit behind it should be the concern for needs of society, its well being and understanding among the people.

Professional ethics indicate the principles, guidelines and norms of morality, which a professional has to follow in his her profession. The code of professional ethics is a set of self imposed professional ideals and principles necessary for the attainment of self-satisfaction and professional excellences.

Teaching in its true sense is not mere instruction but an attempt to influence the behaviour of pupils. In this task, most important thing is the personal examples of the teachers, which commands the respect of pupils, the parents, colleagues and the community at large. His/her dedication towards own profession influences the society. The teacher like other professionals has to acquire three characteristics (Chopra, 1998):

(a) Expert knowledge of their subject.
(b) Special training in core teaching skills and methods.
(c) Continuous in-service growth to do full justice to their work.

The National Policy on Education, 1986, emphasizes the need for preparation of a code of professional ethics for teachers to ensure that teachers perform their duties in accordance with acceptable norms. It should enhance their commitment towards profession on one hand and improve their effectiveness on the other. The need of developing a code of professional ethics for teachers was emphasized due to several reasons. Some of them are as follows:

(a) Enabling teachers to meet the demands of the teaching profession.
(b) Enabling teachers to do justice to the roles and responsibilities assigned to them.
(c) Providing guidelines to teachers for establishment of school community linkages for academic and social relationships like of the school.
(d) Providing guidelines to teachers for establishment of school community partnership.
(e) Guiding teachers to be protected from the unfair and unjust treatment.

Prasad and Prasad (2005) also emphasized the need of professional ethics among teachers for self correction, self satisfaction, to guide the conduct and behaviours, to shape the personality, to set up the ideals for students, to improve the relations with human beings, for the development of society, for the professional excellences, to improve professional environment and to follow the norms and principles of the profession.

Earlier, teaching was not considered a profession. The assumption that the teacher possessing content knowledge can teach well is not merely accepted. There has been a continuous growth and development in the standards of professional preparation of teachers, because of changing roles of the teachers in present day society. No occupation can be rated as high as teaching because its social value lies in its contribution to the welfare of student community, which in turns leads to welfare of the society. Hence the professional ethics must be developed among teachers. Under this circumstances teacher education curriculum needs renovation for developing professional ethics among teachers through both in-service and pre-service teacher education programmes.

Professional Obligations of Teachers

Obligation is a responsibility which an individual imposes on himself. It is ethical and in the line of duty. A professional when follows rules, regulations and correctly interprets it for the progress of humanity, it creates a sense of brotherhood, which makes one to respect fellow professionals and own profession. A person who chooses teaching as a profession accepts the obligation to conduct himself/herself, in accordance with the highest standards of the teaching profession. It is essential for a teacher to aim at quality and excellence in his/her work and conduct. A professionally committed teacher takes pride in up bringing this noble profession. S/he strives to follow the code of professional obligations. Pride in the profession, appreciation of desirable qualities of colleagues and understanding of aims and objectives of the professional creates a desire to attain excellence in the professional performance. Teachers are expected to perform their professional activities in the following five major dimensions (NCERT, 1997):

(a) Teachers in relation to pupils.
(b) Teachers in relation to parents/guardians.
(c) Teachers in relation to society and the nation.
(d) Teachers in relation to professional colleagues and other professional organizations.
(e) Teachers in relation to management and administration.

Professional Obligations of Teachers in relation of Pupils

Teachers at all stages are concerned with pupils. They may be children in the early years of schooling or youths in schools, colleges and universities. Teachers' obligation to bring about learning translates into the need on their part to understand the learner both as a person and as a learner (Seshadri, 2003). Teachers are concerned with students not just in ordinary sense. Their life is intimately bound up with their students. Their professional lives acquire meaning only with reference to the relationship that exists between the two, hence it is expected that teacher of today will have to go beyond limit for the betterment of pupils. Major professional obligations of a teacher towards learners are:

(a) Effective and sincere teaching.
(b) Motivation of learners.
(c) Handling the emotional situations.
(d) Consciousness in works
(e) Developing the decision-making capacity, and
(f) Developing the leadership quality.

To carry out these obligations of getting children to learn, to develop and to make them capable in many aspects, teachers have to understand the art and science of teaching and learning. They have to acquire necessary skills of effective communication with learners. S/he has to learn the skills to develop sense perceptual experience, reason, institution, imagination, creativity, memory and problem solving. This means that teachers have to keep enriching their repertoire of pedagogical skills. *A good teacher is a constant student. He is a child leading children and a light kindling other lights (Joshi, 2001).*

Teachers' Obligations towards Parents/Guardians

Parents send their children to school with a hope that their children will do better, learn every required language and ability along with the subjects. Not only this, parents also feel that the teacher will develop the social and moral values in their children and make them good citizens. So it is now obligatory on the part of the teacher to establish friendly and cooperative relationship with parents/guardians of learners. Teacher should remain in touch with the parents for well-being and educational growth of the child. Some professional obligations of a teacher towards parents are as follows:

(a) Reporting about academics and behaviour of child.
(b) Discussing about future professions/educational options for child.
(c) Informing about interest, attitude and aptitude of child.
(d) Providing guidance regarding the conducive home environment.
(e) Getting suggestions about school and teaching environment.
(f) Developing a healthy relationship between parents and schools.

It is not for a teacher to say; my job is only to teach. In our traditional system teacher is not just an instructor, she is a caretaker, a gardener, a spiritual guide. The mutual understanding of teacher and parents is highly desired. The teachers should train in helping to pupil's confidence in their parents. They should be trained in organizing parent-teacher meeting to understand and solve many personal and scholastic problems of children mutually.

Teachers' Obligations in relation to Society

The teacher is closely associated with his social environment. The teacher's obligation to society manifests itself in many forms; the most important among them is to bring into educational fold the children who have no healthy tradition in their families. In the community/society at large, it is necessary for a teacher to establish good social relationships. The obligations of teacher towards the society are:

(a) Providing good citizens.
(b) Developing the feeling of responsibility towards rights and duties;
(c) Training the students to follow the norm;
(d) Setting up of ethical standards;
(e) Developing religious harmony and cultural understanding;
(f) Making the students capable of living in harmony with nature; and
(g) Developing the feeling of integration, secularism and national pride.

It may be pointed out, however, that in the past community activities were not compulsory for the teacher but now they are. Teachers must participate the community activities along with children and act as their leaders. ,Beyond the boundaries of the community, a teacher is expected today to play a role in the wider society to achieve inter group cohesion and national integration. It is the teacher who as a craftsman craves the futures of the society and the nation. She should be trained in organizing different social awareness and community service activities in the society, of which she is a responsible ingredient. The development of society and nation is among the primary social responsibilities of a teacher.

Teachers' Obligations towards Profession

Teaching profession remains as an oasis of idealism, devotion to duty and love for humanity amidst a vast desert of materialism, competitiveness and concern for others' good. Undoubtedly, with the fast development of education, an element unless imbued with a sense of sacrifices and self-abrogation that characterizes this profession, can keep on continuing this profession. Teaching is a developing profession and the teachers are still fighting for attaining a professional status. They also seek the professional comfort, professional growth etc., therefore obligations on the part of teachers also increase to a great extent.

(a) Developing mannerism and professional ethics;
(b) Creating respect about the profession;
(c) Continuous professional growth and enrichment;
(d) Contributing towards the development and betterment of profession;
(e) Maintaining a healthy work culture and working environment at workplace; and
(f) Developing and participating actively in professional organization.

Being a teacher, it is his/her responsibility to develop a rapport with other colleagues. If s/he wants to be respected as a teacher, s/he should project himself/herself as a good teacher. S/he should be trained and encouraged to participate in conferences, professional body meetings for the betterment of his/her professional quality.

Teachers' Obligations towards Management and Administration

It is the moral duty of the teacher to co-operate with the head of the institution, the management and the educational administration in running the institution in accordance with the stipulated norms. He should also strive for the development of mutual respect and trust through her professional activities. Teachers are the executives who enforce or execute the programmes for effective functioning and development of any institution. It is important that a teacher co-ordinates own action with the higher authorities as per changing need and situations. The major activities for a teacher to perform for coordinating with the higher authorities are:

(a) Binding himself/herself with rules and regulations;
(b) Becoming a link between students and management;
(c) Helping the management in developing strategies;
(d) Sharing policies and organizing programme; and
(e) Being respectful (courteous) to higher authorities.

Apart from the above-mentioned obligations there are other obligations, which a teacher has to take care of. These obligations change their face with time, situation and people. Different authorities, academicians, governing and regulating bodies in the fields of education, develop these obligations but the implementation part remains on the shoulders of a teacher educator.

Conclusion

A teacher can become a professional in real sense if s/he fulfills all the obligations and remembers that a profession is above the professionals and in no case s/he should allow his/her human instincts and feelings to come in the way of his/her profession. It can be said that a teacher has greater duties and responsibilities to perform for the betterment of society. Faith in the profession, appreciation of desirable qualities of colleagues, and understanding of aims and objectives of the profession act as a foundation stone to attain excellence in the professional performance. It is a process that each one involved, influences the other, but, teacher does it more and in a better way, because of his/her knowledge, skills and authorities, s/he enjoys. Naturally s/he shoulders more responsibilities. In the modern context, to honour the obligations, the teachers must have a sound social philosophy characterized by social sensitivity, concerns for social justice and human rights. Professional ethics and mannerism should go hand in hand so that the teacher is able to move ahead as a real professional in changing time.

REFERENCES

Azad, J.L. *(2003). Professional Commitment and Accountability of Teachers.* New Delhi: NCERT.

Chopra, R.K. *(1998). Code of Professional Ethics for Teachers.* New Delhi: NCERT.

Dave, R.H. *(2003). Teacher Commitment.* New Delhi: NCERT

Durcharne, E.R. *(1993). The Lives of Teacher Educator.* New York: Teacher College Press.

Joshi, K. *(2001).* Sri Aurobindo on Education in *Experiences in School Education.* New Delhi: NCERT.

NCERT, *(1997). Code of Professional Ethics for Teachers.* New Delhi.

NCERT, (2004). *Curriculum Framework for Teacher Education.* New Delhi : NCERT.

NCTE, (1998). *Curriculum Framework for Quality Teacher Education.* New Delhi: NCTE.

Prasad, H. and Prasad, H. (2005). Towards Professionalisation of Education. New Delhi: *University News,* 43(18).

Seshadri, C. (2003). *Primary Obligations of Teachers.* New Delhi: NCERT.

Singhal, R.P. (2003). *In Search of Teacher Commitment.* New Delhi: NCERT.

Vachharajani, B. (2005). Some Innovations for Professional Development of Teachers. New Delhi: *University News,* 43(18).

Walia, K. (2003). *Perception of Teacher Commitment.* New Delhi: NCERT.

17

Value Inculcation Intensive Teacher Education

G.N. Prakash Srivastava

The Value Education is becoming increasingly prominent in educational discussion at all levels for devoting more time and effort to achieve greater understanding and awareness of human values. In our pluralistic society education has to foster universal values as well as orient people towards unity and integration. The National Policy on Education (NPE, 1986) envisages the need to make education a powerful tool for the cultivation of social and moral values. The National Curriculum Framework for School Education (NCFSE, 2000/05) highlighted the need for inculcation and nurturance of significant human values among students. The 81st Report on Value Based Education (1999) submitted to the Indian Parliament has emphasized on the inculcation of core universal values viz. Truth, Non-Violence, Righteous Conduct, Love and Peace, The Preamble of the Indian Constitution, the fundamental duties enshrined in the Constitution, and a number of Education Commissions and Committees in India since independence have emphasized on the need for formulation of programmes on Value-based Education through educational institutions.

Concept of Value and Value Education

Value is what is desired, liked or preferred. Values refer to those things what men desire, like, prefer. Values pre-suppose conscious beings with likes, and prejudices. Value may be defined as a concept of standards. It may be cultural or merely personal, by which things are compared and approved or disapproved related to one another. A child is not born with a set of values. Values have to be acquired through the process of education.

Value education intends for desired modifications in the individual's behaviour patterns which apparently involves society, environment, individual and school. Environment and school together play a significant role in building value patterns which grow from purposes, aspirations, beliefs, attitudes feelings, interests, convictions etc. Education has to aim at multi-faceted development of human beings—their intellectual, physical, spiritual and ethical development. Education should aim not only at information based knowledge but also the holistic view of turning the student into a perfect human being. We must have career-building, man-making, character-making assimilation of ideas. The five cardinal values represent the five domains of human character i.e. Intellectual (Truth, *Satya*), Physical (Righteous Conduct, *Dharma*), Emotional (Peace, *Shanti*), Psychological (Love, *Prema*) and Spiritual (Non-violence, *Ahima*) corresponding to five major objectives of education, namely knowledge, skill, balance, vision, and identity. These core universal values can be identified as the foundation-stone on which the value-based education programme can be built up. The social values aimed at are friendliness, cooperativeness, compassion, self-discipline, courage, love for social justice etc. Besides curriculum, schools have to develop the key qualities like regularity and punctuality, cleanliness, self-control, industriousness, sense of duty, desire to serve, responsibility, enterprise, creativity, sensitivity to gather equality, fraternity, democratic attitude, sense of obligation to environmental protection, work-culture, concern for others and tolerance. All religions are to be treated with equal respect (*Sarva Dharama Sambhav*) and there has to be no discrimination on the ground of any religion (*Panthnirapekshata*).

Human Values

Following kind of values are most relevant and important from the points of human values. These are:

Intrinsic values/Root values/Absolute values/Moral values/Ultimate values/Core values which imply ultimate good, ideal or worth whileness as an end in itself. Intrinsic human values are eternal and universal which have been conceived since time immemorial. Accordingly, religions of the world have been shaping spiritual aspects with a view to inspiring and indoctrinating man to be good human being in his journey of life towards the goal of attaining perfection.

Mundane values are social, economic, political and cultural by nature. For example the Indian Constitution is the prime source of mundane, socio-cultural, political and economic values for Indian citizens.

Intrinsic human values transcend all values and behaviour and all varieties of situations and diverse examples of human conduct. Root values should always act as a guiding light. Spirituality, religion, morality, ethics and culture are often referred to as foundation sources of human values. Intrinsic human values are indeed concerned with the inner world. A harmonious and sustainable human society and its institutions depends on right action in the physical world with a right mind inspired by human values of the inner world. Values also act as the base for judgement, preferences, choice on rejection. The fact that different cultures have different value systems and these value systems are conditioned by the developments taking place in a cultural set up proving thereby values have a strong social and cultural base.

Ways to Cultivation of Values

Values may be nurtured through direct and indirect methods. The direct method attempts to instill virtues by centring attention directly upon them through discussing and illustrating them, memorizing and reciting creeds, verses, slogans, oaths, pledges, golden texts, etc. that suggest analyzing actions and events in order to discover them and applying them directly to the lives of pupils. It aims at changing the thought process through the development of thinking and reasoning. In direct method there are fixed periods in the classes where systematic and deliberate instructions are given on value education. But value-education is not to be taught as a subject for the fact that the essence of values are to be realized and appreciated rather than being learnt. Values are to be infused indirectly so that the school atmosphere, the personality and the behaviour of the teacher, the facilities provided in the school will have a large sense of values. The consciousness of values must promote the whole curriculum in the institution. It is not one teacher but each and every teacher in the school should take the responsibility for imparting values through teaching their subjects and for building character of students. The teacher can indirectly make an impact on the minds of students and a sense of value should inspire all activities and must be reflected in the life, tone and atmosphere of the school.

Inculcation of Values

School activities should develop strong moral courage among children. School environment has to provide rich experiences to students for inculcation of values. The textbooks and other learning materials should be related with the learning of values. The steps for inculcation of values may be identified as (i) Knowing, (ii) Believing, (iii) Making Judgement, (iv) Practice, (v) Spontaneous Action. Under knowing the child must be made aware of the values through activities and programmes. Then the child must develop faith in those values (Believing). Again the child must be provided conflicting situations to judge the implication of related values (Making Judgement). The child is to be encouraged to practice these values in real life situations (Practice). Thus, the various programmes of the schools must take the child to that stage where the practice of values may become spontaneous and immediate.

Modelling

Parents, teachers and peers become personal models to children for emulation and initiation. Identification with great personalities and hero-worship trigger off introjections of qualities and initiation of behaviours consciously or unconsciously. A 'crush' for or attachment to such chosen personalities can also be a source of persuasive influence. These tendencies can be exploited by the elders in the family and teachers presenting themselves as impressive models. Other models can also be pointed out or presented from real life or through stories. A model can be live, but a movie presented from real life or illustrated story may also function well. A model can be provided by an oral discussion in which a teacher asks a series of questions. In the ultimate analysis learning by examples rather than precept, is relevant to all social-moral learning.

Value-loaded Behaviours and Experiences

Value-loaded behaviours and principles can be effectively presented through folk tales, stories, comics, cartoon strips, skits and other dramatized presentations with human, animal and other characters for a powerful appeal in early childhood, and even later. It can be followed up with initiative and analogous behaviours and proper reinforcement. Powerful media provided by modern educational technology can be exploited for making impressive presentation. While positive instance should induce appreciation and promote introjections (taking in), 'negative instances' are appropriate to produce aversion depending on the quality of the presentation. Appropriate discussions following presentations may clarify and stress things in their proper perspective. Role-playing, participation in dramatized presentations, etc. can also be useful in experiencing and imbibing attitudes and values. Especially later childhood and adolescence prove quite powerful in moral development. Good groups and good leaders (potential models) can contribute to the wholesome development of the members. Formulation of congenial groups and their guidance along healthy channel can, therefore, be an effective means for proper value development. Generalisation and conceptualisation of value can start in a systematic way in later childhood when the norms and rules of conduct are made by children themselves.

At stage beyond childhood inspiration generating talks by skilful persons can be quite productive. Presentation through articulation and logic made by committed persons and accepted leaders, participation in discussions and debates, opportunities for open minded critical analysis and independent judgement should lead to better understanding, sound rationalization or justification and acceptance. 'Experiencing of values': especially aesthetic and spiritual is effective and necessary. Beauty, compassion, harmony, peace etc. have to be experienced; and not only communicated and conceptualized.

Value attainment can be facilitated by adequate internalization of faith, feelings and commitment. It requires consistent adherence to values and autonomous functioning with internal locus of control and wholesome conscience. It is also necessary to prevent suffering from guilt feelings and pangs of conscience to promote sound mental health, and a strong value system (NCERT, 1992).

It is desirable that educational instructions imparted by teachers should be so directed and oriented as to allow finer values to be adopted and practiced in the course of daily lessons or parts thereof. The lesson of values in educational instructions always demands a quest for excellence to crystallize virtues in reasoning as well as appreciation. Impulses associated with values which must be sought and cultivated in course of education in an intensive manner necessitate a careful approach to education for values.

Curricular Activities

The textbooks in the language courses: Hindi, English, and Sanskrit may be so designed as to contribute in the right attitudes and interest. While teaching poetry at all levels, teacher should use the skill stimulus variation.

The language teachers can teach through association methods, e.g., by singing, chanting versions, relating stories and thereby create enjoyment and satisfaction among students. The instruction in social science should promote values and ideals of humanism, secularism, socialism and democracy. While teaching science, developing scientific attitudes is the main aim apart from realizing the importance of ability, consistency etc. There is scope for unlimited innovations and experiments in teaching science.

Co-curricular Activities

The basic aim for fostering values upto secondary stage may be to get self confidence, self satisfaction, self realization and self sacrifice. This could be achieved by developing certain systematic approaches through morning assembly, interviews, discussions, in-house meeting, cultural programmes, participation in national celebrations, organization of mock parliament, debate on local and regional problems, organizing scout guiding camps etc. Clubs are the means of social education, helping students to participate in decision making, exercise, self discipline and thinking about the world around them.

While organizing morning assembly following points should be kept in mind:

(i) Punctuality
(ii) The way of conducting the assembly
(iii) Pledge-Loyalty to the nation
(iv) News of the day
(v) Thought of the day

Either before or after the morning assembly there should be some time kept for self meditation and peace of mind. Value Education should become a central goal of schooling i.e. helping younger learners to be smart and also helping them to be good citizens.

The process of value education is highly complex that the individual learners are influenced by varieties of hereditary and environmental factors. In a school set up, a "Comprehensive Value Education Programme" is the need of the hour. This would result in an approach that is both conservative and progressive in nature. It basically revolves round the children and their ability to choose right values, realizing them and to live in accordance with them. It is a lifelong process. It is noteworthy that the role of teachers is sought to be determined during the next decades not only in the context of providing the dimension of values in our present system but also in the context of providing more effective methods of education. The teacher should necessarily be not only a good educator but a good person possessing basic moral and aesthetic values. Teacher's influence is not confined to what s/he does during teaching hours but in reality s/he teaches all the time.

Models for Value Education

Values can be inculcated through various models. Some of the models are described below:

(i) ***Role Playing Model:*** The role of the role player is patterned in sequence of feelings, words, attitudes and emotions of self and other persons. Here the role player explores human relations, virtues, values, attitudes, emotions, feelings, perceptions, subject matter, problem-solving skills etc. by enacting real problem situations. It depends on the quality of enactment, role-player's perception of the role and analysis. There are various steps in the Role Playing Model viz., warming up, selection of participants, setting the stage, preparation of observers, enacting, discussion and evaluation, and relating problem situation to real life experiences.

(ii) ***Jurisprudential Inquiry Model:*** It helps students learn to think systematically on contemporary issues. This model has six phases such as orientation to the case, identifying the issues, taking a position, exploring the stances, refining and qualifying the position, and testing factual assumptions behind qualified position.

(iii) ***Value Clarifying Model:*** This model has seven steps viz. (i) freedom to make choice, (ii) critical examination of available alternatives in their choice, (iii) analysis of alternatives and reflecting on consequences of each choice, (iv) reason for choosing a particular alternative, (v) getting public affirmation for the choice, (vi) acting and behaving according to the choice, and (vii) examining the choice in their real life. This model is an attempt to help learners to decrease value confusion and promote a consistent set of values through varying process. The teacher should help students at every stage since discovery learning approach is difficult for students and values are abstract in nature.

There are a number of other models in developing the various aspects of human values such as Rationale Building Model, Consideration Model, Value Analysis Model, Cognitive Moral Development Model, Social Action Model, and Value Discussion Model etc.

Approaches to Value Education

There are many approaches to value education. Some significant approaches are as follows:

(i) ***Incidental Approach* (IA):** This approach is applied incidentally by elders, administrators and teachers to correct the child then and there for his/her moral lapses. Here value inculcation is resorted to an event actually occurred.

(ii) ***Life Line Approach (LLA):*** It is concerned with educating students to live well. It consists of a variety of materials and methods. The curriculum materials have been named as 'In Other People's Shoes', 'Providing the Rules', and 'What Would You Have Done'. The major aim of LLA is that every boy and girl should become morally mature and involved in related activities. This approach should be related to the needs, interests and abilities of students. In LLA, books, teacher's guide and sets of classroom instructional materials are used. Various life situations ranging from simple to complex are also identified for value classification and value inculcation.

(iii) ***Reward and Punishment Approach (RPA):*** RPA helps to remove obnoxious habits and develop desirable behaviours.

We can prepare charts containing desirable behaviours and undesirable behaviours. These charts are given to students and they are asked to put some marks in space provided against each behaviour every day. Credit/marks may be given for each right behaviours and negative credits/marks may be given for each wrong behaviour. Thus it strengthens the student's behaviour pattern.

(iv) ***Critical Inquiry Approach (CIA):*** It helps children to discover what is right through constant critical inquiry and thus harnesses their inherent energies for the pursuit of sound values. Thus it is value focusing approach. Here the problem is given to the student in the form of a dilemma. Even the students may test the new principle in this approach. It is possible that the students may open the new line of thought. At the end they will express their views. These views may be questioned by others for clarification.

(v) ***Total Atmospheric Approach*** (TAA): Moral atmosphere is essential for this approach. The teacher must get examples in schools. 'Morality is caught and no taught' is best suited to this approach. Moral atmosphere is created in the schools only when morality is within all the components and organization of cuhiculum in the school.

(vi) ***Integrated Concurrent Approach (ICA):*** ICA is the synthesis of CIA and ICA. In this approach units in value education should be identified in the beginning. Core virtual values and key questions should also be marked. Concrete examples must be integrated. Experiences must be provided to inculcate the desired values among the students.

(vii) ***Experimental Approach (EA): EA*** focuses on the students' experiences and their work on values/virtues. It has six stages. They are subject matter, message, interest, interactive session, emotional response and celebration.

(viii) ***Value Sheet Method (VSM):*** VSM focuses on the group. It requires a stimulus to initiate. The stimulus may be in the form of a printed or cyclostyled sheet. The sheet contains the following information: (i) Excerpts from literature, (ii) short stories, (iii) quotations, (iv) poems, (v) cartoons, (vi) controversial statements and vii) thoughts of eminent persons.

(ix) ***Case Method (CM):*** A problem faced by an individual/group or an experience gained by an individual group is called a 'case'. Here the case material will be provided to the students to interact with the case material. The students cogitate on issues involved. They reread the material and find out problems. Discussion will be drawn on the strongest argument.

(x) ***Attitude Development Technique (ADT):*** Education is for all-round development of an individual. But most of the classroom techniques are restricted to the cognitive domain whereas an attitude falls in affective domain. Therefore ADT has proposed different techniques such as precept ideal, parables, psycho-drama, and role play which are used to develop desired attitudes in students.

Practice of Yoga for Cultivation of Values

Yoga is science as well as method that allows human beings to live a harmonious life while favouring their spiritual progress through the control of mind and body. The objective of yoga is to enable us to rich our knowledge. It is a method designed to reveal the sources of creative inspiration hidden inside the human psyche and thus involves the manifold expression of our being. It lays the foundations for a higher level of self development and deeper self awareness. The *Asanas* (Yogic Postures) and *Pranayama* (breath control) are the practices in Yoga which not only help one acquire perfect health, stay young and live longer, but is designed to develop inner force that enables us to overcome our feelings, withstand stressful situations and bring serenity. The various 'Yogas' represent all the means allowing learners to come out of ignorance and illusion ('*Maya*'), so that their mind may reflect the light of ultimate reality.

The word 'Yoga' comes from the Sanskrit root 'Yoke' meaning 'to join'. It designates the joining of the lower human nature to the higher in such a manner as to allow the higher to direct the lower 'or' union with the Self. It also signifies communion with the Supreme Universal Spirit to obtain relief from pain and suffering. In this regard the *Bhagavad Gita* explains,

"One who controls his mind, intellect and ego, being absorbed in the spirit within him, finds fulfillment and internal bliss which is beyond the pale senses and reasoning".

Yoga should be taken as a method to obtain mental perfection. It is further supported by self-control and preservance of positive attitude towards life. It is in this way that Yoga leads us towards universal love and brotherhood.

The different forms of Yoga are adapted to the different natures and temperaments of men. It can be classified in the following ways:

1. *Karma-yoga*: The manner in which a man realizes his own divinity through works and duty.
2. *Bhakti yoga*: The realization of the divinity through devotion to, and love of a personal god.
3. *Raja yoga*: The realization of divinity through the control of mind.
4. *Jnana yoga*: The realization of a man's own divinity through knowledge.

Astanga Yoga for Nurturing Values

Understanding the secrets of nature, and the nature of internal and external environments of energy our great *Rishies* (Nature Scientists) put forth the science of Raja Yoga. For this they designed a concrete method of *Astanga Yoga* in view of attaining an 'integrated personality'. The eight stages of mind-process under *Astanga Yoga* are as follows:

(i) **Yama** (Restsraint) consists of (i) *Ahimsa* (non-violence); (ii) *Satya* (truthfulness), (iii) *Brahmacharya* (celibacy); (iv) *Asteya* (non-stealing) and (v) *Aparigraha* (non-covetousness). It emphasizes on abstaining from killing any living being or hurting any one by thought, word or deed; to liberate oneself from untruth and dishonesty by sticking to truth; abstaining one self from stealing, gross animal instinct, the brute passion, lust by self-restraint (Brahmacharya); and not accepting gifts for undesirable ends. All these factors purify the mind

and develop the value of self control and piousness or piety.

(ii) ***Niyama*** (observance) consists of (i) *Shouch* (cleanliness); (ii) *Santosh* (contentment); (iii) *Tapa* (fortitude); (iv) *Swadhyaya* (self-study); and (v) *Ishwara Pranidhana* (complete surrender to the will of God). These practices transform vulgarity of human nature into divine by external cleanliness and intetrnal purity and thus develop the value of cleanliness. Apart from external cleanliness of body and environment it also emphasizes on internal cleanliness of imagination, thoughts, feelings and motivation. *Santosh* or contentment is a weapon to eliminate domination of sensual pleasure and appetite. *Tapa* mortifies all organs through scheduled activities. *Swadhyaya* or self study stresses on transforming, illumining and awakening of new ideas and develops the habit of self study and reading of good literature. Complete surrender to the will of God develops devotion towards teacher, knowledge and almighty. These consolidate basic perceptions, stops negative direction of mind and facilitates the positive upward direction.

(iii) ***Asana*** (Yogic Posture) is the posture for meditation. It is the science of 'Yoga' to prepare a person to meditate physically, vitally, and mentally for speedy evolution. The role Asanas play in the protection of vital energy and the maintenance of good health is quite remarkable. Asana supports in fostering perfect health, which is a requirement to attain the highest level of spiritual development. Asanas make people more active and alert as well as cheerful, free and joyous all the time. By developing an erect posture one gets the power necessary to act well in life and solve most of the every day problems that one faces in the modern society.

The body must not be forced or fatigued during the execution of postures. One should stop the practice as soon as there is any pain. Each posture should be performed slowly, carefully, gradually and patiently.

Postures may be simplified according to individual needs. *Asanas* should be practiced on an empty stomach.

(iv) ***Pranayama:*** The Sanskrit word *'Prana'* means 'vital force' or 'cosmic energy'. It also signifies 'life' or 'breath'. *'Ayam'* means the control. Hence *'Pranayama'* means the control of the vital force by concentration and regulated breathing. With controlled yogic breathing we are able to store a large quantity of *'Prana'* in the brain and nervous centers. For thousands of years Hindu psychologists have studied breath. They examined it from the practical, physical and mystical point of view. To them, breathing was more, much more, than just a necessary element of life. People normally, indeed always, breathe out and breathe in but inhalation is more and exhalation is less. This imbalance causes many physical and emotional problems. It is, therefore, imperative that breathing should be corrected first. *Pranayama* helps slow inhalation filling the lungs with fresh air and equally slow exhalation emptying lungs of all carbon dioxide, thus bringing equilibrium conducive to health and happiness.

Breathing is connected with mental and emotional behaviour. During anger breathing becomes faster. If we control breathing we become cool. Those who are calm breathe deeply. Those who are emotionally disturbed, breathe very fast. By controlling breathing other actions can be controlled easily. By *Pranayama*, emotions can be controlled and with that, concentration increases and other things become simpler. *Pranayama* therefore holds a high place in the science of life. Patanjali believes that thinking power is dependent on breathing. Faulty and disturbed breathing obstructs clear thinking. When breathing is deep and long one thinks well and also meditates well. It means *'prana'* is the vital key to control mind and all thoughts. A continuous *Sadhana* will give a state of stability and steadiness. *Pranayama* improves mental concentration and brings cheerfulness.

(v) ***Prathyahara:*** It is related to introspective nature of mind. Its purpose is controlling the sense from their wayward and outward travel and turning them inward in order to channelize all the faculties towards contemplation of the Self, which is the center of higher values. Control of senses gives immense strength to the psyche. If the senses can be arrested and dissipation of vital energy prevented, one can develop tremendously in all ways—physically, mentally, emotionally, intellectually and spiritually. One can realize the noble purpose of his life and also be of great benefit to the community for which s/he develops altruistic values which emerge from one's higher self. In fact this is the foundation stage which consolidates all moral values.

(vi) ***Dharna:*** It means concentration, i.e. holding the mind fixed at one point, at one place, and keeping it for a sufficient length of time. This brings concentration of mind which results in higher mental abilities. It gives specific exercise and process to the mind. This is the beginning stage of introspective process and bringing value of concentration and development of higher mental abilities.

(vii) ***Dhyana* (Meditation):** This is the solution for all the disorders in learning. This gives proper direction to the mind. There may be (a) meditation with *pranayam* and (b) meditation without *pranayam*. The meditation improves learning. Meditation helps up to get rid ourselves of emotional conflict, inner discord and psychological tension. It completely purifies the mind and frees it from unconscious obstruction. Meditation enables the inner light to manifest itself. One may penetrate to the very center of life's highest values through *Dhyana* or meditation.

(viii) ***Samadhi:*** This is the highest transcendent super-conscious stage of mind. This is the stage of the realization of the 'self' where ego merges in the supreme self and duality between 'self and 'ego' comes to non-existent. For the realization of the super consciousness or spirituality *Samadhi* is the last stage. The highest aim of life is to be one with the Supreme Being. *Samadhi* delves 'self' into the Supreme Being, the *'Sat' 'Chit' 'Ananda'*.

Precautions in Yoga and Meditation

Avoidance of Extremes

(i) Extremes should be avoided. Too much fasting or too little sleep weakens the body and are detrimental to the nervous system. If, we practise moderation and discipline, balance of eating and sleeping habits along with our work and the time we spend, we shall reach perfect harmony and equilibrium. We must have control of both mind and body.

(ii) Practice of *yoga* be done under the guidance of competent *'Guru'* or teacher. Ignorance of the practices and its requirement may prove harmful to both mind and body.

Environment

The best time for *yoga* and meditation is early morning and evening (twilight) with clean body and mind. The place should be neat and clean (better if it is surrounded by nature i.e. plants, grass, flowers etc. with fresh natural air). Flowers are the best surroundings for a *yogi*; also pictures that are pleasing. The practice of *yoga* should be of a supported atmosphere with fragrance of burning incense and non-existent of quarrelling, anger and unholy thoughts at that place. The idea is that by keeping holy vibrations the place becomes and remains illuminated. One should salute ancient *Yogis,Guru* and God and then begin the practice of *Yoga* or meditation.

Mental Attitude

(a) Negative mental attitudes are dangerous and lead to illness. They may act directly and indirectly, in the form of heart attacks or failures, or illness which may be traced back to the accumulation of uninterrupted tension.

(b) Alcohol or tranquilizers are destructive, they accelerate the ageing process and leave one depressed and demoralized, and lead to serious illness.

If we use mental energy positively, we change our attitude and outlook. A positive mental attitude coupled with faith, sweep away all our doubts, we seem to possess an inner force to overcome all our difficulties.

Physiological Factors

(i) A comfortable and firm posture, in such a way that one is conscious of the body, must be adopted in meditation. One should choose the position that allows one to remain still for long time without feeling discomfort;

(ii) The spine and head should be kept very straight without being strained;

(iii) The mind can be directed inwardly in complete tranquility.

The Practice of Pranayama

Pranayam must be practiced in a state of relaxation. It should neither require abrupt movements violent inhalations exhalation, nor should it provoke a feeling of suffocation. *Prana* should be mastered slowly and gradually, according to one's own capacity and physical limitations. One should never hurry over *Pranayama.*

It is recommended to carry out breathing exercises in a well ventilated room on a wide open window. The best posture to practice *Pranayam* is the lotus (*Padmasana*). If it is difficult to adopt, one can sit cross legged or on one's heels. The important point is to keep the back, neck and head in a straight line from the base of the spinal column upwards, without feeling at all tired. It is essential to breathe regularly and according to a set rhythm. In rhythm breathing inhalation should take exactly the same time as exhalation.

Each of *Yogas* is fitted to make individual perfect even without the help of the others, because they have all the same goal in view. Non attachment is the basis of all the *Yogas*, *Vairagya* or renunciation is the turning point in all the various *Yogas*. The utility of the science of *yoga* is to bring out perfect individual and not let one wait and wait for ages, just a play thing in the hands of the physical world, like a log of drift wood carried from wave to wave, and tossing about in the ocean. This science wants individual to be strong, to take the work in one's hand, instead of leaving it in the hands of Nature.

Realization of Self and Consciousness for Inculcation of Higher Values

Self has been conceived as Empirical, Physical, and Transcendental. Self-realization in empirical sense is the unfoldment of all the abilities and potentialities for worldly prosperity. Realization of the psychological self is concerned with the understanding of the laws, forces and processes of mind. The realization of the transcendental self is the spiritual realization i.e. realization of the Self. This 'Self' is the Reality, the Eternal, Ever Blessed, Ever Pure and Ever Perfect. It is the *Atman*, the Soul. The Vedas say that the whole world is a mixture of independence and dependence, of freedom and slavery, but through it all shines the Soul independent, immortal, pure, perfect, and holy. The realization of this *Atman* is the highest goal of human life. It is knowledge, it is happiness, it is God. It is Infinite, Absolute Bliss and Existence. All glory, power and purity are within the soul (self). Besides mind and body, the soul that reigns within is independent, and creates the desire for freedom. This *Atman* or self is not to be reached by too much talking (*Saastrartha*), nor is it to be reached by the power of the intellect (*Budhi*) , nor by much study of the scriptures (*Sastra Adhyayan*) but by dissolving one's ego in the universal being by the practice of *Yoga* and Meditation. The study of consciousness has been approached by Indian seers, saints, philosophers, yogis and metaphysicians from the point of view of the development of consciousness, its expansion, and its ultimate reach and goal through *Sadhana* the spiritual discipline to probe into its depth and its ultimate limit. Sometimes we call consciousness as mind, sometimes *Chitta* and so on. Our Vedic *Rishis* in *Upanishad* look upon to this *Chitta* or consciousness as some power so subtle that it can concentrate itself on a single point, a pin-point or it can expand itself to the whole of the cosmos: *Anoraniyan mahato mahiyan.* It dwells in some secret chamber of the brain and called *Atman.* It can very well be described as the *'chitkan'* a point of consciousness, the coordinating force, the *Spiriton.* It coordinates all the experiences and activities of a personality of a person or a *Purusa.*

The study of the states of our consciousness is meant for the healthy growth of consciousness with a view to attain the highest state called *'Moksha'* or *'Anand'* or causeless joy and delight, the supernatural and blissful condition which a man can attain by *'sadhana'* that is the highest attainment of the present humanity. The approach of the ancient seers and saints was always for trying to attain the highest state of consciousness within themselves, apart from the mastery that they wanted to have on material life, on their body and on other forces. Man has been trying for both these masteries: mastery over what exists outside his own body and his own mind, and mastery over the inner force which makes him live and conscious.

Man has reached in the evolutionary process a stage where he has become conscious of his own consciousness, i.e. state of self-consciousness. Self-consciousness always gives man a kind of lever for developing the power of improving the functions of his consciousness. He can see what is going on in his mind and judge right from the wrong. Even conscience is the result of a development along that line. This development of conscience is itself the result of self-consciousness and maturity.

Thus self-consciousness leads to self-introspection. Conscience which is the faculty of discrimination between right and wrong, good and bad is the result of introspection. The 'will' to follow our conscience as the guide in all matters gives us the power to control our inner powers and mastery over ourselves. The proper use of the knowledge or information received through senses depends upon our faculty of conscience (*'antaratma'*) and our control over our inner urges and elemental tendencies. It is in this sense that knowledge is power and self-knowledge leading to self-control or *'Samyama'* which is the highest power for the preservation and advance of the humanity.

In the *Mandukyopanishad*, our states of consciousness have been enumerated, namely, *Jagrit, Swapna, Susupti* and *Turiya*. *'Jagrit'* means the waking state when our mind and intellect are active and we have the full awareness of our surrounding. The second state, *'Swapna'* is somewhat between the waking and the sleeping state. It is a dream state. *'Susupti'* is supposed to be deep sleep where there are no dreams and no wakefulness. There is a kind of restfulness. Then there is *'Turiya'* a *Yogic* condition. *Turiyavastha* is described as a state of supreme joy in which individual is merged in the universal. There is no consciousness of one's self separate from the universal self. According to all systems *'Jivatma'* experiences a kind of union, a communion and oneness with *'Parmatma'* in *Turiyavastha*. So *Turiya* is that state of consciousness in which individual consciousness merges into universal consciousness which is one and indivisible. No doubt our ancient predecessors came to this conclusion by intuition, by *Sadhana*, by *Dhyana* (meditation) and by experience of a unique kind of ecstasy.

Turiyavastha is really that state of condition of consciousness where separateness is not experienced, but only oneness is experienced. *Saksatkara* i.e. seeing God face-to-face is *Turiyavastha* and its experience. This is an *Avastha* which really the *Sadhus* and *Saints* try to attain by meditation or *Yoga*.

There might be a *'Turiyatitavastha'* a state of consciousness beyond *Turiya*. In the *Taittiriyopanishad*. *Panchakosas* (five sheaths) have been described as existing in man. One is *'Annamayakosa'* which means the material and physical body;

another *'Pranamaya kosa'* means the vital sheath third is *'Manomaya kosa'* that sheath which causes cerebration, thinking, then *'Vijnanmaya kosa'* is responsible for pure objective thinking and the grasp of direct Truth, then *'Anandamaya* kosa' which is the sheath of pure joy. At the end in the *Taittiriyopanishad* there is an attainment which is beyond the *Anandamaya kosa.* That is the possibility of *'Turiyatitavstha'.*

In this *Turiyatitavastha* there might be a simultaneous double consciousness of being one and at the same time many. In this simultaneous consciousness there could be pure delight, joy and supernal bliss of merger in the Universal along with the creative ecstasy of manifestation.

Conclusion

The study of the states of our consciousness is very important if we want to make conscious progress in our evolution. Unconscious progress and evolution is going on as a part of the cosmic process. The study of one's own consciousness, its potentiality, its power and operation are required to participate in the cosmic evolution as a conscious and a self-conscious being so as to know the laws of its evolution and to be able to control and master the powers within oneself. The *Integral Yoga* of Sri Aurobindo, one of the best minds, the great seer and the great teacher of modern India, concerns itself not merely with the maintenance of health of the human mind but leads man in further progress towards the highest reaches of one's consciousness. *Integral Yoga* is a pointer to Life Divine through the establishment of a link between the consciousness of man and the super-conscious forces presiding over the destinies of cosmic evolution.

REFERENCES

Chakraborti, M. (1977). *Value Education—Changing Perspectives*, New Delhi: Kanishka Publishers.

Chilana, M.R. and Dewan, M.L. (1988). *Human Values: A Task For All.* New Delhi: Concept Publishing Company.

Das, R.C. (1988). Teacher Preparation for Education in Values. *The Indian Journal for Teacher Education;* Vol. 1, No. 1.

Goyal, B.R. (1979). Documents in Social, Moral and Spiritual Values in Education. New Delhi: NCERT.

Gupta, N.L. (1986). *Value Education—Theory and Practice.* Ajmer: Krishna Brothers.

Kohlberg, L. (1981). The Development of Moral Judgement and Moral Character. In L. Kohlberg, R. De Vries, et al. *Developmental Psychology and Early Education.* Unpublished manuscript.

NCERT (1992). *Education in Values : A Source Book.* New Delhi: NCERT.

Pandey, J.L. (1999). Value Education: Challenges for the Future. Mimeograph. New Delhi : NCERT.

Rokeach, M. (1973). *The Nature of Human Values.* New York : The Free Press.

Ruhela, S.P. (Ed.) (1986). *Human Values and Education.* Delhi : Sterling Publishers Pvt. Ltd.

Srivastava, G.N.P. (2002). *Teacher Education for Value Inculcation.* Bhopal : Regional Institute of Education.

Srivastava, G.N.P. (2003). *Nurturing Human Values Through School Education.* Bhopal : Regional Institute of Education. New Delhi: NCERT.

Wilson, J. (1972). *Practical Methods of Moral Education.* London: Heinemann Education Books.

18

Teacher Education from Value Perspectives

C.S. Shukla and S.K. Joshi

As pointed out by the Parliamentary Standing Committee on HRD (1999), "There exist inadequacies in the teacher training system which does not prepare the teachers to either assimilate or disseminate values in their teaching. Therefore, the most important intervention that has to be made is in the area of teacher education. All methods and techniques, both direct and indirect, for inculcating values, in tune with the different stages of students' psychological development should be an essential component of teacher training programme." The Kothari Commission (1964-66) also had rightly observed, "The expanding knowledge and the growing power (Science) which it places at the disposal of modern society must, therefore, be combined with the strengthening and deepening of the sense of social responsibility and a keener appreciation of moral and spiritual values." Inculcation of desirable values in the pupils is felt essential for meeting out the crisis of character. In the situation that is rapidly developing, it is equally important for us to give a proper value orientation to our educational system.

The National Policy on Education (1986) also highlights the urgent need for value education in view of the growing erosion of essential values and increasing cynic society. With a well designed system of curriculum, it is possible to make education a forceful tool for the cultivation of desirable ethical, spiritual and social values. Education should foster universal and eternal values. Value education should help to eliminate violence, superstition, fatalism and religious fanatism. Education which inculcates universal and eternal values like honesty, tolerance and truthfulness etc., will help in developing balanced individuals and in creating a humane society.

Though school teaching has been predominantly devoted to cognitive skills, teaching of values remains a very crucial educational aim. We are not just going to the content with development of knowledgeable and skilled individuals. The society desires that the schools help in developing good citizens. The society through education carries out enculturation of the young to shoulder the obligations and the responsibilities of the society. So, education has a normative function. It is through education that the culture of the society is sought to be preserved or conserved. The most essential part of a culture undeniably is its value system. Education has, therefore, a very important function of inculcating the desirable values in the pupils. Thus, teaching, imbibing and enhancing the values becomes a crucial function of the school and the classroom.

In India, value teaching is often avoided in classrooms or is not understood by the teacher with proper perspective. Hill (1991) has rightly observed and which is also true in case of India that value education is the poor cousin of other core areas in the curriculum. The openness of values, in which clinching proof of a position is often hard to pin down, easily leads to the view that such studies are 'soft' and 'vague' ... Value education remains a vague and hollow notion. This state of affairs is reflected in the nickname given by students (at a school) to social studies—they call it 'social slops' (Hill, 1991).

There is, then, an urgent demand to provide for educators a theoretical perspective so that they may themselves selectively and critically construct a theoretical foundation for their practice in the area of values.

Why Values in Teacher Education?

1. The aim is to make teacher educators aware of the human quest for ultimate and ability to dialogue with

persons of different persuations without feeling threatened or hostile, while at the same time working with them to make the democratic community function morally.

2. Through value education, teacher educators will develop a critical awareness of the value domain and assume personal responsibility for the values they embrace.
3. With the growth of electronic communication systems, barriers of distance, nationality, culture and ideology are being challenged and recast. The values which previously have been attributed to a specific locale, now would be reformulated within a more global perspective according to the space and time.
4. With the rise of multinational companies and the changing international aspects of social, economic and political life, it is the system of values which undergoes a process of globalization through examination, critique and explanation.
5. Value education is a matter of concern for both teachers and teacher educators because it relates to their future careers. The question whether the beliefs and practices of teachers in training colleges, and the values they seek to inculcate match those to be found or demanded by the social system remains a burning issue and it needs thorough research.
6. One of the major tasks of teacher education, both at pre-service and in-service level, should be to present theoretical and practical perspectives to teachers and to facilitate their critical reflection on them as a basis for classroom practice.

Perspective of Value Education

The ancient Greeks and Socrates in particular, seem to be an accepted starting point for considering theoretical perspective on values. Central to Socrates' philosophy were the two elements of 'morality' and 'logic'. Socrates based his theory upon the notion that we all want and seek 'the good' but a lack of logic leads to our doing things which we ought not to do. Therefore, in order to avoid acting immorally, people are required to clarify their thinking logically. Thus, from a Socratic perspective, value teaching may involve such strategies as value clarification in which value positions are articulated and critically appraised.

Aristotle, however, was concerned with moral virtues which included friendliness, honesty, justice and courage. For Aristotle, people were able to decide upon a moral course of action by considering the extremes of two action or attitudes for example honesty-dishonesty, patience-impatience, courage-cowardice, hard work-slothfulness etc. After considering the extremes people were then able to arrive at an understanding of a middle or appropriate course of action.

Taking Aristotle as a basis for teaching values, strategies may include comparing and contrasting behaviours and actions, role plays of situations where opposite action are taken in a given situation, debates and activities where choices are provided and options are available.

For John Dewey the context was the central concern rather than direct instruction in values. Dewey was not opposed to moral education so long as it was seen in the whole context of the environment and so long as morals were viewed as social relationships. For Dewey, then, there should be no separate area of the curriculum for dealing with values and moral education. Rather these areas of development of individual should be an integral and inevitable part of all of the experiences and activities a learner passes through. It is also pertinent to note that, for Dewey there could be no predetermined curriculum in a learning context as it was necessary for the learner to earn through experiences, and thus the curriculum was emergent and non-prescriptive. Thus, if an educator takes a stance based upon Dewey's thought, "the value dimension would be seen as part of all teaching and learning activities".

In late 1930s the 'emotivist' perspective came into prominence as discussed by Ayer (1936) and Stevenson (1944). The 'emotivist' stance feels that 'all moral utterances are essentially an attempt to persuade other to share one's own attitude'. Stevenson concludes that "the purpose of moral discussion is to reach agreement through persuation". This view involves a belief that moral reasoning is not subject to logic, reason or rationality nor it is grounded in fact or knowledge. If this perspective is to provide the basis for the teaching of values in school, activities may include debates, persuasive presentations and writings and development of techniques to expound a position or opinion lucidly.

On the other hand, Durkheim (1858-1917) shifted emphasis from the individual in society to the group as a social entity. "If we begin with the individual", Durkehim maintained, "we shall be able to understand nothing of what takes place in the group". If Durkheim's views are the basis for the teaching of values in schools, then it is upon group interactions and group decision-making strategies that the syllabus would focus. Activities might include team building where all members have a specific role to play in the successful product of a group action; group projects and assignments; and heterogeneous classroom groupings across the curriculum where the views of all are negotiated and incorporated.

The moral and developmental thinkers such as Kohlberg, following the work of Piaget in 1960s, has exerted an influence upon the teaching of values in schools. Drawing on Piaget's stages of cognitive development, Kohlberg (1975) articulated a theory of the stages of moral reasoning. The environment plays an important role in the framing and construction of the values in an individual. Each individual will pass through a series of stages in moral development though place of progress will vary according to the individual. Moral reasoning is thought by Kohlberg to be based upon educator to create an environment which enhances an individual's movement through the stages of moral reasoning. Kohlbergs' stages of moral reasoning (Kohlberg, 1966) are given below :

Pre-conventional Level

Stage 1: Avoidance of punishment and unquestioning obedience to supervisor are valued.

Stage 2 Right action consists of that which instrumentally satisfies one's own needs and occasionally the needs of others.

Conventional Level

Stage 3 Good behaviour is that which pleases or helps others and is approved by them.

Stage 4 Authority, fixed rules and the maintenance of the social order are valued.

Post-conventional Level

Stage 5 Values agreed upon by the society, including individual rights, determine what is right.

Stage 6 Right is defined by one's conscience in accordance with self-chosen ethical principles.

Kohleberg claims that the highest stage of moral reasoning is to be desired and thus he established a hierarchy of moral reasoning. The strategy involves the creation of scenario which involve a moral dilemma about appropriate choice for action. Discussion between students in a group occurs, perhaps following the role-play in the dilemma situation, and alternative approaches to the dilemma are raised, and considered. This conflict situation is all together to stimulate students to form opinions and to be able to articulate their reasons for such opinions.

Some critics such as Rest (1975) and Fraenkal (1977) raise some issues about Kohlberg's approach on pedagogical grounds in terms of their implications for the skills of matching and sequencing and the need to sequence dilemmas more rigorously than is traditionally the case.

Other strategies which have been evident in classrooms have focused upon the Value Analysis Approach of Hunt and Metcalf (1968) Banks (1973) and Fraenkel (1977). In this approach a series of stages for decision-making and moral reasoning are outlined as the basis for discussion and student activity in the areas of value education.

Indian Perspective of Value Education

Gandhiji wrote in 1926, "Everybody is right from his own standpoint". Hence the necessity for tolerance, which does not mean indifference to one's own faith, but more intelligent and purer love for it. Tolerance gives us spiritual insight which is as far from fanaticism as the North Pole is to the South. The question is how to prevent intolerance particularly religious intolerance through education, in schools and elsewhere. Swami Vivekananda once told that each religion is a path towards the same goal of salvation and, therefore, each religion must be given utmost respect. Indeed, no one religion can claim monopoly and said that it is the only way to the truth. Every religion reflects but a facet of the divine splendour, *vedahamedham purusham mahanttam adityya Varanam tamasah* as Indian civilization teaches us. Indian Vedic philosophy maintains that the sole purpose of human birth is to attain liberation (*moksha*) from *samsara*. Lord Krishna says in the *Bhagwat Gita*, "one who sees intelligent among men, and he is in the transcendental position, although engaged in all sorts of activities."

Nobody can deny the fact that education in itself is value inherent. In schools morning assembly is a very effective medium of imparting values in students. Prayers sung in chorus are bound to create faith in a supreme power in young minds and help to inculcate belief in secularism and patriotism in the students. Special emphasis should be given on a particular value everyday during the morning assembly. As suggested in Parliamentary Committee's report, "In morning assembly, students may also be encouraged to make presentation on different subjects with special focus on patriotism, national integration, humanism, cultural unity in diversity, service and sacrifice, secularism and prevailing social problems". It will definitely have an impact on all students.

Meditation can also play a key role in enhancing values in students. According to J. Krishnamurti, meditation can (and probably should) take place in a bus, or walking in a park or even looking at the faces of your loved ones. Students can sit silently and reflect about their conduct and behaviour; they can learn to develop concentration and they can be made aware of the quiet strength lying within one's body and mind. Meditation begins with the mind, not the body. Concentration and a rigidly held posture makes it difficult to practise constant awareness, the kind of awareness that is beyond imagination or desire. It is good that there is no success and no failure in meditation. It is only a constant state of total awareness. Meditation during and before examination is also bound to enhance the concentration of students resulting thereby better results.

It seems that scouting-guiding and community awareness programmes which earlier used to be a major activity in most higher secondary schools and training colleges now seem to have lost its charm. Besides that, due to burden of syllabus and limitation of time, pupil teachers, students are not generally inclined to participate in sports and other cultural activities. There is a need for promoting these activities which can prove to be effective in promoting discipline, brotherhood and creating a healthy attitude towards life.

Value education must encourage pupil teachers to:

- Develop their own personal moral codes and have concern for other;
- Reflect on experiences and search for meaning and patterns in those experiences;
- Have self respect and respect for commonly held values such as honesty, truthfulness and justice;
- Make socially responsible judgments and be able to provide justification for decisions and actions.

Religion and Values: Are they interrelated?

Although formal religion, as part of education, appears in the curriculum of most countries, this is not always reflected in the attitudes expressed by the teachers in their approach to value teaching in the classroom. The fact that religious beliefs form part and parcel of every day thought and living is, however, acknowledgement by the people who talk about faith in religion. Therefore, unless the necessity of religion is felt, there can be no proper planning of teaching

Religion tells us how to control passions (anger, pride, attachment, greed, fear, etc.), it means practice in developing the power of control. Non-belief is possible with regard to the invisible or the unattainable. But to exercise control over one's emotions is good for life. It is necessary for leading a peaceful life and getting rid of tension. The question of non-belief just does not arise here. People who often talk about lack of faith in religion, do so without understanding its nature. One may display want of faith in respect of imponderables like God and Soul, inaccessible to the intellect, but when we talk of religion on the mental and emotional level, there is no room for disbelief there. Dislike can be changed into liking. An awareness of utility and right values can transform aversion into fondness.

Although Sri Prakasa Committee (1960) observed that leaving religious education entirely to home and the community would result in the neglect of ethical teaching and spiritual values. This unfortunate ignorance of other faiths has bred prejudices and disunity. Therefore, an objective, and sympathetic study of all the major religions of India, without their myth, dogma, and rituals, should be provided for. "In ancient times of *Gurukulas,* emphasis used to be primarily on building the character of a student. Today right from the schools up to professional colleges, emphasis is on acquiring techniques and not values. We seem to have forgotten that skills acquired on computers tend to become outdated after some time but values remain forever. In other words, present day education is nothing but an information transmission process.

Hope for the Future

The worst days of a serious threat to Indian society are over. Under foreign domination and western influence we had developed the foolish notion of degrading everything, morals, ethics and spirituality and were easily swept off our feet by the glamour and glitter of the exotic. The wonderful phenomenon that is taking place now is that we are returning to these things which have lent stability and strength to our culture over the centuries. Because the various educational programmes launched by the NCTE, NCERT, UGC and other higher education organizations (like Sri Sathya Sai Institute of Higher Learning, Puttaparthi) ranging all the way from nursery to post-graduate level, are bringing into proper focus the valuable ingredients of our culture. By far the most important aspect of these programmes is that besides giving a theoretical and conceptual base in the curriculum they also seek to transform the quality of life through inculcation of human values of truth, right conduct, peace, love, *ahimsa* and, above all, national character which, in effect, represent the highest and the noblest in our culture system.

The most important aspect of the value oriented programmes is that the teachers should set examples of good conduct and behaviour which the students may imbibe in themselves. Swami Vivekananda says "The life is short, the varieties of the world are transient, but they alone live, who live for others the rest are more dead than alive".

REFERENCES

Kohlberg, L. (1975). *The Cognitive-Development Approach to Moral Education,* Phi delta Kappam, 56 (10).

Mathur, P.N. (1986). The Problem of Values in S.P. Ruhela (Ed.) *Human Values and Education.* New Delhi : Sterling Publishers Pvt. Ltd.

Ministry of Human Resource Development (1986). *National Policy on Education.* New Delhi : MHRD.

NCERT (2000). *National Curriculum Framework for School Education,* New Delhi, NCERT.

NCERT (2000). *Journal of Value Education,* Vol. 2, Number 1, New Delhi: NCERT.

Rao, S . (2004). *Education Psychology,* New Delhi: Wiley Eastern Ltd.

Rajya Sabha, Parliament of India (1999). Department Related Parliamentary Standing Committee on Human Resource Development. *Eighty-first Report on Value-Based Education,* New Delhi : Rajya Sabha Secretariat (mimeo).

Rajput, J.S. (2000). Culture and Continuity-Putting Spirit Back into Education, *The Times of India* dated 18 August 2000.

19

Teacher's Role in Imparting Value Education

J. Sthapak, H. Dinkar and M. Sthapak

Value education has been increasingly prominent in educational discussions at all levels during recent times. This issue is projected as one of the national priorities in the National Policy on Education (NPE, 1986). The NPE declares: "the growing concern over the erosion of essential values and an increasing cynicism in society have brought to focus the need for readjustments in the curriculum in order to make education a forceful tool for the cultivation of social and moral values. According to National Curriculum for Primary and Secondary Education (1985), the crisis of values our society is passing through "demands more explicit and deliberate educational efforts towards value development". The first term of reference for the National Commission on Teachers (1983) was "to lay down clear objectives for the teaching profession with reference to the search for excellence, breadth of vision and cultivation of values...". The Working Group to review teachers training programmes in the light of the need for value orientation set up by the Government of India in 1983 recommended for the inclusion of a value education component in the teacher education programme besides spelling out details of curriculum, methodology and teachers rule (Burnes et al. 2000).

Need for Value Based Teacher Education

Today we are in a technological world where things are happening fast. Parents and teachers would like to be getting results fast. India has kept pace in science and technology with advanced nations. But we have shown slower pace in our value system even when we have a strong heritage of human values. India was quoted by great visionaries and saints as a *Punya Bhumi*. Swami Vivekananda reiterated in his powerful words: "If there is any land on this earth that can lay claim to be the blessed *Punya Bhumi,* to be land to which souls on this earth must come to account for *karma,* the land to which every soul is wending its way Godward must come to attain its lost home, the land where humanity has attained its highest towards gentleness, towards generosity, towards purity, towards calmness, above all, the land of introspection and of spirituality—It is India." Thus value Education has been elucidated by Swamiji. From such a state, we are in the pythonic grip of deepening value crisis. How unfortunate it is!!!

In the National Policy on Education (NPE) and the Programme of Action (1992) emphasis was given to value oriented education, and ten core elements were made an integral part of the school curriculum (Fyfe, 1993). But their transaction has continued to remain fragmented. What is now required is to use the instrument of pre-service teacher education for ensuring that entrant teachers understand holistically the concept of education in human values, and are able to use direct and indirect techniques in formal and informal education for the development of values through the schooling process.

The NPE (1986) and subsequently the POAs have been emphasising the faith in *vidya dadati vinayam, vinayat yati patratam, patratwat dhanamapnoti, dhanat dharmam tataha sukham.* It is learning and knowledge that gives capability to earn, and earning the ability to do dharma for a noble cause and this results in gaining peace. All the commissions, reports and recommendations have one thing in common and that is, changing curriculum at different levels for capacity building among teachers. Further, recent studies and analysis of evaluation of achievements at different levels have clearly shown the quality concerns and that teacher factor and his/her performance is poor but responsibilities are more. There is need to train teachers several new techniques and bring them to the frontline in this task of building a national system of education with a focus on Value Education. Thus educating the whole child and developing values assumed importance in recent years. Considering value education in a broader and more comprehensive way, the NCERT Curriculum Framework (2000) has explicitly mentioned that "Value education and education about religions would not form a separate subject of study or examination at any stage of the curriculum. These would be so judiciously integrated with all the subjects of study in the scholastic areas and all the activities and programmes in the co-scholastic areas to achieve the objectives." Thus values would be essential component of any curriculum. It was Swami Vivekananda whose vision was to educate the whole man. "Education is manifestation of perfection already in man." Again it was Swamiji who spelt this idea as "man-making and character building education." These thoughts of the philosopher clearly gives the direction to the reconstruction of the curriculum at several stages of education. These ideas are also reflected in the principles of curriculum. (Martin, 1990; Parker, 1999)

Educational objectives refer to explicit formulations of the ways in which students are expected to be changed by the educative process. That is, the ways in which they will change in their thinking, their feelings and their actions. The Objectives whether of value education or of any other curricular area depend on a variety of factors, psychological, sociological and epistemological, indicating thereby appropriate tools and processes in changing contexts.

Changing Value in Education

As the world has entered the Information Age another dimension to value education concerns information itself. This is to do with the nature of information. Information is received by human beings through five senses—the sense of seeing, hearing, touch, taste and smell. Information as any one of us receives it is value neutral. Information of seeing is carried by electro-magnetic waves, which consist of vibrations of electric and magnetic fields. These vibrations when received by our eyes are transmitted as signals to the brain. The response of brain to information received is determined by sub-conscious mind. A person may feel happy, threatened or worried by what he sees. A piece of rope when perceived as a snake can cause feeling of fear and a snake when perceived as a piece of rope gives the feeling of dealing with a harmless object (Verter et al., 2000, Zigler, 1998).

Similarly, when information is received as voice, it comes in the form of physical changes in the medium that carries the sound waves, which generally is air. It comprises of condensation and rare faction of density of the medium. The audio information through the eardrums reaches the brain. When an audio information reaches the brain response of a listener to that information is also determined by its sub-conscious mind. A listener may perceive it as music and get a feeling of happiness, or may perceive it as noise and become aggressive or get emotionally disturbed. Different types of reactions to an information have nothing to do with its nature. Information can either be an electromagnetic wave or an acoustic wave or even some molecules that may reach the nose. Information does not carry emotions. It is a common reaction to blame the information for the way an individual reacts to it. It is possible to change the quality of response to an information by raising the level of sub-conscious mind to a level of higher consciousness.

We do agree that the technology has developed in a multi-faceted manner. Especially the Information Technology has reduced the gap between man and machine. Just being self-sufficient is not enough for an overall growth of an individual, but it should also mean the characteristic growth of an individual. All technological advancement should result in the reorientation of new trends and goal-oriented values. Unless we revamp the education system with these inclusions along with enlighted thoughts and sentiments, we cannot boast of our trends and values. If it is essential, only then formal education is to be replaced with non-formal education. Some universities and academic institutions are updating their curriculum with non-formal syllabi and courses just to attract the students. Instead of improving the value of the education, it only spoils the atmosphere of education. Some foreign establishments and universities are thriving in our nation just for this purpose. Their rigorous campaigning and attractive course materials are attracting a good number of Indian students. Though the fee structure is very high in these institutes, the parents are not worried about placing their wards for a foreign degree. Instead of being creative and competitive, the students are becoming just degree oriented. Ultimately, the urge to become instant leaders spoils their future. The degrees and diplomas offered by these institutions have formalised the system so much that our whole society is swelling up with the educated unemployed. This slowly degrades our values of education.

Objectives of Value Education in Present Context

Objectives, especially in value education, have a temporal dimension. Traditionally the objectives of value education were based on religion and philosophy. There was no secular value education and very little scope for the development of moral thinking and the capacity for independent moral decision. In the modern world it is expected that every individual must possess certain minimum social skills. S/he has to establish decent relationship with people with whom s/he may come across for a short while or for a long duration. S/he may have to transact business in his private or public capacity. S/he has to function as a citizen of his state, or his country and to the world, all at the same time playing appropriate roles in each of these contexts. There are also many other demands made on him/her that need not be enumerated. Value education therefore, is pointed out to prepare an individual in meeting these demands. That these cannot be accomplished in the form of a few do's and don'ts of the traditional form is quite evident.

The Working Group on value oriented education has identified five dimensions on value education, these being physical education, emotional education, mental development, aesthetic development and the moral and spiritual domain. The values to be pursued in the moral and spiritual realm, according to them are: sincerity, faithfulness, obedience to what one conceives to be the highest, gratitude, honesty, benevolence, generosity, cheerfulness, selflessness, freedom from egoism, equanimity in joy and suffering, in honour and dishonour, success and failure, pursuit of the deepest and the highest of the absolute and ultimate and the progressive expression of this pursuit in thought, feeling and action (Richardson, 1995; Rokeach, 1973).

In many countries today the emphasis is on socio-economic reconstruction with the declared intention of a more equitable distribution of the benefits brought about by modernisation. Traditional cultural values have had little time to adjust to certain attributes of modernisation. Planners of value education curriculum then are faced with the problems of identifying values and character traits that will best equip the individual in modern society. The objectives of value education should be such that the curriculum should recognize the tensions that are brought about by the conflicts between tradition and change. The planned programme should aim at developing a critical value perspective in our pupils that will enable them to employ modern skills for the betterment of mankind while helping them renew their commitment to fundamental traditional values. ,

Role of Teacher

Each teacher has to be a value educator and a role model. The teacher has to be a living example of desirable values that s/he wants the students to imbibe. S/he should realize that "Teaching is not a Profession but a Mission". In this Mission the teacher should be a source of inspiration. The teacher should create right situation, activities and environment for development of specific values. Following actions are suggested to be undertaken by the teachers :

- Practicing those values which are expected to be inculcated among children.
- Consciously avoiding manifestation of undesirable values in his/her behaviour and actions.
- Identifying the potential areas and situations in different subjects for inculcating values and be sensitizing these values as role model.
- Integrating values with learning of contents and skills in all curricular activities—classroom, laboratory, workshop, on-the-job training, project work etc.
- Organising visits and field trips to develop cultural and aesthetic values in children.
- Motivating students for participation in social events and practical classes.
- Identifing and recording various behaviour and attitudes of students which depict desirable values. Same may be suitably recognized and appreciated during curricular and co-curricular activities in the school.
- Organising parent-teacher association meetings to highlight the specific role of parents towards inculcation of values in their children.
- Organising competitions in production of quality goods or in rendering quality services to develop confidence, skills and value for time, excellence and perfection.
- Organising activities to develop leadership qualities, service mindedness, teamwork and cooperation among students.
- Conducting visits to industry/work situation to observe not only performing skills but values inculcated in relation to the work.
- Involving other stakeholders in curricular and co-curricular activities to demonstrate certain values.

Teacher-Pupil Relationships and Values

Teaching-learning processes and interactions among teachers and pupils have unlimited potentials for value generation. The teacher conveys value through personality as role models, presenting knowledge in ways leading to development of selective cultural position among pupils as well as their interaction with pupils. Teacher therefore is a very essential instrument of preparing for value education. Teacher preparation for value education has three clear cut faces. First of all their own context of values and cultures has to be broadened to include the universality of culture and society; they have to be familiarised with the agent of education in human values, and human development. This calls for flow information which sensitises them to these issues.

Secondly, action has to be initiated for development of their own interaction skills for facilitation of interpersonal interaction which includes skills of listening, responding, empathy and genuineness. Development of these skills require availability of reading materials, training modules and organisation of training programmes. Action on these issues has to be expedited for our vast nation using all possible strategies supported by technology. However, before putting in practice intervention ought to be examined and assessed. Lastly, the competencies related to teaching of subjects have to be situated in the multi-cultural context.

This would make it imperative that teachers have awareness of link between transaction strategies and their impact on values. Ignorance of the linkages and issues may result in their inadvertently causing harmful influence in the minds of students about cultural issues. Teaching of science organised in different ways has implication for the method and approaches of science that students will learn, some of which work against science (Bonnet M. 2000). Language itself being carrier of values, its teaching has an impact on values; geography and history, etc. all could be taught in ways having different influence on pupils about cultural attitudes.

Role of School Management

- The school management should be transparent, honest and sensitive. The conduct and behaviour of key functionaries should be such that it inspires others to practice desirable values.
- Making available relevant books, journals and supplementary reading materials on value education including biographies of great national personalities in the school.
- Deputing teachers and other staff for participation in seminars/workshops/training programmes on value education organised by different organisations.
- Orienting teachers to observe value-based behavioural change in students and appreciate the same.
- Organising value-based literary and cultural activities such as plays, debates, essay and poem competitions, story writing, folk songs and dances etc. which should emphasize, respect for manual work as well as social cohesion and national integration.
- Celebrating important national days, birthdays of great national leaders and freedom fighters and festivals (such as Independence Day, Republic Day, Gandhi Jayanti, Bal Diwas, Teachers Day, Holi, Diwali, Eid, Christmas, Vaisakhi, Mahavir Jayanti, Vivekanand Jayanti, Subhash Jayanti, etc.) with magnanimity and festivity for inculcation of national values and understanding and respect for each other's religion.
- Developing mechanisms of reward to motivate teachers and students for practicing values.
- Organising activities and programmes to inculcate respect for manual work such as cleanliness, plantation, etc.
- Ensuring community participation in this venture (Boyatzis et al. 2000)

Society, Teacher and Values

The role of a teacher in the changing social scenario is becoming very challenging. In the earlier times teacher was the only source of information and commanded respect on this count. Any one desirous of gaining knowledge had to bow down before *guru*. Today, we have multiple information centers. There are books, coaching centre, the audio visual aids such as audio cassettes, video tapes, microfilms and internet services that provide a flux of information to those who need it. Thus teacher's role as the only source of information is marginalized. The society is becoming more materialistic and values appear to be pushed into the background. There is nothing unusual about it. Each era throws up a role model and the whole society tries to emulate this model. Consider the Vedic times when wise man or a *Rishi* was an icon. Even the kings and the princes came down to his hermitage, sat at his feet to get Knowledge. When one looks into the period of *Mahabharata,* the role models had changed. The heroes of this era are undoubtedly the mighty warriors such as Bhishma, Drona, Karna, Arjuna etc. The Brahmin Dronacharya was teaching the princes warfare instead of philosophy. Even the god incarnate, Parshurama was also teaching the princes warfare instead of philosophy. Every one wanted to be a great warrior. Before independence of India, our role models were Gandhi, Patel, Bhagat Singh, Rajguru and other freedom fighters. It was the dream of every youngster to be a freedom fighter and every school in the country was a training ground for freedom fighting. All school campuses vibrated with the chanting sounds of *vande mataram.* After independence, unfortunately, the icon of the society has been a rich man. Every one in the society is aspiring to become rich, as much as possible and as quickly as possible. Getting rich at any cost has been the motto. Invariably this process of getting rich instantly is at the cost of values (Sharma ,1995).

The situation would not remain like this forever. There are enough indications that our country would awaken once again to those eternal values for which this land has stood for many centuries. We are at a transition time during which it is essential that the values are maintained and nurtured. Only an ideal teacher whose life itself is a beacon light of values can lead a society in the right direction. S/he has to demonstrate the essential values such as optimism, motivation, willingness to learn and teach, truth, non-violence, never to speak and think ill of others, creativity and ability to demonstrate un-addressed love. This is a tall order. But, that is the responsibility that the teacher must take in order to be an effective catalyst for social change.

School processes and activities which includes the conduct of morning assembly, games, board displays, organisation of parent-teacher meetings, cultural and the other related activities, all have implications for integrating practical aspect of value education relating to persona, social and moral values. The activities have great potential for creating awareness of issues which leads to development of understanding and sensitivity for other cultures. However, the potential inherent in all the processes could be realised for value education only with orientation of staff, teachers and out of school systems by exposing them to appropriate culturally sensitizing information and experiences (Prahalada, 1994).

Values as Culture

The Indian culture is deeply rooted in spiritual values and unless these values find their way into the life of students, education will lose its significance and will not fulfil its function of endowing the students with a vision to live by and with the ideals to work for. Therefore, in deference to the cherished goals of democracy, socialism, humanism and secularism, it is very essential that our education system should evolve a new positive morality, which could effectively be built into the social curriculum.

It is essential that, the teachers also should be exposed to the traditional values and ethics of education through training programmes time to time. They should not confine to their job to a mere matter of completing syllabus and following the curriculum. There should be a platform for teachers to deliberate on any sensitive issues or topics as and when the need arises. They should also explore the ideas of accepting modernisation, globalisation and liberalisation from the academic point of views. They should also learn while imparting their duties for which they are meant. By creating a conducive atmosphere for intellectual rigour and freedom of expression and thought, one can practice values and thereby developing a value culture.

REFERENCES

Barnes, M. Clarke, D. and Stephens, M. (2000). Assessment: The Engine of Systematic Curricular Reform? Journal of Curricular Studies, 32(5), pp. 623-650

Bonnet, M. (2000). Value Issues in Developing Children's Thinking. In Leicester, M. et al. (series ed.) *Education, culture and values.* Vol 111, New York: Falmer Press.

Boyatzis, R.E. Murphy, A.J. and Wheeler, J.V. (2000). Philosophy as a Missing Link betwen Values and Behaviour. *Psychological Reports,* 86, p. 47-664.

Fyfe, A and Figueroa, P. (Eds) (1993). *Education for Cultural Diversity: The Challenge for a New Era.* London: Routledge.

Martine, J.R. (1990). Filing the Gap the Goal of American Education (Revised); *International* 36(2) pp. 145- 157.

Parker, W.C. Ninomiya A. and Cogan J. (1999). Educating World Citizens: Towards Multinational Curriculum Development *American Educational Research Journal* 36(2) pp. 117-145.

Prahalada, N.N. (1994). Contemporary Significance of Value Education *University News.* Richardson, R. (1995) The Hidden Message of School Books *Journal of Moral Education* 15 (1), 26-42

Rokeach, M. (1973). *The Nature of Human Values.* New York: The Free Press.

Sigler, R.E. (1998). The Four Domains of Moral Education. The Contribution of Dewey, Alexander and Goleman to a Comprehensive Taxamony. *Journal of Moral Education* 27(1), pp. 19-33.

Sharma, L.S. (1995). Role of Education in India Modernisation in Uberoi N.K (ed.) *Professional Competency in Higher Education,* UGC, New Delhi

Venter, E. Franzsen, K. and Heerden, E.V. (2000). An Analysis of the Effect of Recent National Policy Changes of Values and Education in South Africa. In Lecisester, M. Modgil, C. and Modgil, S. (Series. eds). *Education, Culture and Values,* Vol. I London: Falmer Press.

20

Values in Teacher Education

H.S. BAJWA

Our society has undergone sea changes due to political, social, economic and technology pressures. The worship of false values and false heroes has assumed great importance. At no time in the living history did we witness this worship of wrong values as we do today. Honour and virtue are not a familiar currency in modern life and thought. Contradictions in living is the order of the day. We find economic competition of the extreme on the one side and talk of brotherhood and affection on the other. A double moral standard is the reality which is no healthy setting for decent pupils' growth. Reality does not seem to them (youths) to reflect the values taught in the books. It puzzles them to find if values are so important to life and living why they are not reflected in the life of most people in society.

The Social Context

It is a well accepted fact that modern age is the age of materialism. The mundane felicity is leading towards the increasing complexities of modern society. Man has become an economic animal in the context of technological advancement. The never ending race after materials in the absence of channeled and moralized way of life has maligned the minds of men by stirring in various impurities of selfish motives. Our society today is in the throes of moral and cultural crisis. The existing education system has failed to create a decent society. Value system in the present day academic set up takes a back seat. Professional competence is given priority but a professionally competent teacher without values cannot contribute to the cause of a healthy society. The greatest need of today is that man in his mad race and in pursuit of transient materialistic gains and objectives, should, at least occasionally, pause and reflect on the real purpose and value of human life and give a fresh orientation to his view of life based on such introspective reflection. If this were done one should have no difficulty to realize that amongst all living species the human being occupies a special and exalted place by reason and discrimination aided by a discerning intellect and faculties of analytical thinking, assimilation and recollection. From time immemorial these special gifts have generated in man a keen sense of inquiry in search of truth, wisdom and bliss, which are the source of basic human values. The importance of imparting education in human values to youngsters has always been felt and emphasized by all great religious teachers, educationists, social reformers and all other sorts of humanists in varying degrees, in one way or the other, throughout the world in all ages. But at present juncture of the history of human civilization its importance has become extremely acute and critical due to riotous interplay of diverse economic, technological, political, cultural and social disorganization. The educational systems in India and almost everywhere in the world are miserably failing to work for the spiritual, moral and social upliftment of human being.

The Developmental Context

The present age is an age of Globalization, Liberalization and Information Technology. The global economic developments give rise to both competition and interdependence between the countries. In the present century our education will face the issues of enhancing competitive ability on one side and cultivating human and cultural potentials on the other side. Information technology cannot humanize an individual. It does not help to elevate the moral values, but a teacher does. Because of the free access to the information on the internet, users may be exposed to a volley of incorrect information and hostile propaganda. The government will not have any control over the information transmitted through internet, media etc. which may lead to cultural degradation. The possibility of virus attack through internet is a source of constant menace to the users of information technology. Teacher can suggest good websites to the student from where they can get healthy literature. Imparting of values by the teacher will always continue inspite of IT revolution. Values required for humanity and harmony will have to be taught by the teacher. He is required to inculcate human values of integrity, uprightness, truthfulness, compassion and culture and educate students about the environment and other living being.

If the teacher, who is kingpin in the schooling process, is personally committed to the values and practices them in his/her own life, it is a foregone conclusion that his/her student will imbibe the values for which teacher stands. Teacher must have value oriented outlook. Values cannot be taught through lectures. Values are inculcated in students through daily life of teachers and students.

Identifying Values

Of all the countries in the world, we in India have the richest cultural and spiritual heritage. India was known for higher values of life. It is a said irony of fate that we have been denying students of this country even the barest opportunity to imbibe the great moral, cultural and spiritual values that form part of this heritage by imposing a taboo on all moral and spiritual instructions in the educational institutions in the name of secularism. It is imperative to distinguish value education from religious education. Teachers, parents, social workers, in fact every responsible citizen of India are concerned about erosion of values. Some people say there is no erosion of values, rather there is just a change of values. Whether it is erosion of values or change in values, it is pertinent to identify values.

The contemporary Indian society is also passing through a state of turmoil. As someone has said, "the tricolor fluttering all over the country is black, red and scarlet-black money, red tape and scarlet corruption (Chittibabu, 1997). There is an all-round chaos, disorder, hatred, pain, misery, violence, injustice, corruption, conflict, despair and so on. The list is endless. The problem is not purely Indian in nature as the collective injustices are on the rise everywhere.

A crisis situation arises, when we make an attempt to identify values that could be universally accepted. In a 'pluralistic contemporary world, each culture has its own identity and their autonomy is well regarded. However, each culture is constituted by several sub-cultures. Further, each man has not only his own identity but he is an independent source of values. On the other hand, no culture, sub-culture or individual, can live in isolation. Mutual interactions and interplay are inevitable. So the question arises, whether values depend on individual choices? To answer it, Agrawal (1998) stated, "By their very nature, values in general must be independent of individual whims and fancies, and some, the more basic ones must in principle be universal." He further added that the values can be personal and private but they can exist only, if there are some values, which in principle, are universally accepted.

In an attempt to identify values that need to be inculcated through education, the Education Reforms Commission, Punjab, organized a seminar in 1983 at Chandigarh. The seminarians identified 10 values, which if successfully integrated with the content and process of education, would help in the realization of value-education goals. These include: excellence (truth, beauty and goodness); scientific temper and spirit of inquiry; national unity and integrity; justice; freedom; equality; fraternity; secularism; empathy; and maintenance of harmony.

Transaction of Values

The intellectualization of moral education puts one in quandary as to relate moral education with other intellectual studies. This leads to a conflicting situation in decision making as to whether values can be taught as a separate subject or these need to be taught through the instrumentality of a number of subjects. It is equally pertinent to think that any casual treatment of values would lead to disintegration of personality rather than its integration. For the content of value education we will have to adopt the instrumentality of integrating values with other subject areas and educational programmes.

Value Orientation in Teacher Training

Inspite of the recommendations of several commissions on education that education on human values be treated as an integral part of curriculum, there is continuous erosion of values. The reasons for this state may be that their transaction has continued to be fragmented. It has compelled to use the instrument of pre-service teacher education for enabling future teachers to develop values through the schooling process.

Parameters for Training of Teachers

Any task force for training of teachers for better imparting of value education should be primarily concerned with the following parameters:

- Identification of essential values to be cultivated by learners.
- Principal causes for erosion of values.
- Avenues of elimination of disruptive forces leading to erosion of values.
- Identification of values contributing to national cohesion.
- Specific thrust towards prominent aesthetic and moral values like tolerance, goodness, integrity etc.
- Abiding and endearing approach to values glorifying heritage and culture, civilization and progress.
- Certain insistence on upholding values like truth, beauty, austerity, non-violence etc. to ensure advancement in character formation.

While emphasis should be given on the above, teacher education should be forewarned with the following guidelines in dealing with value education as suggested by the National Policy on Education (1986) that the growing concern over the erosion of essential values and an increasing cynicism in society has brought to focus the need for readjustments in the curriculum in order to make education a forceful tool for the cultivation of social and moral values. In our culturally plural society, education should foster universal and eternal values oriented towards the unity and integrity of our people. Such value education should help in eliminating obscurantism, religious fanaticism, violence, superstition and fatalism.

Integrating Values with Teacher Training Programmes

The question before the teacher education is whether for imparting value orientation of pre-service teachers a new course would have to be introduced or the entire programme of preparatory teacher education should be given a value orientation? The answer to this question could be given through a metaphor. If sweetened milk, sugar is not visible but its presence is felt by its taste. Sweetened milk is preferred to have unsweetened milk and eating sugar afterwards. Therefore, for giving value orientation to the curriculum of teacher education instead of adding to the existing course a separate additional subject, it would be more appropriate to inseparably integrative value education in it. Just as A and B loose their properties and become a different compound after going through a chemical reaction, teacher training programme and value education need to meet and become value oriented teacher training programme.

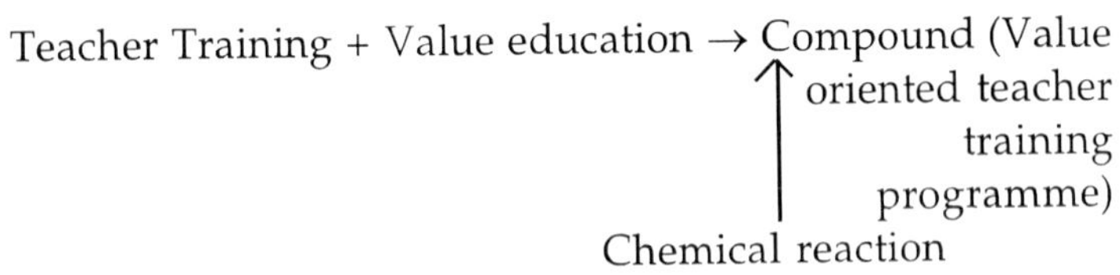

Fig. 20.1: Values in Teacher Education

There are two challenges that may have to be faced in providing value orientation to teacher education—stability and change. Stability demands preservation of culture and change demands technology. The National Council for Teacher Education (NCTE) is well aware of this challenge. The foci of its recent initiatives have been on developing resource materials on indigenous thoughts on education and promotion of use of information and communication technologies in school education through teachers. It has been playing the role of an innovator and that of a facilitator at the same time. Hence, the thrust of its recent efforts have been on production of multimedia resource materials on education in human values and conduction of orientation programmes for teacher educators with the help of experts and of institutions, which have specialized in the field of value education.

The NCTE has been conducting orientation programmes on education in human values for teacher educators and repackaging electronically the contributions of the experts and those of the participants. The outcomes of its programmes are distributed to each of its recognized institutions on multimedia CD-ROMs and through the World Wide Web of the Internet. Full texts of publications on value education in easily downloadable form have been made available on the NCTE web site (http://www.ncte-in.org). Titles related to value education available form the NCTE web site are: *Education for Character Development; Education for Tomorrow; Report of the Working Group to Review Teachers Training Programme; Role and Responsibility of Teachers in Building up Modern India; Gandhi on Education; Sri Aurobindo on Education;* and *Tilak on Education.* The titles of the NCTE CD-ROMs on value education are *New Education for New India—Integral Education of Sri Aurobindo, Jeevan Vigyan and Teachers as Transformer.* A CD-ROM based on the workshop that was organized by the NCTE jointly with the Chinmaya World Centre will be released shortly.

Conclusion

It may be appreciated that the role of the NCTE in bringing any curricular change in teacher education programme, even providing facilitation in integration of education in human values in it, at best, is that of a catalytic agent. What NCTE trying is to make available a basket ful of resource materials on education in human values to teacher education institutions. Training of teachers is of paramount importance in the process of cultivating values among students. Prospective teachers in their pre-service programme need to be provided rigorous training to imbibe desirable values. Further appropriate experiences need to be provided to them to acquire competencies to develop values among students. There is a need to prepare teacher educators to be adept in training teachers for imparting instructions on values to pupils in an ardent and all-embracing way. Then these teachers and their pupils (teacher trainees) forming a force in society could bring about changes needed to establish value education as a practice for all.

REFERENCES

Agarwal, M.M. (1998). *Ethics and Spirituality*. Shimla: Indian Institute of Advanced Studies.

Chakrabarti, M. (1988). *Teacher Education Modem Trends*. New Delhi: Kanishka Publishers, Distributors.

Chhitbabu, S.V. (1997). *Value Orientation of Education*. University News, New Delhi 35(18).

Delors, J. (1996). *Learning:* The *Treasure Within* Paris: UNESCO.

Morris, Charles (1956). *Varieties of Human Values*. Chicago: The University of Chicago Press.

Natarajan, V. and Kulshrestha, S.P. (1983). *Assessing Non-Scholastic Aspects of Learning Behaviour*. New Delhi: Association of Indian Universities.

Puri A. (2005). *Value Orientation in Teacher Education New Horizons*. Amritsar: Khalsa College of Education.

Ruhela, S.P. (1986). *Human Values and Education*. New Delhi: Sterling Publishers Private Limited.

IV

ICT and Context Specific Competencies

21

ICT Innovations in Teacher Education

D.N. SANSANWAL

The destiny of India is being shaped in her classrooms (Indian Education Commission, 1964). The shaping is being done by the teachers. It is believed that teachers are born. It might be true today too but teachers can be trained. This view has gained weight and momentum. Consequently researchers started investigating the best strategy of training the teachers. It has given different models of training teachers. Some of the models were in the form of innovations. Even today also researchers are trying to design the training strategy that best equips the teachers to deal with different situations and perform at his/her best competency level. Today, in general, schools do not get the competent teachers to teach. The quality of shaping is not being achieved at the school level. This has drastically affected the quality at the university level. Further, the unplanned expansion of teacher's training programme is also contributing in degradation of quality of teacher's preparation. The main cause is non-availability of quality teacher educators. Under such circumstances, Information and Communication Technology (ICT) can play an important role in the preparation of quality teachers. Researchers from different parts of the world are trying to use ICT in training of teachers. Looking to the potentiality of ICT, National Council for Teacher Education (NCTE) has put lots of emphasis on its use. Even NCTE organized ICT orientation campus for training the teacher educators. Not only this even the CDs were developed and distributed free to each teacher training institute. National

Assessment and Accreditation Council (NAAC) has put ICT as one of the criteria of grading the teacher-training institutes. At this stage, thus, it becomes imperative to make teacher educators aware of the ICT related innovations in teacher education.

Assumptions for Innovations

Different people have defined innovation in different ways. Innovation is the introduction of new ideas, goods, services, and practices that are intended to be useful (though a number of unsuccessful + innovations can be found throughout history). The main driver for innovation is often the courage and energy to better the world. An essential element for innovation is its application in a commercially successful way. Innovation has punctuated and changed human history (consider the development of electricity, steam engines, motor vehicles, et al.). .... One of the attributes of innovation is the newness attached with it. After its wide use, the newness fades away. Whenever the researcher puts forth the innovation to the users, it might be having the following assumptions.

- **Usefulness:** The innovation must bring out the desired change in the target group. This change should be visible and measurable.
- **Economical in terms of Time and Money:** The innovation should be affordable by majority of users.
- **Easy to Implement:** The implementation should be easy and smooth. It should not take lots of time in its implementation.
- **Availability of Infrastructure:** The implementation of any innovation will require some physical infrastructure. If the infrastructure required is too costly then the innovation may not be implemented in the field or only a few can use it.
- **Availability of Human Resources:** Any innovation will require manpower to use it for the benefit of the people. If the trained manpower is not available then the innovation will die its natural death.

- **Trainable:** The innovation should be such so that people can be trained to use it.
- **Acquired Skills should be transferable to schools:** The skills acquired in the use of innovation should be such so that these can be transferred to the schools. Without transferability there is no sense of innovation.
- **Environment Friendly:** The innovation should be environment friendly. The people should not fear to use it. People are not threatened. Innovation should be able to attract and motivate people.
- **Socially Acceptable:** Each society has its norms, values and traditions. Innovation should be able to safeguard them.
- **Matches with the Philosophy of the Nation:** Each nation has a philosophy. The innovation should be able to match with the Philosophy of the Nation. If it does not happen, then the social acceptability will not be there. Hence, it will be difficult to implement.
- **It breaks the monotony:** The system does not produce desirable result due to its monotony. The people also loose their interest. Thus, the innovation should be able to break the monotony of the system.

Web Based Instruction

According to WBT Information Centre (1997), Web Based Instruction (WBI) is an innovative approach to distance learning in which Computer Based Training (CBT) is transformed by the technologies and methodologies of the World Wide Web (WWW), the Internet and Intranets. WBI presents content in a structure format that allowing self-directed, self-paced instruction on any topic. WBI is media rich learning fully capable of evaluation, adaptation and remediation, all independent of computer platform.

Ron Kurtus (1998) states that, in its strictest sense, Web Based Training (WBT) is the communication of information over the WWW or Web with the objective of instructing or training the user. WBT is actually a form of Computer Based Training (CBT) that uses the Web or company intranet as the delivery medium instead of using disks or CD-ROMs. Both CBT and WBT are part of a larger classification called Electronic Performance Support System (EPSS) that includes such communication forms as online manuals and Windows Help. Instead of holding to the strict training definition of WBT, the tools and techniques explained will include other form of EPSS on the Web, such as, work procedures, service manuals, help and guides.

Fig. 21.1: Comparison between Traditional Instruction and WBI

Characteristics	*Traditional Instruction*	*Web-Based Instruction*
Instructional philosophy	Instructivist	Constructivist
Teacher's role	Didactic lecturer	Facilitator
Student's role	Passive learner	Active learner
View of collaboration	Cheating	Constructing knowledge
Learning paradigm	Content-driven	Concept-driven
Problem solving	Algorithmic	Situated and relevant
Time on task	Limited by class period	Asynchronous and synchronous
Pedagogy	Abstract to concrete	Concrete to abstract
Sequence and duration	Bounded by college term	Flexible entry and exit points
Communication	Teacher-directed	Student-initiated
Adaptivity	Not individualized	Individualized for learner

Sansanwal and Nawayot (2001) defined Web Based Instruction as a hypermedia-based instructional programme that utilizes the attributes and resources of the WWW to create a meaningful learning environment where learning is fostered and supported. They developed WBI for facilitating the reasoning ability of people. It was a website put for three weeks and 72 people belonging to countries, like, Australia, Africa, America, France, Germany, India, Japan, Laos, Malaysia, Nepal, Singapore, Thailand and UK visited the developed website. Out of 72 visitors, 55 took the pretest and 45 took both pretest and posttest. The reason of not taking the test was that the WBI was in English and visiting people did not know English. So language can be the barrier in WBI. The WBI was found to be effective in facilitating reasoning ability amongst people belonging to different countries and age groups.

WBI is an innovation in Teacher Education as it has all the attributes of an innovation and can be implemented in the Indian situation. It can go a long way in improving the quality of existing teachers' training programme. Even the teacher-educators can use it to bridge the gap in their understanding and knowledge. This can also help in meeting the shortage of quality teacher educators. Not only this even it can also be used for improving the teaching and other competencies of the existing school teachers. Teachers can be trained at their workplaces. It will be cost effective as well as time effective. It is more flexible. Thus, the teacher education institutes can move use of it for the benefit of trainees as well as teachers.

Cross Cultural Studies

So far, the researches conducted in India and abroad are limited to a narrow population. Due to this the findings of the studies do not have wider implications. This boundary can be widened with the help of ICT. The study conducted by Sansanwal and Nawayot (2001) has clearly demonstrated that without expenses the cross-cultural researches can be conducted. The researcher needs to learn some basics of designing required website. ICT has not been used extensively for conducting researches. The use of ICT can help in widening the coverage of population, proper selection of sample, data collection, data analysis, sharing the findings, etc. At present the researchers find it difficult to decide the appropriate technique to analyze the data, interpret the results, write the discussion as well as implications of findings. This can be taken care of with the help of ICT.

Computer Based Diagnostic Testing

The common observation is that the quality of teaching in the classroom is on the decline. More and more students are depending on the private tutorial classes. The private tuition also has become a business. This phenomenon is not only prevalent in India but also present in other countries too. There are about 800 students from USA who have enrolled themselves for private tuition in Mathematics. It means tuitions are also being outsourced. This is being done through the use of ICT. These students fail to understand certain concepts or retain certain information. This can be improved by introducing the diagnosis and remediation in the process of teaching - learning. However, such practice is not adopted in usual classroom teaching. The reasons might be large class size, non-availability of diagnostic tests in different subjects, lack of training, money and desire on the part of teacher, etc. This is the age of technology. These difficulties can be easily overcome with the help of ICT. Sansanwal (2005) has developed and tried out Computer Based Diagnostic Testing in Mathematics in CBSE affiliated schools situated at Indore, M.P, India. It works well and has helped the teacher as well as students in identifying the gray area of each and every student. This can be put on the website of the school and the student can access it from home also. The student can prepare the topic/chapter and can take the test to find exactly what he has not understood? The teacher cannot do this manually. The student progress can be monitored and his/her performance can be improved. This will develop confidence in students and may change their attitude towards the subject. It may also help in reducing the suicidal tendency among students. Students may start enjoying learning. Similarly, Sansanwal and Dahiya (2006) have developed computer based diagnostic test in Research Methodology and Statistics. It has been titled as Test Your Understanding: Research Methods and Statistics. Thus, ICT can be used to improve the quality of pre as well as in-service teacher training programmes.

Curriculum Development

At present some of the Universities are able to improve and update their curriculum. Each university has its own procedure of developing curriculum. This is quite old and too narrow. In this digitalized world, the universities should change some of their procedures related to curriculum development, examination, evaluation of doctoral work, etc. Each University must have its website. The curriculum can be put on the website and suggestions can be invited for its improvement. It broadens the scope of receiving the suggestions. At present in India, in spite of efforts made by UGC as well as NCTE, many universities are still not in a position to update the teacher education syllabus. In many universities microteaching is incorporated in teacher education curriculum just for name shake. Models of Teaching have not entered in the syllabus at all and ICT is just a formality in many universities. Even the schools that employ the trained teachers have felt this gap. Thus, there is a scope to use ICT in improving the curriculum of teacher education.

Digitalized Instructional Material

As pointed out earlier, there is a shortage of qualified teacher educators. Not only this even the instructional material available in the print form is not of quality. This is because many authors have written on those topics that they have never read and/or done research. Sometime the information given in the books is also wrong. The book reading is not very enjoyable and does not help students in understanding the concepts and retaining the information. There are many teacher educators who are well known for the specific subject. Their lectures should be digitalized and made available to all the users. It will enhance the quality of instruction in the classrooms. The teacher educator can use them in the classrooms and can organize discussion after it wherein the new points can be added both by the teacher as well as students. It will make the teaching effective, participatory and enjoyable. In this context, Sansanwal (2006) has developed digitalized lectures on Research Methodology and Statistics and has used it for teaching this subject at Master's level. Other researchers are also using it. Of course, digitalized lectures will have their limitations of revision and inbuilt interaction. Another form of digitalized lectures is e-content. The Consortium for Educational Communication (CEC) is making efforts to develop e-content material in different subjects for the benefit of diverse users. The teacher educators should also start using it for developing e-content in their own areas of specialization.

This has lots of potentiality to bring quality in teacher education.

Selection of Teacher Trainees

It is a well known fact that the quality of the output of teacher training programme depends to a great extent on the quality of its input. At present different states adopt different mechanisms of selecting students for the teachers training programme. Some procedures of selection are very good and are in a position of screening students very well. The entry level of test should assess those characteristics that are necessary to being a teacher. Entry test must serve the purpose of IIT or CAT or NET examinations. To improve the quality of selection, ICT can be made use in selecting students for the teachers training programme. It can be centralized like other entrance examinations. This will make the entry uniform. At present ICT is used in conducting GRE examination. It is Online. It indicates the feasibility of the use of ICT in the selection of teacher trainees. Like this ICT can be used in improving different quality of different aspects of teacher education.

REFERENCES

GOI (1964). Indian Education Commission, Government of India, New Delhi.

Ron Kurtus (1998). Web Based Training, WBT Information Centre.

Sansanwal, D.N. and Nawajot, (2001). Web Based Instruction, Indore: School of Education, DAVV.

Sansanwal, D.N. (2005). Computer Based Diagnostic Test in Mathematics, Indore: School of Education, DAVV.

Sansanwal, D.N. and Dahiya, S. (2006). Computer Based Diagnostic Test in Research Methodology and Statistics, Indore: School of Education, DAVV.

Sansanwal, D.N. (2006). Development of Digitalized Lectures on Research Methodology and Statistics, Indore: School of Education, DAVV.

WBTIC (1997). Web Based Instruction, WBT Information Centre.

22

ICT Towards Better Teacher Performance

L.C. Singh and Surender S. Dahiya

Social, economic and technological changes of the past decades are making teaching more crucial than, ever. The information and knowledge society needs a continuous change in the role and the working of teachers. Being a teacher in the Knowledge Society, one has to deal with (i) new knowledge and new ways for accessing knowledge; (ii) a networked world and with new types of co-operation and collaboration; (iii) a society in which knowledge plays a crucial role and lifelong learning.

Information and Communication Technologies (ICTs) have brought new possibilities into the classroom. At the same time, they have placed more demands on teachers. Information and Communication Technologies exemplified by the internet and interactive multimedia are obviously of great significance for teachers. It needs to be effectively integrated into the formal classroom teaching and learning conditions. ICTs integration in teaching in general and teacher education in particular is need of the day. Its adequate recognition and fulfillment of relevant needs are crucial for integration and effective utilization for quality education programmes. The use of ICTs can make substantial changes both for teaching and training mainly in two ways. Firstly, the rich representations of information change in learner's perception and understanding of the context. Secondly, the vast distribution and easy access to information can change relationships between teacher and learner. ICTs can also provide powerful support for educational innovations.

Every day newer technology emerges. The latest technologies have capacity to integrate with older analog technologies and retrieve information stored in older technologies and to develop link between the old and the new. So the choice of technology is important for a specific purpose of classroom teaching.

Why do we need ICT?

The face of the classrooms is changing. The teachers should prepare to cope up with the technology utility in the classroom. ICT is not only an essential tool for teachers in their day to day work, but also it offers them opportunities for their own professional development.

In *conventional teaching,* most of the time is consumed for input-output and less time left for process. But, in *teaching through ICT,* the input and output time is reduced and thereby increasing more time for process parts. When the process time is increased, the time of students' activities, discussion, correlation with other subjects, brain storming, learning etc. is enhanced. When we do teaching with the help of ICT, we get more time to process phase which is more important in a period of 45 minutes or one hour.

Form of ICT in the Classroom

ICT can be used in many forms in classrooms. We can organize teaching learning via ICT. It can be used as a core or a complementary means to the teaching process (Collis and Jung, 2003).

There are three main possible approaches to ICT which can be adopted in the classroom teaching learning situations.

Integrated Approach

This aims at planning the use of ICT within the subject to enhance particular concepts and skills and improve pupils' attainment. This involves a careful and considered review of the curriculum area, selecting the appropriate ICT resource which will contribute to the aims and objectives of the curriculum and scheme of work, and then integrating the ICT use in relevant subjects.

Enhancement Approach

This focuses on the use of an ICT resource to enhance the existing subject matter through some aspect of the lessons and tasks e.g. using an electronic whiteboard for presenting theory about a topic. In this approach, the teacher plans to complement the lesson with an innovative presentation method to promote class discussion and the visualization of problems.

Complementary Approach

This aims at using an ICT resource to empower the students' learning, e.g. by enabling them to improve their class work by taking notes on the computer, or by sending homework by e-mail to the teacher from home, or by word processing their homework.

All the three approaches can enhance attainment, but the effects may be different. In integrated approach, students' learning is enhanced because they are confronted with challenges to their existing knowledge and given deeper insights into the subject being studied. The enhancement approach could improve students' learning through presenting knowledge in new ways, promoting debates among pupils, and encouraging them to formulate their own explanations. The complementary approach suggests that learning can be supplemented by reducing the mundane and repetitive aspects of tasks such as writing essays and homework by hand, supporting the learner to focus on more challenging and subject-based tasks.

How ICT can be implemented in teaching-learning?

The effective and efficient use of ICT depends largely on technically competent teachers. They should be able to appreciate the potential of ICT and have positive attitude towards ICT. Four phases are conducted to implement ICT content in the classroom. These phases are as under:

- ICT Literacy
- Use of ICT hardware and software for teaching-learning activities
- Integration of Pedagogy and ICT (Integration of ICT in subject content, teaching, online support, networking and management)
- Innovative practices in the use of ICT.

How does ICT help in better teacher performance?

In new technology era, the role of teacher has changed and continues to change from being an instructor to a constructor, facilitator, coach and creator of learning situation. A teacher will be able to integrate the use of ICT into teaching effectively if he has acquired various competencies like creativity, flexibility, logistic skills, skill for project work, administrative and organizational skills, and collaborating skills. The ICT will help in better teacher performance in following ways.

Knowledge Enhancement through use of ICT

'Access to information' is considered to be one of the most important benefits of the use of ICT in education. There are several levels on which ICT can improve the cognition boundaries. ICT tools allow us to represent in rich and diverse ways. They enable us to traverse the boundaries of art, science, language and senses. They allow us to represent and simulate experiences. The interactivity capacity of ICT provides more

opportunities for students and teachers to involve as creators. It supports teachers in bringing together aesthetic as well as scientific consideration. Through use of ICT, teachers' knowledge can be improved. It helps in tailoring learning resources to meet the particular needs of students at every stage of his/her education. Some ICT tools are: Internet, software CD/DVD, e-books, e-content, learning objects, multimedia representation and simulations. Learning materials in electronic format are most useful when they are directly linked to the curriculum. Digital clearing houses and evergreen curricula are useful in teaching and learning.

Strategies for Teachers

ICTs provide many opportunities to use variety of pedagogies. As a tool, ICT can support didactic or facilitative approaches, interact and collaborate across time and distance. ICT enables us to interact with students over a physical distance. It enables to access on-line libraries, journals and research to support individual learning. Didactic software/courseware and intelligent tutoring systems can dramatically reduce the cost of teaching and learning. It enables to deliver information or to communicate with a mass of students in quite individual ways, opens up the possibility of tailoring pedagogy to the needs of teachers and students. Multiple uses of technology are interesting and effective. ICT can provide the valuable tools to align the system to promote students' learning. ICT enables to instructional designs to follow constructivist approach by using hypertext and hypermedia because it allows for branched design rather than a linear format of instruction. Hyperlinks allow for student control, which is crucial for constructive learning. ICT enabled teaching facilitates sharing of ideas, experiences as well as collaborating on projects, exchanging materials through discussion groups etc.

Management of Learning

ICT enables to provide individual instruction with individual pace. Self-pace learning is only possible through didactic CDs,

DVDs and On-line learning. ICT enables to pay attention for gifted or talented students. Individual self-paced learning is possible through e-books, virtual laboratories, concept formation animations (learning objects), flow diagram and pictures, developed media aids through On-line and Offline resources.

Evaluation of Learning

ICT enables to give feedback and testing objectively and quickly without biases. It enables self testing and large group testing easily. It makes formative and summative evaluation easy and can evaluate learners in remote location also evaluate through Internet. Subjective evaluation may be done through recording and sent for evaluation to subject experts easily. Recording can be evaluated by self and peers also. ICT tools like e-mail, Internet, CDs and DVDs of evaluation programmes, Online access of evaluation software etc. can be effectively used for evaluation.

Guidance to the Learners

Diagnosis of individual is also possible through ICT using specific software. Remedial teaching for each and every student is not possible by the teacher but with the help of ICT it may be made possible. Individual self-paced learning can play a role for remedial teaching through e-books, virtual laboratories, concept formation animations (learning objects), flow diagram and pictures, developed media aids through Online and Offline resources. Video conferencing can also provide a diagnosis and remedial teaching by experts in remote places.

If teachers are to cope with the challenges of the rapidly changing society and make use of new opportunities offered by ICT, the teachers and students must have access to necessary equipments. The most important competence building is the development of pedagogical methods. That can happen only when long-term competence programmes can work along with real-life experiences where teachers and students can make use of ICT in their daily work and learning experiences. Integration of ICT in education is still far from desired in classrooms. Highly interactive multimedia or hypermedia are not yet being used. Online activities are used to a limited extent. Special emphasis must be given on the use and integration of Online resources in classroom.

REFERENCES

Cameron, Richards (2003). ICT in Teacher Education: Some Common Misunderstanding and Dilemmas.

Dahiya, Surender S. (2005). Educational Technology—*Towards Better Teacher Performance.* Delhi: Shipra Publications.

Dellit, Jillian, Using ICT for Quality in Teaching-Larning Evaluation Processes. South Australia: Adelaide.

Delors, J. (1996). Learning the Treasure Within: Report to UNESCO of the International Commission on Education for the Twenty First Century. Paris: UNESCO.

Hary, K. and Khan, A. (2000). The use of technologies in Basic Education. In Yates, C. and Bradley, J. (eds.). *Basic Education at a Distance.*

Heddad, Wadi D. and Draxler, Alexandra (2002). *Technologies for Education: Potentials, Parameters and Prospects.* Prepared for UNESCO by Knowledge Enterprise Inc. Paris: UNESCO.

Peace Crops (2002). *Information and Communication Technology (ICT) Training of Trainers—Computer and Internet use for Development.* Facilitator Guide and Reference Manual. Information Collection and Exchange Publication No. *T0122.*

Vaa, R. (2000). *Appropriate Telecommunication and Learning Technology for Distance Educatzon in South Pacific.* Report of a project funded by the New Zealand Overseas Development Agency. Suva Fiji.

Vancouver, B.C. *Commonwealth of Learning.* London: Routledge Falmer.

http://www.wgu.edu

http://www.crtvu.edu.cn

23

Empowerment of Teacher in ICT Supported Teaching

JYOTSNA AMIN AND R.L. MADHAVI

Now a days 'Information and Communication Technology' (ICT) is a synonymous term which is used to refer to a wide range of services like telephony, fax, internet; applications such as distance education and management information systems, and technologies from 'old technologies' such as television to 'new technologies' such as cellular phones, using various types of equipment and software, often running over telecom networks. The ICT revolution has radically changed the way people share information. Governments, NGOs, businesses, institutions, and individuals have re-modified their working mechanisms to make ICT a part of their day to day organizational processes.

Use of ICT in education has many useful applications. Technology facilitates important curricular processes; as a result of its interactive and multi-media capabilities, it can be used to engage and stimulate all students, and compensate for specific learning difficulties. ICT can bring an enormous range of educational sources and resources into the classroom, support autonomous, group and whole-class teaching and bring to life topics and concepts in a way which enables teachers to teach and learners to learn.

In a highly populous country like India, where classrooms are crowded, making it impossible for teacher to take care of individual differences ICT becomes a very handy tool. Use of audio-visual aids and computer aided instructions in classroom makes the teaching learning process more interesting, attractive and comprehensive. Particularly in the era of computer domination in educational domain as a technological tool with all its hardware and software revolutions, teaching learning process becomes successful if proper efforts are made. Learner's knowledge about content is more comprehensive, broader as learner can use various media available to gather knowledge than simply depending on teacher's lecture. Improvements made in areas of teleconferencing, preparation of television aided instructional materials, using television as a medium of education for masses, revolution in the area of satellite telecasting etc. made it possible to cover marginalized groups of the country. This helped in improving adult and continuing education programmes, open university programmes and various distance and correspondence education programmes aimed at spreading literacy and life skills education in the country. Not only for teaching learning, but also administrative, management level work can also be done with speed and accuracy using this technology. So admission, examination, evaluation programmes at many institutions are improved in the recent times on many aspects.

Whatever may be advancements in the use of technology in education, when it comes to classroom interactions or teaching-learning process one cannot overlook the importance of teacher in the process. Teacher as a facilitator, has to introduce the student into the process where technology is gaining importance in today's global classrooms. For this process to carry on smoothly, teacher needs proper training on skills and knowledge about technology and more so empowerment to implement the process.

Empowerment

Empowerment is a construct shared by many disciplines and arenas: community development, psychology, education, economics, and studies of social movements and organizations. How empowerment is understood varies among these perspectives. In recent empowerment literature, the meaning of the term empowerment is often assumed rather than explained or defined. Rappoport (1984) has noted that it is easy to define empowerment by its absence but difficult to define in action as it takes on different forms in different people and contexts. Even defining the concept is subject to debate. Zimmerman (1984) has stated that asserting a single definition of empowerment may make attempts to achieve it formulaic or prescription-like, contradicting the very concept of empowerment. A web definition of empowerment defined that concept as, how individuals/communities engage in learning processes in which they create, appropriate and share knowledge, tools and techniques in order to change and improve the quality of their own lives and societies. Through empowerment, individuals not only manage and adapt to change but also contribute to generate changes in their lives and environments.

A common understanding of empowerment is necessary, however, to allow us to know empowerment when we see it in people with whom we are working, and for programme evaluation. According to Bailey (1992), how we precisely define empowerment within our projects and programmes will depend upon the specific people and context involved.

As a general definition, however, we suggest that empowerment is a multidimensional social process that helps people gain control over their own lives. It is a process that fosters power (that is, the capacity to implement) in people, for use in their own lives, their communities, and in their society, by acting on issues that they define as important. We suggest that three components of our definition are basic to any understanding of empowerment. Empowerment is a multi-dimensional, social process. It is multi-dimensional in the sense that it occurs within sociological, psychological, economic, and other dimensions. Empowerment also occurs at various levels, such as individual, group, and community. Empowerment, by definition, is a social process, since it occurs in relationship to others. Empowerment is a process that is similar to a path or journey one that develops as we work through it. Other aspects of empowerment may vary according to the specific context and people involved, but these remain constant. In addition, one important implication of this definition of empowerment is that the individual and community are fundamentally connected.

The worthwhile concept of empowerment too frequently fails to achieve its intended results, unless the following points are taken care of:

- Establish a long-term purpose and vision for employees and organization;
- Carefully select those to be empowered and define what they are empowered to do;
- Recognize and build upon the existing base of experience in the oganization;
- Train adequately those expected to assume power and responsibility;
- Create genuine trust between management and employees; and
- Convey to the empowered a true sense of stewardship for the organization's future.

Teacher Empowerment

Teacher empowerment is not entirely providing them some incentives which act as reinforcers and motivate them. To empower teachers' means they should be motivated to reach the highest strata of the hierarchy that is reaching the top of need hierarchy. It is not just providing them with monitory benefits, working conditions etc. but also providing them opportunities to grow, get recognition, advancement in professional life etc. According to Tate (1991) teacher empowerment is a domestic reform that yields wider participation i.e. democratization. It is a bottom up as well as top down reform (inversion of the hierarchy) with teachers reclaiming their right to have a say in policies affecting them. It includes the professionalism which means that teachers should be able to provide good judgments about educational issues. Empowered teaching should also be characterized by reflection, self-fulfillment and decentralization.

Teacher empowerment therefore includes the following elements: decentralization, professionalism, enablement, democratization and inversion of the power hierarchy as depicted in the figure below:

Fig. 23.1: Elements of Empowerment

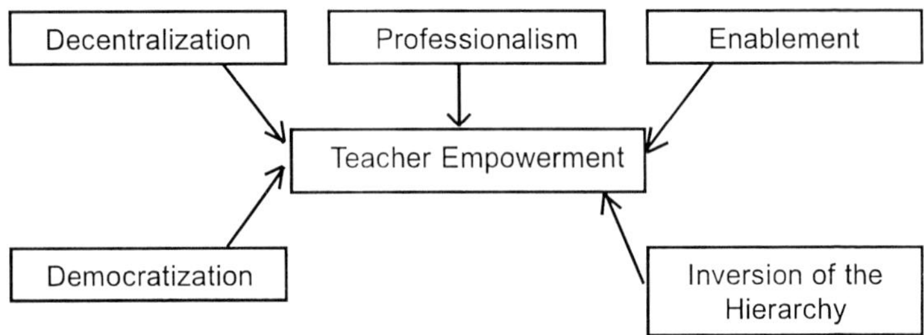

This figure demonstrates that the five elements are inevitable for teacher-empowerment to be a reality and functional. It is a process whereby a teacher is motivated to reach the higher level of career with a filling of self-esteem and job satisfaction. For teacher empowerment to materialize, the college administration, persons in administration at various levels are to be involved in the process. (Manu, 2001)

ICT Needs of Teachers

In the present scenario of techno-savvy classrooms, teacher has to be a master in use of technology in the teaching learning process. For this the important needs can be broadly related to training, access, support and advice.

Training Needs

To be skilled and knowledgeable is of course the key to effective implementation of ICT in teaching and learning and there is no doubt that teachers are motivated and interested in developing their own skills and knowledge. There is a need for training to develop knowledge and skills. Conversely, no matter how good the quality of the training is, if it is not related to the ICT resources available in school it is likely to be seen by teachers as a waste of time and effort. It is important, therefore, that training opportunities for practicing teachers remain flexible enough to cope with the varying pace of development.

Similarly, it is important that there is ongoing provision for staff development to enable teachers to move on once they have acquired the basic technical skills which many still feel they need and so that they can keep pace with the introduction of new resources into school. Teachers need to be encouraged to integrate self-development of ICT skills and knowledge within their normal development planning. If teachers are to be able to make informed decisions about the relevance of ICT resources to meet their own and their pupils' needs it is important that they become aware of a broad range of ICT resources and their potential. Training is a felt need to develop more confidence in teachers for using the technology as a necessary prerequisite to exploring more effective ways of using ICT in the classroom. Teachers' own priorities should be for more technical skills and knowledge despite the fact that they may have already received some basic ICT training.

The effective teacher, as in any other profession, plays a number of roles: s/he is not only a **classroom practitioner** but is also a **manager,** a **planner,** and a **learner.** The role of life long learner is particularly important in underpinning all other roles. For the teacher this means updating their subject knowledge as well as their skills and knowledge of new approaches to teaching, managing and planning. In other words, the effective teacher must also be an effective learner. This implies that teachers are to 'personalize' ICT as a learning tool for themselves. In relation to their roles as planners and managers, teachers should develop some knowledge related to the selection and general management of ICT resources. Teachers have to relate ICT to any great extent to different facets of their professional life, e.g. in professional development, or administration.

Access to ICT

Simply providing training facilities is not enough. Providing proper access to the system is also one of the important needs. Systems are required in each school to publicize and inform all teachers about the availability of ICT resources: teachers need to be made aware of the existence of ICT within their own school (e.g. location and availability), as well as its potential. All schools need to seek ways of sharing relatively expensive ICT resources. This could take the form of centralized sorting of resources even if the resources that are held in different departments or centralized citing of multipurpose, cross-curricular resources, such as the Internet, in the school library. There is a need to build ICT into strategic planning and budgeting in each school: this has immediate implications for those already in managerial positions who will benefit from mechanisms which encourage the sharing of knowledge and experience, and the provision of advice from education authorities; it should also be built into the longer-term staff-development of all teachers whose careers progress along a management path. Education authorities, should consider providing computers for use by teachers at home: access to a computer at home will encourage those who are motivated towards ICT to make greater use of ICT in school, by providing the space and time for development which is often lacking in a busy school time schedule.

Support and Advice

Support is an essential component: mechanisms need to be put in place to ensure that teachers have adequate access to technical support and advice, and to ensure that teachers do not feel that they have to become technical experts themselves. The support need not only be in the form of an in-school technician, but could take the form of one designated individual who also networks with others with similar roles. Mechanisms should be put in place to support teachers in identifying, selecting and evaluating the ICT resources appropriate to their needs. Methods which allow teachers themselves to disseminate their knowledge and critical appraisal of materials are likely to be particularly effective.

Problems and Challenges

No provision for needs of teachers adequately is one of the main issues in use of ICT in classrooms. Teachers identify a range of issues which they regard as inhibitors to effective use of ICT, like:

- Lack of access/availability of hardware/software;
- Lack of familiarity, skills and knowledge;
- Lack of support during times of crisis; and
- Lack of management guidelines from organization

While it cannot be assumed that if teachers had greater access to, or were more familiar with a broader range of ICT they would tend to use it. It is clear from the situation that many teachers are currently not in a position to make judgments about the suitability of ICT. They are not in a position of taking any independent judgment regarding any matter of ICT related teaching due to lack of authority and knowledge. Some of the problems faced by teachers while using ICT in classroom situations are as under.

- Classroom management issues are the focus of much concern in relation to ICT; providing fair and equal access for all pupils when hardware is limited is seen as a major challenge. Teachers have to work in small groups, to take care of entire class, which is not possible for an average school.
- The perceived expense of ICT, relative to more traditional resources, creates tensions in terms of prioritizing budgets for hardware and software; the problem of hardware becoming obsolete within no time, raises concerns in relation to long-term planning, training and budgeting. The feeling amongst many

related personnel in the organizations is that there are other more important priorities than investing in ICT at a time when resources are scarce. For some, the cost of software is prohibitive. Opinion surveys also indicate that ICT spending has to take second place when there are more important priorities: Cost and prioritization are also seen as issues in relation to training.

- Dissemination of knowledge related to various aspects of ICT among teachers is rare. This brings in the feeling of gap among teaching faculty, which is not conducive for achieving goals. Moreover, if one trained teacher can teach the same to other colleagues, it helps in reducing the budget on training. Teachers felt confident that there were mechanisms for ensuring that those who have been on courses could disseminate their knowledge to others.
- The priorities for teaching learning at different levels say primary, secondary etc. are different. When this point is not given consideration, teachers may feel that administrators possess biased priorities in the allocation of ICT resources.
- Lack of proper evaluation procedures related to ICT use in classrooms is another problem. Proper guidelines are not there for use, access to different varieties of resources available in the organization. Proper rules and regulations regarding these matters help in proper managing, utilization of available resources within the purview of the organization. People can also devise their own strategies for evaluation, selection of resources if guidelines are provided from the authorities.
- The other problem which surfaces is that of incompatible hardware. This can hamper the transfer of ideas and skills. Incompatibility of hardware within a school also limits the value of information resources. Proper advice by some expert who can guide people properly all through is the need.

- Absence of support during times of crisis is the serious problem in organizations. If something goes wrong whom to consult is the question. Technical support and advice on selecting ICT resources are barely needed; Teachers value support provided by other teachers but it may place additional burdens on colleagues. Often help of a special computer teacher, technician or other skilled person available in the organization is sought. Availability of support within organization, and in local community is an important matter. Resource centers can also offer advice and support. Business relations with the organizations can make resource centers provide a help in these matters.

Keeping in view all these issues and many more that may arise with time and changing needs, there is a need for providing proper empowerment to teachers by framing conducive rules and regulations by authorities. Different roles of institutions, administrators, principals and teachers themselves in enhancing the use of ICT in classroom situations are discussed here.

Role of Institutions (Administrators)

- Objectives of ICT programme must consider the following points need for safe-guarding values like academic freedom; the need for continued attention to quality in teaching-learning; the need to protect student involvement and influence etc.
- Develop and continuously update institutional ICT policies in order to align educational objectives with technology.
- Place equal emphasis at all levels of education in institution in using ICT technology.
- Provide all members of academic and non-academic community with skills to use up to date ICTs.
- Sufficient and on-going financial support should also be allocated to ensure that all students are provided with the relevant ICT skills.

- Provide for a variety of educational and technological material in accordance with the heterogeneity aspects arising out of globalization, enhanced by ICT use.
- Maintain socializing aspect of classroom, critically examine the use of ICT in teaching learning and try to avoid excessive reliance on technologies.
- Try to develop networks or partnerships with other institutes in areas of courseware, development of technology and ICT expertise. It helps to bridge the gaps between institutions in established ICT facilities, knowledge and skills.

Role of Principal

There is a need for all head teachers to be ICT literate. The school principals need to be aware of the potential of ICT, to be aware of issues relating to the planning and management of ICT within schools, and to be able to develop effective ICT strategies in schools.The head teachers must have to play in encouraging the use of ICT—they in turn need to be aware of the benefits of ICT across the schools, in all contexts, and can set examples by being seen to be using ICT themselves. The school principal has to encourage teachers in ICT based teaching on the following lines:

- Actively participating as an equal in the programme designed for the organization.
- Being enthusiastic and energetic in providing support to teachers.
- Ensuring inclusion of all teachers in the programme.
- Providing opportunities to meet and discuss various problems to find amicable, possible solutions time to time.
- Encouraging team spirit and supporting risks.
- Being flexible in building trust in teachers to develop professionally. Implementing professional development programmes with knowledge about various programmes, qualities, capabilities of teachers;

respecting teacher's opinion; seeing to provide a variety of programmes.

- Encouraging autonomy by trusting, listening to and encouraging teachers. Making teachers take their own decisions.
- Encouraging innovations by respecting new ideas; allow them to try out new ideas.
- Encouraging teachers to take responsibility and solving problems along with colleagues.
- Behave as a model for others to follow.
- Providing for proper rewards, recognition patterns for excellence shown by people in the organization.

Role of Teacher

The teachers need to understand their role in the present day techno-savvy classrooms. Teacher plays the role of leader, guide, facilitator and manager of the entire process of classroom teaching learning. A teacher must be a life long learner of rapidly changing ICT resources, in order to facilitate effective use of ICT in teaching 1earning. He must act as a disseminator, supporter, and advisor to all colleagues. In order to accommodate properly to the changing situation a teacher should possess autonomy and accountability issues related to ICT use in classrooms.

Co-ordination, co-operation among all persons is the key issue in enhancing use of ICT for effective classroom teaching learning. Everyone involved in the process need to be aware of their roles, responsibilities and various other things related to the issues. Teacher has to understand the importance of self empowerment through knowledge development, work empowerment from organizations and authority . ICT plays a significant role in this perspective.

REFERENCES

Charles, J. Latino, (1998), www.unesco.org/education/educprog/lwf/doc/portfolio/definitions.htm

International Association of Universities, IAU Policy Statements http://www.unesco.org/iau/p_statements/itc_statement.html

JESU 'S MARTI' NEZ-FRI' AS, "The importance of ICTs for developing countries", Centre for Astrobiology, Madrid, Spain and UNCSTD, Geneva, Switzerland (www.scidev.net)

Manu Patrick, (2001). "Empowering Teachers: How Successful Principals can promote it", University News, 39(33)

Nanette Page, http://www.joe.org/joe/1999october/comml .html

Rappoport ,(1984) http://www.encounters.jp/mike/professional/publications/tchauto.html

Tate, (1991). In Manu Patrick, (2001). "Empowering Teachers: How Successful Principals can promote it", University News, 39(33)

http://www.scotland.gov.uk/library/ict/appendsection4.htm

http://www.scotland.gov.uk/library/ict/appendsection7.htm

24

Attitude and Anxiety towards Computers among Secondary School Teachers

TARA SABAPATHY

Information and Communication Technology comparises information technology and other media. These technologies are playing important roles in education and training at all levels. Multimedia, Internet, World Wide Web and Online tools are being used to a greater extent in education. Between 1989 and 1992 the use of computer technologies had increased by nearly 50 per cent jumping 2.9 million units to 3.5 million units at school level and today there are an estimated 5.8 million computers for instructional use alone. The growth of technology as an instructional tool has influenced teachers' attitude, towards these technologies and their ability to use them successfully. Planow, Bauder and Sarner (1993) found that many teachers are struggling to make efficient and effective use of today's technologies. A number of studies conducted by Kay (1989); Koohang (1987) and Marshall and Bannon (1986) have concluded that teachers' attitude towards computers is affected by computer anxiety. Computer anxiety as defined by Howard and Thomas (1986) is the fear of impending interaction with a computer that is disproportionate to the actual threat presented by the computer. According to Gvangenett computer anxiety is a specific anxiety that regularly occurs in a specific situation. Those who are computer anxious may experience fear of the unknown, feeling of frustration, possible embarrassment, failure and disappointment. Teachers may exhibit classic signs of anxiety reaction such as sweaty palms, heart palpitations and headaches.

There is a growing concern that computer anxiety may lead to negative attitudes towards computers among secondary school teachers and will prevent them from reaping the pedagogical, social and economic benefits of computer technology. Many researchers have spent the greater part of the past two decades in verifying the existence of the construct of computer anxiety (Cohen and Waugh, 1989; Dukes, Discenza and Couger, 1989; Francis and Evans, 1995; Kerman and Howard, 1990; Lloyd and Gressard, 1984b; Marcoulides, 1989; Marcoulides, Mayes and Wiseman, 1995). There exists positive relationship between computer anxiety and factors such as gender, age and level of familiarity with computers (Ayersman and Reed, 1995-96; Gilroy and Desai, 1986; Gos, 1996; Igbaria and Chakrabarti, 1990; Lloyd and Gresard, 1984a); and seeking ways to predict who will experience computer anxiety and subsequently how to reduce it (Dupagne and Krendl, 1992; McInerney, McInerney and Sinclair, 1994; Szajna, 1994; Woodrow, 1991). Several scholars (e.g., Dupagne and Krendle, 1992; Maurer, 1994; Rosen and Maguire, 1990) have also attempted to make sense of this massive body of literature so as to provide directions for further research and practice.

Unfotunately, the foci and results of different studies within this body of empirical literature lack an element that would optimize their usefulness and consistency. In other words, different researchers come to different conclusions about computer anxiety in different studies, rendering them ultimately unable to make meaningful statements about how to address computer anxiety. Researchers who have attempted to understand the literature often suggest that more research is needed.

In view of the above discussion it is imperative to study the computer anxiety and attitude towards computers among secondary school teachers.

Objectives

The following objectives were formulated:

1. To find out the relationship between the Attitude towards Computers of Secondary School Teachers and their Computer Anxiety.
2. To find out whether differences in Computer Anxiety of secondary school teachers would account for significant differences in their Attitude towards Computers.
3. To find out whether differences in biographical variables namely, sex differences, type of management, subject specialization and teaching experience of secondary school teachers would account for significant differences in their Attitude towards Computers.

Hypotheses

The hypotheses were formulated for empirical validation:

1. There is no significant relationship between Attitude towards Computers of Secondary School Teachers and their Computer Anxiety.
2. There is no significant difference in the Attitude towards Computers of Secondary School Teachers experiencing high and low Computer Anxiety.
3. There is no significant difference in the Attitude towards Computers of Secondary School Teachers experiencing high and moderate Computer Anxiety.
4. There is no significant difference in the Attitude towards Computers of Secondary School Teachers experiencing moderate and low Computer Anxiety.
5. There is no significant difference in the Attitude towards Computers of Secondary School Male and Female Teachers.

6. There is no significant difference in the Attitude towards Computers of Secondary School Government and Private Aided Teachers.
7. There is no significant difference in the Attitude towards Computers of Secondary School Private Aided and Unaided Teachers.
8. There is no significant difference in the Attitude towards Computers of Secondary School Private Unaided and Government Teachers.
9. There is no significant difference in the Attitude towards Computers of Secondary School General Science and Social Science Teachers.
10. There is no significant difference in the Attitude towards Computers of Secondary School General Science and Mathematics Teachers.
11. There is no significant difference in the Attitude towards Computers of Secondary School Mathematics and Social Science Teachers.
12. There is no significant difference in the Attitude towards Computers of Secondary School more experienced and less experienced teachers.

Methodology

For the present study, the investigator used stratified random sampling technique. In order to get a fairly representative and unbiased sample, the investigation was carried out on a sample drawn from three different types of schools, namely, private aided, private unaided and government schools. In total, the sample comprised 101 male teachers and 173 female teachers.

The following gives details about the number of sample teachers from each type of school.

Type of School	*No. of Teachers*
Private Aided	84
Private Unaided	100
Government	90
Total	274

The following tools were used in the study:

- Attitude towards Computers Scale constructed and standardized by the investigator.
- Computer Anxiety Rating Scale developed by Chupe and Spires (1991) and modified by the investigator.

Analysis and Interpretation of Data

The data was analyzed by using Pearson's Product Moment co-efficient of correlation and t-test.

Table 24.1: Relationship Between Attitude Towards Computers and Computer Anxiety Among Secondary School Teachers

Variables	*N*	*df*	*'r'*	*Sig. level*
Attitude towards Computers and Computer Anxiety	274	272	-0.462	Significant at .01 level

Findings and Conclusions

1. There is a significant and negative relationship between the Attitude of Secondary School Teachers towards Computers and their Computer Anxiety (r = -0.46).
2. There is a significant difference in the Attitude of Secondary School Teachers towards computers experiencing high (M = 81.47) and low (M = 88.58) Computer Anxiety.
3. There is a significant difference in the Attitude of Secondary School Teachers towards Computers experiencing moderate (M = 81.47) and low (M = 86.53) Computer Anxiety.
4. There is a significant difference in the Attitude of Secondary School Teachers towards Computers experiencing high (M = 86.53) and moderate (M = 88.58) Computer Anxiety.

Table 24.2: Table showing the Mean, SD and 't'-value of the Attitude towards Computer score of secondary school teachers as per their levels of Computer Anxiety, Sex differences, Type of School Management, Subject Specialization and Teaching Experience

Variables	*N*	*Mean*	*Std. Deviation*	*t-value*	*Sig. level*
High Computer Anxiety	69	81.47	11.06	-3.528	**
Low Computer Anxiety	75	88.58	13.11		
Moderate Computer Anxiety	130	81.47	8.72	-2.980	**
Low Computer Anxiety	75	86.53	13.11		
High Computer Anxiety	69	86.53	11.06	-1.334	NS
Moderate Computer Anxiety	130	88.58	8.72		
Male	101	84.96	12.75	-0.754	NS
Female	173	86.07	9.80		
Government	90	85.46	9.65	-1.041	NS
Private Unaided	100	87.15	12.71		
Government	90	85.46	9.65	0.908	NS
Private Aided	84	84.11	9.90		
Private Aided	84	84.11	9.90	1.824	NS
Private Unaided	100	87.15	12.71		
General Science	43	85.30	11.06	-0.338	NS
Social Science	60	86.30	10.51		
General Science	43	85.30	11.06	-0.246	NS
Mathematics	64	85.81	9.62		
Social Science	60	86.03	10.51	0.122	NS
Mathematics	64	85.81	9.62		

5. There is no significant difference in the Attitude of Male and Female Secondary School Teachers towards Computers.
6. There is no significant difference in the Attitude of Secondary School Teachers working in Government and Private Unaided Schools towards Computers.
7. There is no significant difference in the Attitude of Secondary School Teachers working in Government and Private Aided Schools towards Computers.
8. There is no significant difference in the Attitude of Secondary School Teachers working in Private Aided and Private Unaided Schools towards Computers.

9. There is no significant difference in the Attitude of Secondary School General Science and Social Science Teachers towards Computers.
10. There is no significant difference in the Attitude of Secondary School General Science and Mathematics Teachers towards Computers.
11. There is no significant difference in the Attitude of Secondary School Social Science and Mathematics Teachers towards Computers.
12. There is no significant difference in the Attitude of Secondary School Teachers with more or less teaching experience towards Computers.

Educational Implications

Correlational analysis of data reveals that there was a significant and negative correlation between Attitude of Secondary School Teachers towards Computers and their Computer Anxiety. In other words teachers with high positive attitude possess low computer anxiety and the vice-versa. The t-test analysis also reveals that teachers with low computer anxiety had better attitude towards computers than teachers experiencing high computer anxiety. This clearly implies that teachers who experienced high anxiety had a negative attitude towards Computers. This necessitates that educational institutions identify methods of reducing computer anxiety thereby promoting positive attitude towards computers. Training programmes which concentrate on equipping teachers with necessary computer knowledge and skills would definitely lower the anxiety levels of teachers. Recognizing that many teachers have trouble acclimating themselves to computer equipment, managements must plan relevant teacher training programme. When the new computers are unpacked and set up in the classroom, teachers feel threatened, afraid, or just remain apathetic towards them. A technology training programme must tackle this grassroot challenge.

Strategies for Reducing Computer Anxiety

Turn them On

To the uninitiated, computers can often be a source of anxiety. That's why, before attempting any technology training, you must first get teachers excited about the prospect of using computers. The trick is to appeal to teachers at a personal level. Show them how computers can improve the quality of their lives, both inside and outside the classroom with one or more software applications.

At the core of every teacher lies a passion for a particular subject or discipline, perhaps it's world history or the environment or creative writing. Whatever the teacher's personal passion, find out what it is and then introduce the teacher to a computer programme that can help develop and nurture that passion. That is the single most important step in the teacher training process.

Never underestimate the power of first impressions, particularly with regard to technology. Even hardboiled anti-technology teachers will succumb if they get some hands-on experience with software programmes that are personally relevant to them. Indeed, unlike other forms of staff development, technology training has to be hands-on from the very beginning.

Begin at the Beginning

Like students. teachers learn at different rates and have specific needs when they come across acquiring new information and mastering new skills. That means teacher technology training should be flexible. Yet coverage of a comprehensive set of skills be emphasized within the framework of training curriculum.

Take Plenty of Time

Technology training takes a great deal of time. For adults, the learning curve for developing technology skills is like learning a new language—and it's a very unforgiving learning curve. Having learned the basics, teachers need roughly six months or more to practice their skills and, more important, to learn problem-solving strategies for those frustrating moments when the computer doesn't do what they want it to do. At this stage, many teachers become tempted to throw in the towel, convinced they'll never truly master that "dang machine". The danger here is that they'll resign themselves to using computers for rudimentary tasks only. Printing classroom banners and having students use drill-and-practice software might be all they'll ever attempt—unless you can help them overcome their frustrations.

Personal consultation with technical staff is the best way for teachers to become confident about troubleshooting the computer difficulties they encounter. To make this a manageable proposition, consider enlisting the help of computer-literate teachers to provide support and guidance to their inexperienced or techno-phobic colleagues.

The key is to assign enough one-on-one instructional assistance in each stage that teachers will begin asking questions and start taking a few risks. Otherwise, many teachers will just quietly accept that a particular software application is not going to work for them.

Individual tutoring is crucial for getting past reluctance or fear. Watching seasoned computer veterans find solutions to computer problems and then practicing the problem-solving techniques under the veterans' guidance also help teachers in making the connection between their technology training and real-world problems.

After receiving this kind of technical support several times, teachers will naturally begin to experiment, solving problems on their own by using the resources available to them through the computer's help files and manuals. Once teachers develop the confidence to troubleshoot independently—even if they are unsuccessful at first—they will never again be satisfied to use computers at only a rudimentary level.

Offer a Carrot

Encourage teachers to engage in independent study and curriculum development by offering them the necessary time and money. Finally, continue to offer ongoing troubleshooting assistance to even the most advanced teachers, but let them take the lead in solving problems while they are receiving technical advice.

Conclusion

In most of the developed nations of the world, there has been a paradigm shift in understanding the teaching-learning process with the accent on learning rather than teaching. There is a growing awareness in academia that a teacher is less 'the sage on the stage' and more of 'a guide on the side'. With the increasing emphasis on the learning process, teachers have to recognize and harness the awesome power of technology to take this giant leap into the future.

The use of computers in education opens a new area of knowledge and offers a tool that has the potential to change some of the existing educational methods. The teaching community can no longer afford to have a blinkered outlook and will have to recognize that information technology is very much a part of their lives. The teacher is the key to the effective exploitation of this resource in the educational system. As computer use continues to increase in society, educators must also prepare themselves for the use of computers within the classroom. Positive attitude towards use of computers as an educational tool would go a long way in successful implementation of technologies in school.

REFERENCES

Cohen, B.A. and Waugh, G.W. (1989). Assessing computer anxiety, Psychological Reports, 65, 735-738.

Delcourt, M.A.B. and Kinzie, M.B. (1993), Computer technologies in teacher education: The measurement of attitudes and self-efficacy. Journal of Research and Development in Education, 27(1), 35-41.

Dupagne, M. and Krendl, K.A. (1992), Teachers' attitudes toward computers: A review of the literature, Journal of Research on Computing in Education, 24(3), 420-429.

Gilroy, F.D. and Desai, H.B. (1986), Computer anxiety: Sex, race, and age. International Journal of Management Studies, 25, 711-719.

Glass, C.R. and Knight, L.A. (1988), Cognitive factors in computer anxiety. Cognitive Therapy and Research, 12(4), 351-366.

Gordon, H.R.D. (1993), Analysis of the computer anxiety levels of secondary technical education teachers in West Virginia, ERIC #ED357218.

Gos, M.W. (1996), Computer anxiety and computer experience: A new look at an old relationship. The Clearing House, May/June, 271-276.

Honeyman, D.S. and White, W.J. (1987), Computer anxiety in educators learning to use the computer: A preliminary report, Journal of Research on Computing in Education, Winter, 129-138.

Igbaria, M. and Chakrabarti, A. (1990), Computer anxiety and attitudes towards microcomputer use. Behaviour and Information Technology, 9,229-241.

Kelley, C.L. and Charness, N. (1995), Issues in training older adults to use computers. Behaviour and Information Technology, 14 (2), 107-120.

Kerman, M.C. and Howard, C.S. (1990), Computer anxiety and computer attitudes: An investigation of construct and predictive validity issues. Educational and Psychological Measurement, 50, 681-690.

Koohang, A.A. (1987), A study of the attitudes of pre-service teachers toward the use of computers. Educational Communications and Technology Journal, 35(3), 15-149.

Laguna, K. and Babcock, R.L. (1997), Computer anxiety in young and older adults: Implications for human-computer interactions in older populations. Computers in Human Behaviour, 13(3), 317-326.

Loyd, B.H. and Gressard, C. (1984a), The effects of sex, age and computer experience on computer attitudes. Paper presented at the Eastern Educational Research Association annual meeting, West Palm Beach, Florida.

25

ICT Awareness among Prospective Teachers

NAMITA SAHOO and B.C. DAS

There has been a technotronic gap between the progress of the society and instructional activities managed by the teacher. This can be said an educational wonder. On the one hand technology has revolutionized our society; on the other the teaching learning activities at school level have remained untouched of technology. In classroom, the knowledge is imparted by the teacher in a linear/didactic mode, which is most of the time boring and not to the interest or liking of the learners. Consequently it makes differences between students' experience at school and the experiences they gain outside the school. This felt gap needs an educational reform so that the modern classroom can be brought to the path that the technologically advanced society has been longing for. It is imperative for our education system to prepare teachers and facilitate students in acquiring skill based knowledge through learning with technology.

A host of studies in preceding couple of decades have experimented technology as the better medium of acquiring classroom knowledge. The major studies in this area can be identified in the works of Irving (1991), Kulik (1994), Ferneding-Linert and Harris (1994), Chun (1994), Jonassen (1996) and Means and Olson (1997). These studies found technology can support teacher's efforts to engage learners in long term, enhancing students' motivation and self esteem, instigating greater collaboration and giving teachers additional impacts to take on a coaching and advisory role. Most of the studies have highlighted the teachers have to be well-equipped with many technotronic competencies related to instructional process. Besides, Jonassen's study (1996) pointed out with technology drives much of the current thinking about the use of technology to support learning and when students learn with technology it becomes a mind tool facilitating higher order learning.

Several Indian studies conducted by Mallick (1995), Mohapatra (1992), Sahoo (1993) have highlighted the effectiveness of technology supported learning at primary, secondary and higher education stage respectively. Mallick's and Sahoo's studies experimented the educational television (ETV) while Mahapatra's study was related to the experiment of computer assisted instruction (CAI). Sahoo (1993) in her study on effectiveness of ETV with and without talkback found that ETV integrated with a talkback by the teacher was more effective than ETV without talkback. These findings are akin to the emerging idea that learners must actively construct and inter-relate knowledge by learning in more' authentic way.

The technology support in education has been termed as Information and Communication Technology (ICT). The relevance of ICT in education is being increasingly felt by the experts in 2lst century. The ICT comprises of information technology and other media. Research experience in India has witnessed the use of ICT based educational delivery modes in formal as well as non-formal education system. These include one-way TV broadcast, inter-active TV via phone-in, inter-active TV with computer support through e-mail, video conferencing, tele-conferencing, web based instruction etc. Adoption of these technologies is feasible with appropriate kind of satellite support. The launching of Edu-Sat on 20th September, 2004 has acted as a trend setter in popularizing all the stages of education i.e., from pre-primary to higher education. The UNESCO Global Monitoring Report (2007) has reported Edu-Sat as a revolution launched to meet the demand for greater access to education.

The major challenges ahead in this respect shall be ICT awareness among teachers, motivating and empowering experts and effective teachers in content development and transaction related subject specific competencies along with relevant other technotronic competencies and preparation of educational software enabling teachers in making appropriate use of interactive mode virtual classroom presentations in a real classroom situation. Intregrating such opportunities in curricular practices at school stage shall require specific abilities to be developed among school teachers ,such as innovation proneness, technology friendliness, adoptability, encouraging learners' participation in teaching-learning activities, empowering learners to learn, motivating learners to take self-initiatives in making use of various kinds of learning resources available in the forms of real and virtual situations. The in-service as well as the prospective teachers need to be aware up and equipped with adequate technotronic as well as subject specific competencies at a point of time when the school have been undergoing the technology starved crisis. Now some categories of schools have been flooded with computers. But the work is limited to computer literacy only. Jonassen (1996) observes that the use of technology has been less emphasized in schools. The study pointed out the reasons to 'increasing number of computers in society' that gives students more experience and there is 'lack of understanding to use computer as tool in instructional processes'. Only mere emphasis has been given on memorizing the vocabulary about computers in computer literacy classes. It is obvious that learners' expectations at school stage are to be met. The similar situation is existing at higher education stage. Studies conducted by Santawani (1986), Sonlanki (2002) and Joshi (2002) on teaching strategies and computer awareness found that the use of computer in teaching and research was very less, most of the academics possess computer literacy through informal ways and all the teachers lack mastery over all the skills of using computers for educational purpose. Besides, Joshi (2002) in his study pointed out that teacher-educators are moderately aware of the uses of computers but they have no experience of their use. These findings bring to the light the need for teacher empowerment with updated knowledge and skills in order to support the much debating quality education in 21st century. In this regard, a study carried out by the authors related to the ICT awareness, utilization and problems and constraints among the prospective teachers is of worth noting.

Objective of the Study

The attempt was made to study the awareness of the teacher trainees in terms of understanding of ICT, relevance of ICT in instructional process, use of ICT based instructional materials, understanding the 'use of internet', surfing for teaching-learning materials, understanding 'virtual learning', importance of Edu-Sat in teacher education programme and the problems and constraints faced by the teacher trainees in using ICT based technologies in teaching learning activities.

Methodology

Around one hundred teacher trainees from two teacher education colleges of Allahabad University were the sample for the study. The sample of teacher trainees was both from arts and science background and included both males and females. The author used a self developed ICT Awareness Questionnaire to collect the data. The data were analyzed using percentage and content analysis techniques.

Major Findings

The major findings were given component wise:

Understanding ICT

About 80 per cent teacher trainees possess an informal understanding about information and communication technology in various modes as existing at present e.g., computers, internet, video-conferencing, tele-conferencing, radio and television broadcasts, cell phone, print media and so on. It has been noticed that the student teachers having English medium background possess more clarity in understanding the operational meaning of information and communication technology as compared to their counterpart trainees of Hindi medium background.

Relevance of ICT in Instructional Process

It is a positive signal that about 70 per cent teacher-trainees showed their inclination in fovour of the relevance of ICT in instructional process. However, the experience about the use of ICT as an educational tool was least found among most (82 per cent) of the teacher trainees. The major reason cited by these trainees was that the opportunities, facilities, and proper operational knowledge had not been given to them.

Knowledge of ICT based Instructional Materials

About 18 per cent teacher trainees responded having knowledge of ICT based instructional materials (IMs) that are available through Television, Radio Lesson and on different websites. It was found that neither the trainees have been given training of using ICT based IMs nor they have used ICT based IMs in their teaching practices.

Understanding use of Internet

Around 72 per cent of teachers trainees are aware of the utility of internet in various communications related to on-line chatting, e-mailing, dissemination of information, trading, banking, administration, advertisements, educational counseling, examination results, website based specific information and programmes.

Surfing Web Sites for TLMs

It has been found that only 15 per cent teacher trainees have been surfing a limited number of websites for teaching learning materials at surfing centers. Google.com and Yahoo.com are the most frequently used search engines.

Understanding Virtual Learning

The concepts of virtual learning, smart school and virtual university are yet to be assimilated by the teacher trainees. Most of the trainees (82 per cent) possess inappropriate knowledge about these said concepts.

Importance of Edu-Sat in TEP

About 98 per cent teacher trainees responded that they do not know about the utility of Edu-Sat in Teacher Education Programme.

Problems and Constraints

The major problems and constraints related to operating and utilizing ICT supported teaching learning activities as perceived by the teacher .trainees have been categorized as follows:

- Lack of proper knowledge about the utility of ICT supported teaching learning activities.
- Lack of proper operational knowledge.
- Lack of ICT mediated training facilities in the teacher training institutions.
- Lack of interest among management, personnel and teacher educators.
- Teacher educators have no mastery over all the ICT based competencies and skills related to educational use.
- Lack of ICT related advanced content in Teacher Education Curriculum.
- Lack of provision for adequate number of computers and other media.
- Lack of internet facilities.

- Lack of electricity/alternative arrangement.
- Lack of specific orientation programme for teacher trainees in this regard.
- Surfing constraints such as difficulties in seeking information, information credibility, difficulties in finding the relevance of information and lack of search efficiency.

Conclusion

The study reveals that a large chunk of teacher trainees have their knowledge about various existing modes of ICTs, their relevance in education and especially in instructional process. Likewise, a large number of teacher trainees possess their understanding regarding the importance and use of internet. However, a very few among them have experiences about the ICT based instructional materials and their integration in classroom instructions. The teacher trainees possess inappropriate knowledge about the concepts of virtual learning, smart schools and virtual universities. Further, the teacher trainees have least knowledge about the role of Edu-Sat in Teacher Education Programme. The teacher trainees are not aware of large number of educational websites. In course of surfing they face many constraints like difficulties in seeking information, confronting the credibility and relevance of information and less competent in searching information. The major problems are lack of ICT based infrastructure in teacher education institution, absence of advanced content related to ICT in teacher education curriculum and lack of technotronic competencies among teacher educators to prepare the teacher trainees in ICT related skills. The need is therefore, to develop techno-savvy skills among the teacher educators and the prospective teachers along with the provision of updated content in teacher education curriculum about the trends and developments in ICT and their use in education.

REFERENCES

Chun, D.M. (1994). Using computer networking to facilitate the acquisition of interactive competence. System, 22(1), 17-31.

Ferneding-Linert, K.F. and Harris, J.B. (1994). Redefining expertise and reallocating roles in text based asynchronous teaching learning environments, Machine Mediated Learning, 4 (2/3), 129-148.

Irving, A. (1991). The education value and use of on-line information services in schools, *Computers In Education,* 17 (3), 213-225.

ISRO. (2002). *Educating the Nation.* Ahmedabad: DECU.

Jonassen, D.H. (1996). Computers in the classroom: Mind tools for critical thinking, Englewood Cliffs, New Jeresy: PHI.

Joshi, B. (2002). Teacher Educators' Computer Awareness, paper presented at National Seminar on *ICT in Education: Emerging Issues,* Vodadara: CASE, MSU.

Kulik, J.A. (1994). Meta-Analytic studies of findings on computers based instruction, In E.L. Baker and

H.F. 0' Neil1 (Eds.), *Technology Assessment-in Education and Training,* Hillsdale, NJ: Lawrence Erlbaum.

Mallick. P. (1995). Effectiveness of ETV at Primary Stage, Unpub. PhD Thesis, School of Education, Indore: DAVV.

Means, B. and Olson, K. (1997). *Technology and Education Reform:* Washington, D.C.: US. Dept. of Education.

Mohapatra, B. (1992). Effectiveness of Computer Assisted Instruction for Teaching Science at Secondary Level in MP State, Ph.D Thesis, Indore: School of Education, DAVV. Sahoo, N. (1993).

Sahoo, N. (2005). Television in Higher Education, New Delhi: Kailash. Effectiveness of CWCR Programmes with and without Talk back at Higher Education Stage, PhD Thesis, School of Education, Indore, DAVV.

Santawani, S. (1986). Perception of the MS University Students about their Teachers, M.Ed. Dissertation, Vododara: CASE, MSU.

Solanki, T.(2002). Study of Computer Literacy of Teachers of MS University of Boroda, M.Ed. Dissertation, Vodaders: CASE, MSU.

UNESCO, (2007) *Global Monitoring Report.*

26

ICT Integrated Teacher Education

Sutapa Bose

Rapid developments in the field of Information and Communication Technology (ICT) and its invasion of almost every sphere of our life have been witnessed during the last few decades. The field of education is no exception to such technological invasion and is becoming increasingly dependent on ICT for not only delivery of instructions but also for creating and sharing knowledge. This has been possible not only due to the revolution in the field of 1CT but also due to the widening of its accessibility and above all due to the realization as to its potential in furthering the goals of education. Moreover, the new paradigm of teaching learning process does not suppose the teacher to possess and deliver all information but requires him/her to be a manager and facilitator of learning. It also requires the learner to actively engage in the creation of knowledge than being the passive recipient of the information dished out by the teachers. This paradigm can be successfully implemented only through technology aided instructional system.

Knowledge mediated by ICT has a high value not only in the academic world but also in financial, societal and governmental environments as it is highly flexible, enables fast paced activities and has a ubiquitous distributing power (Gayol, Boubsiland & Hoban, 2005). Therefore, it is required that the teachers are fully equipped with the necessary knowledge, skills and attitude to shift to the new role and are at home in the technology driven teaching learning scenario. Also, the phenomenon of staying connected through telephone, interactive audio-video programmes and internet has now penetrated deep even into rural areas but for this advantage to be used for educational purposes, it is required to equip the teachers to harness the potential of ICT. Hence, teacher education programmes have to take care that pedagogical skills are redefined in the context of increasing use of ICT for imparting instructions.

Teacher education programmes have themselves to provide a culture that encourages the use of ICT as tools for learning so that the teachers in turn are prepared to do so with their learners. The teachers should have the ability to use the latest ICT devices and be well conversant with the current developments in the field of ICT that are reforming the field of education. As underlined by Lee (2005) teachers should learn to use technology, use it to learn, possess basic computer literacy, use ICT hardware and software for teaching-learning activities and learn pedagogy based ICT use, integrated use of ICT in classroom teaching and management, and online collaboration and networking. Although, the teacher education programmes have the responsibility of preparing teachers for the ICT based educational system, the curriculum usually followed is unable to develop these abilities.

Today, professionalism in teachers demands acquisition of knowledge and skills that are being redefined in the contest of ICT based education system. It is not enough to be able to impart instructions but there is a need to undergo a transition from the traditional role of a teacher to that of being a manager who is a system expert and a learning strategist (Bowes, 2003). This need for redefining teachers' roles have led to the launching of professional development programmes to train teachers in the use of computers. However, most of these training activities are crash courses that aim to generate computer literacy per se and do not enable teachers to actually integrate ICTs in day-to-day classroom instruction. Learning to use computers and the Internet is a relatively simple task, but mastering ICT use as an effective tool to improve teaching and learning is certainly not (UNESCO Bangkok, ICT in Education, Issues and Rationale). For developing professional efficiency, the latest skills and knowledge associated with the profession are to be mastered. Therefore, the curriculum of teacher education programmes is to be revised so as to fulfill these needs.

Place accorded to ICT by the ongoing Teacher Education Programmes

The teacher education programmes that are offered today usually have components that tend to inform the trainees about certain aspects related to educational technology such as various types of media, their shortcomings and strengths, use of computer for learning, benefits of using technology while imparting instructions, etc. These components are usually a part of the theoretical component of the teacher-training programme. Practical activities in these areas are usually neglected and Mostly computer literacy generation programmes are included. There is hardly any effort to integrate technology in the ongoing teaching-learning process in these institutions. The trainees who are the would-be teachers are therefore aware of the developments in the field of ICT and their applications in the field of education and some of them may also be able to use some of these technologies but they are not adequately equipped to integrate ICT in their teaching.

ICT is treated usually as an isolated theoretical component in the curriculum followed in teacher education programmes. Technology therefore, remains at the periphery of the teaching-learning process. While the trainees can write essays on computer assisted learning, use of computers for simulated learning, benefits of using multimedia approach to learning, etc. but may lack even the skills of operating these technologies as tools of learning. There is hardly any hands-on training regarding the latest development in the field of educational technology such as computer assisted learning, web based learning, developing softwares for different types of media, development of online courses, etc. Again, while using technology is undoubtedly the prerequisite for integrating technology but integrating it seamlessly in the flow of instructions is different from merely using it. The present day teacher education programmes have to look ahead instead of looking backward with teachers in traditional classrooms, wherein they are imparting instructions mainly orally and using technology as teaching aids. That there has been a shift in the role played by the teacher and the teachers of the modern world have to facilitate learning and allow the learners to use technology as tools to create and share knowledge is yet to be reflected in the present day teacher education programmes.

Hence, teacher education programmes need to provide an environment or more aptly a culture so that teachers are imparted not merely theoretical knowledge and computer literacy but are also trained in the application of various kinds of educational software in teaching and learning. Furthermore, they need to learn how to integrate ICT into their classroom activities and other activities of the school and be aware of the ethical issues that are involved with the use of ICT as learning tools. It has been rightly underlined that in an era where new technologies are becoming an indispensable part of educational systems, the success in expanding and improving the use of technologies in teacher education will directly and strategically benefit Education for All (UNESCO Teacher Education Programme, Use of Technology).

Reforming Teacher Education Programmes for Enhancing Professionalism

Owing to a variety of reasons, allegations are often made against the practitioners of the teaching profession that they are yet to achieve professionalism in true sense. It is felt that there is a need for the members of the teaching profession to be as professional as those pursuing other professions such as law, medicine, nursing, etc. However, instead of shifting the entire blame on the teachers for inadequate professionalism, the causes need to be probed. One of the reasons cited is related to the pre service education provided to the teachers. Questions are raised as to the nature and quality of pre service teacher training programmes and it is being felt that even after attending these programmes, the teachers are not fully prepared for the modern ICT based teaching-learning system while children are today rapidly learning to use the latest technologies. Unlike the trainees of other professional courses such as medicine, engineering, etc, with opportunities to learn and practice using the relevant technologies, the teachers rarely get the opportunity to use them during their training. For instance, they learn about computer-assisted instructions. teaching with the help of audio-video technology, etc. but rarely do they handle the hardware or prepare the necessary software during their training. A service provider can render best possible services only if she has the competence for successfully dealing with latest developments in the field. Teachers of the future have to possess in their repertoire the skills for being a successful broker who can locate and negotiate appropriate learning resources in mixed models of teaching-learning with online teaching, computer discs, web based learning, print medium, etc. (Bowes, 2003). But the teacher education programmes are yet to take concrete steps in this direction.

There is also the need to redefine the pedagogic skills in the context of emerging ICT based education. Activities comprising teaching and learning are changing. For instance, while preparing a lesson plan a teacher still has the mental setup that it would be used for the lecture s/he is going to deliver. Accordingly the content with the questions to be asked, the chalkboard work, teaching aids to be used are considered. But learning centered education with integration of technology, demand a different type of planning. Also new set of skills is required to assess the individualised, independent and technology based learning. Again, skills required for maintaining, updating and sharing records, preparing and using data bases through ICT, need to be practised in the perspective of ICT based education system. As per the findings of a study conducted in parts of Egypt and Africa, new digital technologies have the potential to revolutionize the quality of training and status, self-image, confidence, knowledge and professionalism of teachers within sub-Saharan Africa, thus transforming teacher education *(http://w\\.Vl.comminit.com/Strategicthinking/st2004/thinking-920.html).* Hence, professionalism in teachers can be enhanced not by preparing them for what is rapidly becoming obsolete but by preparing them for the present day requirements.

Reforming the Curriculum

The realization of the potential of ICT for furthering the goals of education, its widening accessibility and its much needed integration in the educational process in the schools around the world are having a profound influence on all aspects of education. Also, this happens to be an irreversible phenomenon. But what are the real implications of this change for teachers and what role will they play in the new knowledge society? What skills do educators need to acquire and develop to respond to these changes within their profession'? These are some of the questions that are being raised (Teacher's Role in ICT Environment, ICT portal for Teachers, UNESCO Bangkok). In the light of these issues that are being raised, the existing curriculum has to be reformed. Some of the measures that can be adopted to bring about reform in the curriculum are discussed below:

Adopting Learning centered Approach

Although it is strongly advocated to adopt learning centered approach in the educational institutions so that the learners are responsible, independent and active in their pursuit of knowledge, yet those who are to implement it and design such learning environments are themselves not trained in this way during their training programmes. If the teachers are to design learning environments that transform traditional paradigm to one in which students construct knowledge, creatively using digital technologies then it has to be assumed that learning is a natural process, unique for every individual, involves engagement of the learners with integration and contextualisation and is a social process requiring collaboration with peers, teachers, parents and others (http://unesdoc.unesco.org/images/0102 /00 1295/129533e.PdQ.). Therefore, the first and foremost requirement for teachers to creatively use ICT is that the approach adopted in the teacher education institutions towards teaching-learning process needs to be based on similar assumptions. This will help the teachers to understand their role in ICT based teaching-learning process and also nurture positive attitude towards it.

Learning to use Technology

The next important requirement is that the teachers are trained to use technology. It is well known that Computer literacy and ability to surf the Internet are the prerequisites for future complex activities such as development of online courses, teaching through multimedia approach, etc. Today for teachers it is becoming essential to be well versed in using desktop technologies for word processing, computing, making presentations, etc. Learning to efficiently use the Internet will also make teachers life long learners, much needed for the emerging knowledge driven societies.

Using Technology for Learning

While the skills mentioned above require only technical know how and are comparatively easier to master, using technology as tools for learning and teaching is more difficult. It is often expressed that computers are provided to even rural schools as a matter of policy of the government but the teachers are still not ready to integrate them while imparting instructions. Learning to use technology in a creative way involves several aspects such as:

Integrating Technology

Integration of ICT into the teaching learning process has been aptly called informatisation of education, which is the necessary component, condition and catalyst for modernization of education that will help the transition from reproductive model of learning to the independent model (http://unesdoc.unesco.orglimages/0012/001295/1295 3 3e.Pdf). Teachers have to be trained to infuse technology in the curriculum for pedagogical purposes. Strategies have to be prepared so that instructions are supported and facilitated by technology by designing developmentally appropriate learning experiences for the learners. As the teachers are preparing lesson plans today for teaching in traditional classrooms, lesson plans have to be prepared that would envisage technology mediated self-learning by students. The students should be able to survey and select information, organize it, analyze it and interpret their findings. Also the planning has to possess the flexibility that would allow scope for creativity while using technology. This requires:

- Selection of content and the choice of appropriate technology (s): The suitability of a particular technology as decided by accessibility to it, economic factors associated with it, its pedagogic strengths and weaknesses, etc. have to be considered. Therefore, the teacher has to locate and thereafter evaluate a technology for its appropriateness for the content. Selection of several types of technologies to adopt a multimedia approach for learning may also be needed. Trainees need to be provided with opportunities in the teacher education programmes so that they can practice such activities.
- Management of technological resources and facilitating student learning: How the technological resources can be put to optimum use for learning and facilitate individual and group learning are to be considered. It has to be internalized during teacher training that

media is used not only for communication of information but also for broadening and deepening experiences of the learners (McNeil and Wiles, 1990). Hence, it is to be realised that ICT should not be treated merely as teaching aids while education remains teacher-centered but should be treated as tools for learning. Management of technological resources also implies that the teachers monitor the appropriateness of the information collected from the Internet by the students, especially its authenticity.

- Evaluation: The use of technology for carrying out evaluation has to be learnt by the teachers so that they can evaluate the outcomes of technology-aided learning. This requires a wide range of skills such as the skills for preparing digitalized records, retrieving them, updating them, their communication, creating databases, analyzing data, interpreting findings, etc. Also there is the need to develop skills such as preparation of tests, quizzes, etc. that can be used for self-evaluation and also for valuation by the teacher.

Using Technology for Collaborative Learning

Teachers have to understand that learning cannot be confined within the four walls of the classroom. The learner is not a passive recipient but an active collaborator interacting with the tutors and peers during the learning process (Dowling, 2003).Neither the teacher nor the textbooks are the only sources of information. Learning involves interaction with peers, teachers and also with those from the outside world. ICT can be put to use for sharing information and exchanging views that help learning. If the teachers are provided with the opportunity for such collaborative learning during their training period whereby they can interact and share information with those within the classroom and those outside, they can realize that learning is a social process and that interaction and collecting information from different sources enrich the process.

Using Technology for Management

Teachers' role, especially in the schools is not restricted to imparting instructions. S/he also has to perform a number of tasks that complement instructions like preparing assignments, preparing instructional plans and schedules, etc. as well as those that are related to administration. Learning to use ICT for such activities will greatly help in lessening the workload and the time spent in these jobs. Hence, training to use ICT for recording data, maintaining data banks, sharing and communicating them effectively, analyzing and interpreting data to create information out of it, etc. are needed.

Using and Preparing Softwares as Instructional Materials

Today a variety of Softwares are available. Locating them and selecting the appropriate ones for instructional purposes is important. Also the teachers themselves must be able to produce some of the softwares. Training to prepare instructional packages for learning, drill, problem solving, games, simulations, preparing scripts, etc. is required. With the growing popularity of distance education it is also becoming necessary that the teachers learn about online courses and receive the training to prepare them.

Awareness about Ethical Issues

The teachers need to be aware of the ethics that are associated with the use of digital technology especially the Internet. Respect for rules governing access and use of information, copyright laws, etc. have to be developed during the training period.

Conclusion

The teacher education programmes to a major extent have the onus for ensuring the professionalism of teachers. As has been rightly mentioned by Childs (1989) every teacher is responsible for mastering those technology skills that will allow effective professional performance. Preparation for ICT based educational system will enable teachers to understand their role of being managers of learning rather than the possessor and dispenser of all information. The teachers no longer are supposed to feed the students with information but are to introduce them to the appropriate sources of information after duly evaluating the source for its pedagogical strength and other relevant issues. For this it is not enough to master the skills of using ICT but more important is effectively integrating it into the curriculum. The present day teacher education programmes treat ICT as a part of the theoretical component about which the trainees are supposed to learn. ICT is thus treated in isolation as an area unto itself and technology is not integrated into the process of teaching and learning. The trainees on the other hand are required not only to know about ICT, but also learn to use them as tools for learning. Unless the teacher education programmes themselves integrate ICT into the curriculum, the teachers of the future may know about ICT but not about integration of ICT into the curriculum they would be dealing with. This requires that the teacher education programme be reformed so that teachers are ready to harness the pedagogic potential of ICT in creating learning centered education.

As rightly underlined by Jager & Lokman, (2003) teacher-training institutes have to anticipate new developments and prepare prospective teachers for their future role. The nature and extent of ICT usage demands that teacher-training institutes shift their focus from dealing with present education to that of future education. Therefore, curriculum of teacher education programmes should be such that ability to use technology especially for imparting instructions, facilitating collaborative learning, evaluation and carrying out administrative work are developed in the teachers of the modern world.

REFERENCES

Childs, J.W. (1989). The Teacher and Technology. In Quina, J. Effective Secondary Teaching. Harper & Row Publishers. New York.

Gayol, Y., Boubsiland, O. & Hoban, S. (3005). Infonnation Technology Fluency of Science Teachers In the United States: A Case Study. In Garg, S., Panda. S.. Murthy, C.R.K. & Mishra. S. (Eds). Open and Distance Education in Global Environment Opportunities for Collaboration. Viva Books Private Limited. New Delhi.

McNeiI, J.D.& Wiles, J. (1990) The Essentials of Teaching. Macmillan Publising Company. New York.

Lee, N.N.M. (2005). Teacher Education: Patterns, Policies and Practices. The Mobile Training Team (MTT) Project in Curriculum and Teacher Education, India. (2005). Paper presented at In-country Training Workshop organized by School of Education. IGNOU and UNESCO (4-6 .May, 2005, IGNOU, New Delhi).

Bowes, J. (2003). The Emerging Repertoire Demanded of Teachers of the Future: Surviving the Transition. Paper presented at IFIP Workings 3.1 & 3.3 Working Conference, ICT and the Teachers of the Future, held at St. Hilda's College, The University of Melbourne, Australia 27th -3 15 1 January, 2003. (http://crpit.comfconfpapers/CRPITV23Bowes.pdf) Retrieved on 10.1.06.

Dowling, C. (2003). The Role of the Human Teachers in the Learning Environments of the Future. Papers presented at IFIP Workings3.1 &3.3 Working Conference, ICT and the Teachers of the Future, held at St. Hilda's College, The University of Melbourne, Australia 27th-31st January)', 2003. (http://crpit.com/confvapers/CRPITV23Bowes.pdf.) Retrieved on 10.1.06.

Jager, A.K. and Lokman, A.H. (2003). Impacts of ICT in education. The role of the teacher and teacher training. Paper presented at the European Conference on Educational Research, Lahti, Finland 22-25 Septernber1999. (http://www.leeds.ac.uk/educol/documents/00001201.htm) Retrieved on 10.1.06.

Teacher's Role in ICT Environment, ICT portal for Teachers, UNESCO, Bangkok. UNESCO, Bangkok, ICT in Education, Issues and Rationale http://www.unescobkk.org/index..php? id=782) Retrieved on 13.1.06.

UNESCO Teacher Education Programme, Use of Technology. http://portal.unesco.org/education/en/ev.php URL ID=32272&URL DO=DO TOPIC&URL SECTION=201 .html: Retrieved on 12.1.06

ICT in Teacher Education Global Context and Framework in ICT in Teacher Education A Planning Guide. Division of Higher Education, UNESCO, 2002.Coordinator: Evgueni Khivilon Editorial Coordinator: Mariana Patru. (http://unesdoc.unesco.org/images/0012/001295/129533e.Pdf.) Retrieved on 12.1.06

ICT Supported Teacher Education: Images and Scenarios in ICT in Teacher Education A Planning Guide. Division of Higher Education. UNESCO, 2002.Coordinator: Evgueni Khivilon Editorial Coordinator: Mariana Patru. (http://unesdoc.unesco.org/images/0012/001295/129533e.Pdf.) Retrieved on 13.1.06

The Communication Initiative (http:// www.commlnit.com/strategicthinkinglst20041th inking920.html) Strategic Thinking. ICT for Teacher Education in the Global South Researching the Issues by Digital Education Enhancement Project (DEEP) June 2004. Retrieved on 12.1.06.

27

Van Hiele Model of Thinking in Developing Teachers' Competencies

MIN BAHADUR SHRESTHA

School mathematics curriculum at elementary and secondary levels faces serious dilemma when it comes to geometry and it is easy to find fault with traditional course in geometry, but it is difficult to come with sound advice on its remedial measures. Except the knowledge of shapes, the geometry knowledge of students at the end of elementary school is spotty and rather minimal (Allendoerfer, 1969; Usiskin, 1987). The situation seems to be further worse when we come to secondary school level *Euclidean* geometry. Most of the difficulties that students face in the classroom are related to the way of construction of logical arguments in the development of proofs (Dreyfus and Hadas, 1987).

If the students are to learn basic geometric knowledge as sound foundation for secondary school geometry, then it is important for teachers to be comfortable with these ideas together with the ways to help them learn the fundamentals of geometry. But the researches conducted have shown that teachers had patterns of misconceptions similar to those of students and the content knowledge in geometry among pre-service and in-service middle school teachers was low and much of their prior learning in geometry had been by memorization and rote. (Mayberry, 1983; Herskowitz et al., 1987; Fuys et al., 1988). Studies conducted on secondary school geometry indicated that teachers held limited views on the nature of proofs and they needed more experiences in logical underpinnings of proofs (Knuth, 2002; Riley, 2003).

Among many attempts made in improving geometry instruction and geometry curriculum, the radical change and far-reaching innovations had been introduced by Russian researches based on Van Hiele Model of thinking (Fuys et al., 1988; Wirszup, 1992). The Van Hiele model of mathematical reasoning has become a valid descriptor of the progress of students' reasoning in geometry and is a valid framework for the design of teaching sequences in geometry as acknowledged by the NCTM's Curriculum and Evaluation Standards for School Mathematics (1989).

The main objective of this paper is to consider the teaching of school geometry (Euclidean geometry) in the line of Van Hiele model of instruction. An attempt has been made to report analytically some of the major features of Van Hiele model that may help teachers to perceive students' difficulties of learning geometry and help to equip them how to guide the students in learning geometry.

A Brief Introduction to Van Hiele Model

Throughout the 20th century, a common recommendation has been to do informal or intuitive geometry in elementary and junior high school level and formal geometry in senior high school level. Such distinction is thought to be clear at the extreme (Usiskin, 1987). The distinction between formal and informal geometry leads one to think that there are only two levels of discourses. Such broad classification make it difficult to sequence geometry experiences in a productive manner. The lack of clear characterization of formal and informal geometry led to ambiguity among mathematics educators and teachers (Usiskin, 1987). He suggested that one of the goal, of teaching formal idea could be to change the learner's perception of the idea from intuitive to formal. He continues that it might be best to avoid the words formal and informal and their analogous abstract and contrite, except as they might apply to the state to an individual learner in encountering a concept.

Van Hiele model of thinking has been found effective in addressing such problems, which has distinguished five levels of thought (as stratification of human thought) in the learning of geometry.

What has become known as the Van Hiele model of thinking was developed by P.M. Van Hiele and his wife Dina Van Hiele-Geldof on the basis of their research dealing with mental development in geometry (Van Hiele, 1957/1984; Van Hiele, 1959/1984; Van Hiele, 1986). Since Dina Van Hiele-Geldof died shortly after her dissertation work was completed. P.M. Van Hiele took a lead to explicate the theory (Usiskin, 1982).

Stratification of human thought into five different hierarchical levels has been fundamental contribution of Van Hiele model of thinking. Research on Van Hiele model has given further clarification on the level theory. The detail characterization of the levels by Fuys *et al.* (1998) and Clements & Battista (1992) have been found more useful in clarifying Van Hiele levels of thinking. The model consisted of five levels of understanding in hierarchical order:

- Level 4: Rigor/Mathematical
- Level 3: Formal Deduction
- Level 2: Informal Deduction
- Level 1: Descriptive/Analytic Level
- Level 0 : Visual Level

According to the Van Hieles, the learner assisted by appropriate instructional experiences moves sequentially from the basic level (Visualization), where geometric figures are observed as a whole in a look-like manner without recognizing properties through the sequence listed above to the higher level (Rigor), where the learners reason formally about mathematical system. The learner cannot achieve one level of thinking without having passed through the previous levels. Van Hiele (1984) states that the levels are characterized by differences in object of thought. At visual level (Level O), the object of thought are geometric figures, while at descriptive/analytic level (level I), the student operates on classes of figures (as the product of level 0 activities) and discovers properties for these classes. At the level of informal deduction (level 2), these properties become the object that the student acts upon, yielding logical ordering of properties. On the basis of level 2 activities of ordering properties and relations, the ordering relations become object that the student acts upon, yielding logical ordering of formal type. At level **3,** the ordering relations become the object of thought. At the apex level (level 4), the object of thought are the foundation of these ordering relations. It is at the apex level, students study different postulational system and the foundation of mathematics as logical interpretation. In particular, student can understand non-*Euclidean* geometry, as a system different from *Euclidean* geometry.

According to Van Hiele (1959/1984), progress through the levels is more dependent on method and organisation of instruction and materials used than on age or maturation. In view of addressing these issues, Van Hieles proposed phases of next level involving five phases are:

Information: Students get acquainted with working domain.

Guided orientation: Students are acquainted with the objects from which geometric ideas are extracted (Clements and Battista, 1992).

Explicitation: Students become conscious of the geometric relations and express in own language and they learn technical language accompanying the subject matter.

Free orientation: Students learn by general tasks to find their own way in the network of relations. Students solve problems whose solution requires synthesis and utilization of previously learnt concepts and relations.

Integration: Students summarize what they have learnt into a coherent network of objects and relations.

For each phase, the teacher plays unique role in providing instruction with appropriate method and materials. The teacher plays the role of acquainting content domain, directing students activities, bringing the object of study to an explicit level of awareness by leading students' discussions, presenting problems with open and multiple solutions and encouraging them to solve, and assisting them to form global survey for the purpose of integration (Van Hiele, 1984). In addition to levels of thinking and phases of instruction, Van Hiele identified some important generalities that characterize the model, especially, the level theory. They are known as characterizing features of the Van Hiele levels. They are:

- The levels are sequential and hierarchical.
- Each level has its own language.
- What is implicit at one level becomes explicit at the next level.
- There are jumps in the learning curve which reveal the presence of qualitatively different levels of thinking.
- Materials taught to students above their level result in the reduction of level.

These properties are particularly significant to educators and teachers because they provide guidance and teaching advice. In particular, they suggest that geometric activities should not reduce level of geometric content. For that, language is considered as an important factor in the development and assessment of geometry understanding.

Due to the above features of the Van Hiele model of thinking, it has emerged as comprehensive and useful model to tackle the problems of curriculum development, and transaction in the field of geometry.

Geometry Courses and Its Teaching

According to Van Hiele model of thinking students progress through a five-level sequence in a particular order and progress through a level is more dependent on method and organization of instruction as well as materials and organization of contents is one of the major characteristics that differentiates Van Hiele model of thinking from Piaget's theory. Van Hieie adopted 0-4 numbering scheme in leveling in the sense that level 0 (basic level) worked as basement in the hierarchy of thinking.

Level 1 i.e., descriptive/analytic level has been taken as the first level of geometry discourse. Corresponding to first, second, third and fourth level of his hierarchy of understanding, Van Hiele proposed four different levels of geometry courses (Van Hiele, 1959/1984). These have been referred as different parts of geometry courses and they have been considered as follows.

Different Discourses in Geometry Course

Corresponding to the levels of thinking, Van Hiele proposed four different discourses in geometry. For the teaching of geometry, a teacher should be oriented with different geometry discourses in school geometry curriculum.

The first part of Geometry Course should allow the attainment of the first level of thought (descriptive/analytic level) (Van Hiele. 1959/1984). Based on the ground of basic level (Visualization), the aim of teaching should be to teach geometric figures such as cubes, squares, rectangles, rhombuses, circles, triangles, etc. not only in a lock-like manner as visual gestalt, but also as the bearer of their properties. This course should develop in students the ability to characterize shapes by their properties. A rectangle is no longer recognized by its appearance in a look-like manner (as in basic level) rather, for example, by the fact that opposite sides are equal, opposite angles are equal and all angles are right angle. The students operate on classes of figures as the product of level 0 (Visual level) activities and discover properties for these classes (Fuys et al., 1988).

The first part of geometry can be interpreted as the formation of visual geometric structures through the analysis of the global structures that are provided by empiricism (Dina Van Hiele-Geldof, 1957/1984) called as the aspect of geometry, Van Hieles recommended manipulation of contrete materials (colouring, folding, cutting, modeling, etc.) so as to characterize figures by their properties.

The second part of the course should allow the attainment of the second level of thought which Van Hiele call the *essence of geometry*. The main aim of instruction is to develop in student the relations which link properties of geometrical patterns. Based on the experiences of first course activities, during this course one is to order properties of figures logically. The transition from first level to the second level only brings about a structuring within the geometric context although global structures of perception has to serve as starting point (Dina Van Hiele-Geoldof, 1957/1984). Organizing the aggregate of geometrical properties is made by so called *organizing principle,* such as the role played by parallelism and equality of alternate angles in showing triangle-angle sum 180°. It is important to note that the role of organizing principles, such as, parallelism and congruence act as *signal character* structuring within geometric context so as to bring students from visual thinking to abstract thinking.

If one takes the geometric relations of a figure itself of object of thinking, then a separation in the relations, namely, into premise and conclusion, evolve after the structure of thinking on the second level of geometry discourse (Dina Van Hiele-Geldof, 1984). Hence, the student identifies premise and conclusion as two parts in implication statement during the second part of the course. Since relations are linked logically, the pupils are capable of differentiating geometrical shapes into definitions and conceptualizing class inclusion (Fuys et al., 1988). During this, the student develops deduction of properties not on the strength of formal logic but on the basis of their working. The deductive sense of understanding is developed during the course of the third part of geometry.

The third part of Geometry Course should allow the attainment of the third level of understanding i.e., formal deduction. The aim of instruction is to guide students to understand what is meant by ordering the properties and why one property precedes another property. This course should help students to perceive geometry from higher perspectives independent of empirical results and it should develop the understanding of necessity of definition, axiom/postulate and basic assumptions in the development of geometric structure. Van Hiele called it *the essence of mathematics* in the sense that geometry should be understood as the system of mathematics. The material (content) of instruction is made up of geometric theorems, the ordering of theorems, the linkage between a theorem and its converse and the role of axioms/postulates and definitions in the development and linkage of geometry material such as theorems. Students' ability to develop proofs on the strength of deductive thinking should be developed during this course, but since the essence of deductive thinking belongs to the uppermost level 4 (rigor), the axiomatic foundation of the proofs in geometry is the matter of its fourth level.

The fourth part of Geometry should be the attainment of the essence of deductive thinking which Van Hiele called *scientific insight into the subject of geometry* (Van Hiele, 1984). The aim of teaching geometry would be to analyze the nature of the discipline, such as the nature of *Euclidean* geometry and non-*Euclikan* geomety which is generally impossible in general education (Van Hiele, 1984).

According to Van Hieles, a student cannot achieve higher level of thinking without passing through each of lower levels in order and students assisted with appropriate instructional experiences passes through the levels. The four different parts of courses in geometry corresponding the first, second, third and fourth level of thinking have been given the flame of references: the aspect of geometry, the essence of geometry, the insight into geometry and scientific insight into the theory of geometry (insight into mathematics/essence of logic) respectively. Each of them carries unique sense about the level of thinking they represent. For example, the fourth part, which is described as insight into mathematics indicates geometry as mathematical system independent of physical interpretation and based on axiomatic foundation. It is also characterized as essence of logic which indicates geometry as a discipline as determined by system of logic independent of its practical implication. The development of thinking from lower level to upper most level and the corresponding geometry discourses have been of great pedagogical importance (Wirszup, 1992) Van HieIe model of thinking and researches conducted on this model have suggested instructional strategy and guidelines for the teaching of geometry as stated in the following.

Instructional Strategy/Guidelines for Teaching of Geometry

The importance of Van Hiele model of thinking lies more in its concern with the problems of instruction and ways to guide students to overcome these obstacles. Unlike many other learning theory which insists guiding students smoothly without having faced difficulties in learning, Van Hiele model of thinking stresses facing difficulties (crisis of thinking) while advancing through higher level of thinking. The characteristics features of Van Hiele model provides teaching advice (teaching guidance) and the phases of learning presents guidelines on the sequencing and delivering geometric activities within a level (Crowley, 1987). The characteristics feature of the model (which is also called properties of the model) provides guidance of more general nature applicable to all the levels. Characterisitcs features of the model have been a matter of great concern in the field of pedagogy. Rest of the portion of this paper has been devoted to the consideration of instructional guidelines based on these features of Van Hiele model of thinking.

The sequence of levels, language, reduction of level, and *adjacency property* of levels are some generalities that characterize the model as well as provide teaching advice.

The sequence of levels tells us that the teacher who deliberately strives to lead his students from one level to another (and help them to acquire activities of preceding levels) gets them ready and to explore faults in a deductive system of geometry (Van Hiele, 1984). Directing instruction too rapidly or skipping a level may result in rote learning. According to Van Hiele (1984) progress from one level to the next is more dependent on instruction than on age or biological maturation. Since students cannot achieve one level without passing through the previous levels, the teacher cannot help students for meaningful learning if s/he skips a level.

The Van Hieles point out it is possible to present materials to students above their actual level, like one can train young children in arithmetic of fractions without developing the concept, or older children in differentiating and integrating without understanding what differential quotients and integrates are (Freudenthal, 1973). Geometric examples include memorization of proportion rather than discovering, or just copying a proof rather than developing. Such situation which is not uncommon in the teaching of geometry (and in mathematics) results in the *reduction of the subject matter to a lower level* (or no level). Van Hieles asserts that secondary school geometry instruction faces problems of reduction of level because of lack of sufficient experiences at lower levels.

Another problem of geometry instruction which is common in mathematics class is that of *mismatch* between the level of teacher's presentation with students' level of thinking. This happens if the student is at one level and instruction is at another level and the result is that the desired learning progress may not occur. With other things, *language* plays a vital role, for each level has its own linguistic symbols and its own system of relations connecting these signs. Language structure is a critical factor in the movement through the Van Hiele levels. Two persons who reason at two different levels cannot understand each other and this is what often happens between teacher and students in teaching mathematics (Van Hiele, 1984). Neither the teacher nor the students can manage to follow the thought process of the other and the dialogue between them can proceed if the teacher uses language at the level of students.

Van Hiele model of thinking seems to be more dedicated in suggesting that geometry teaching should not reduce the level of geometric content and whenever possible, materials should be organized for higher learning. Van Hiele and Van Hiele researchers (Usiskin, 1982; Mayberry, 1983; Wirszup, 1983; Burger and Soughnessy, 1986; Fuys et .al, 1988, and others) have supported the above mentioned problems in geometry instruction. Experimental studies conducted to improve students' understanding in geometry (based on Van Hiele model of thinking) have given encouraging results for the improvement of geometry instruction.

Traditionally, often, geometry is taught in a mechanical way. Let us consider the case of triangle-angle sum. In conducting my teaching experiment, the ninth graders were asked "what is the angle-sum of a triangle?" and "how do you know it?" with many other questions. Many of them said that it could be found 180° by measuring angles and there were some who said that they were simply told the information of triangle-angle sum 180°. The latter tactic is an example of the reduction of the content. Dina Van Hieie-Geldof in 1957 used *tiangular grids and organizing principles* to elevate students' thinking from level 1 to level 2 in case of triangle-angle sum relation. (Similar techniques have been used by Fuys et al. (1988) and other researchers including this author). Level I activities, such as drawing one set of parallel lines and intersecting it with another sets of parallel lines to form triangular 'grid, and identifying and colouring angles to show equality of alternative angles and equality of corresponding angles (Filgure 1), and extension of such activities to show relationship between triangle-angle sum and straight angle, may provide students with a powerful means, both inductively and deductively, for understanding triangle-angle sum relation. Insight into the reason why every triangle-angle sum is equal to straight angle on the basis triangular grid structure provide groundwork for the formal proof at the level of formal deduction. It should be noted that grid structure provide means for ascending level 2 from level I and ancestry mapping of identifying ancesters may lead towards the attainment of formal deductive thinking.

Students should work on many cases like above case which would help them to fill up within a level and advance to the next higher level. Dina Van Hiele-Geldof conducted a year long teaching experiment to develop her students' level from visual to abstract thinking in a continuous way.

According to the Van Hieles (1958/1984) learning progress through *fixed seuence but learning* is *discontinuous* process and the discontinuity reveals the presence of the levels. Citing Van Hieles (1958), Fuys et al. (1988) mentioned that at certain points in instruction the learning process stops and the teacher does not succeed in explaining the subject. The teacher seems to speak a language which is not understood by pupils who have not reached the new level. The students might accept the explanation but the matter does not go into their minds. This author in his teaching experiment (Shrestha, 2005) observed some instances like this while guiding students to conceive inclusion relations, necessary and sufficient conditions, and most apparently in case of conceiving the necessity of axioms, postulates, definitions and undefined terms in the development deductive proofs. It was more apparent in guiding students towards formal deductive thinking). Such situation indicates crisis of thinking. Van Hiele implores teacher to recognize such crisis of thinking that impede students' progress and provide guidance to facilitate transition to higher level of thinking. Dina Van Hiele-Geldof (1984) used family tree and ancestry mapping in guiding students towards abstract thinking in geometry. Similar types of activities together with arrow diagrams to relate and to arrange theorems and properties of geometry have been found effective in guiding students to upper Van Hiele levels.

In one way or in another, Van Hiele model of thinking focuses on development of thinking in geometry along different levels, where the learner cannot achieve one level of thinking without passing through the previous levels. The existence of different levels has been reflected by the features of the Van Hiele levels of thinking. *The sequence of levels, reduction of level, mismatch and language* are the main features in Van Hiele model of thinking which characterize the model and provide instructional guidelines.

More than these features, Van Hiele (1984) notes that at each level there appears an extrinsic way that which was intrinsic at the preceding level. In other word, the inherent object at one level becomes the object of study at the next level (Crowley, 1987). That is, the object of learning implicit at one level becomes explicit at next level. For example, at basic level, a figure is determined by its appearance rather than its component parts, but it is not until level 1 the figure is not recognized in terms of its component parts. Such feature implies that the geometric figures should be presented to students in look-like manner so as to identify and differentiate shapes and after identifying the geometric shapes (e.g., triangle, rectangle, parallelogram, circle, cube, etc.) they are guided to the properties of shapes.

On the whole, the characteristics features of the model deal mainly with the characteristics of the levels and provide instructional guidance applicable to all levels. It provides guidance for organization of instruction to move from lower level to upper level. In providing teaching advice, Van Hiele model of thinking ensures that geometric activities should not reduce the level of geometric content and whenever possible geometry materials should set the stage of further learning (Crowley, 1987). Reduction of level of geometric content has been a common problem and the situation seems to further crucial when we come to secondary school geometry.

Language is another matter of great concern in the Van Hiele model of thinking. Each level has own language and linguistic symbols and language is a critical factor in the movement through the Van Hiele levels. Van Hiele notes that many failures in teaching geometry results from language barrier: the teacher using the language of a higher level that is not understood by students. Language carries mathematical content and the difference in content is also expressed by language and linguistic symbols. So, language and thoughtfully chosen materials plays an important role in the development of geometric thinking. It is important that children talk about their linguistic association for words and symbols and their use. Such verbalization requires students to articulate consciously what might otherwise be vague ideas and serve to reveal immature and misconception of ideas.

According to Dina Van Hieie-Geldof (1984) at the start of the instruction each child possesses his own linguistic style. In course of the teaching process the teacher should try to find the common mental correlate of words and concept which are present in the child, clarify and complement this mental correlate so that it coincides with the meaning of the world in the discipline, and expand the language style in so far as necessary. The concomitant language structure should take place only after concepts have been formed.

Dina Van Hiele-Geldof suggests that before one can proceed to the definition of particuiar figure in the teaching process, it is necessary first to establish a totality of properties and order these properties according to known principles. Only after this has been completed, one can guide students towards the formulation of precise definition in which necessary and sufficient characteristics can play a role in conceiving the necessarily of the definition (level two thinking: informal dedication). But the deductive significance of definition could be realized from level 3 (formal deduction) and onwards. Such situation reveal how language is inseparable from the content.

Researches have shown that teacher's understanding of geometry knowledge together with the knowledge of relevant learning theory (for example, Van Hiele theory for geometry) have been found effective in improving instructional skills. With other things, teacher's use of language and questioning techniques play vital role in directing students thinking. Guiding students using appropriate terms/phrases related to specific level (e.g., *all, some, at least, always, never, sometimes,* for level 1; *If then, It follows that .... It implies that ....*for level 2; and *axiom, postulate, converse, inverse, necessary and sufficient condition* for level 3 and questioning technique in directing activities plays vital role in directing students thinking (Crowley, 1987). Teacher instruction should be directed to that direction which would encourage and initiate students to work on their own, to manipulate materials, to explain their ideas, to list properties and to explain, to arrange properties with some principle, to find examples and non-examples, to shortlist properties and to use in forming definition etc. Unlike frequent questioning style which begins with "What is ...." in traditional teaching, the "What....?" question should be followed by "How...?" question so that students will be challenged to explain and explore under the minimum guidance of teacher. Raising appropriate questions, allowing sufficient response time, providing prompts, hints and clues as needed and discussing the quality of student's responses are methods that take into account the levels of thinking (Fuys et al., 1988). The author in his teaching experiment conducted for doctoral dissertation found such techniques and method useful in raising students' level of geometric, understanding (Shrestha, 2005).

Conclusion

School mathematics curriculum faces serious dilemma when we come to geometry. The situation seems to be further disappointing when we come to secondary school geometry. Geometry curriculum is relatively ignored and the geometry experiences of both students and teachers are inadequate (Usiskin, 1987). Among many attempts made to improve the poor situation in geometry, Van Hiele model of thinking has been found effective. The importance of Van Hiele model of thinking lies on providing schemes for teachers in assessing student's geometric maturity and providing instructional guidance to move through hierarchy of level of thinking. Throughout the past, a common recommendation has been to do informal or intuitive geometry in elementary and junior high schools and formal geometry in senior high school. The distinction made between informal and formal was vague and such distinction leads to two levels of discourses in geometry. The importance of Van Hiele model lies in giving reference to four levels of discourses in geometry course with instructional guidance to move through the hierarchy of geometric understanding.

In addition to levels of thinking and phases of instruction, the model specifies and characterizes itself in the form of characteristics features, such as sequence of levels of thinking, language, reduction of level of thinking in teaching, mismatch between students and teacher, and adjacency of the levels of thinking. As mentioned above, they provided teaching guidance through hierarchy of the levels of geometric understanding from visual gestalt to rigorisation of mathematics which are found very important to teachers in teaching geometry.

REFERENCES

Allendoerfer, C.B. (1969). The dilemma in geometry. *Mathematics Teacher,* 62,165-169.

Burger, W. and Shaughnessy, J.M. (1986). Characterizing the Van Hiele levels of development in geometry. *Journal for Research in Mathematics Education,* 17 (I), 31-48.

Clements, D.H. and Battista, M.T. (1992). Geometry and spatial reasoning. In D.A. Grouws (Ed.), *Handbook of research on matlzematics teaching and learning.* New York: Macmillan Publishing Company.

Crowley, M.L. (1987). The Van Hiele model of the development of geometry thought. In M.M. Lindquist and A.P. Shulte (Eds.), *Learning and Teaching Geometry; K-12: 1987 Yearbook* (pp. 6-13). Resbon, VA: National Council of Teachers of Mathematics.

Dreyfus, T. and Hadas, N. (1987). Euclid may stay and even be taught. In M.M. Lindquist and A.P. Shulte (Eds.), *Learning and Teaching Geometry, K-12: 1987 Yearbook* (pp. *47-58).* Reston, VA: National Council of Teachers of Mathematics.

Fuys, D., Geddles, D. and Tischler, R. (1988). The Van Hiele model of thinking in geometry among adolescents. *Journal of Research in Mathematics Education Monograph,* 3.

Hershkowitz, R., Bruckheimer, M. and Vinner. S. (1987). Activities with teachers based on cognitive research. In M.M. Lindquist and A.P. Shuite (Eds.). *Learning and Teaching Geometry. K-12: 1987 Yearbook* (pp. 222-235). Reston. VA: National Council of Teachers of Mathematics.

Knuth. E.T. (2002). Secondary school mathematics teachers' conceptions of proof. *Journal for Research in Matizemaizcs Education,* 33(5). 379-405.

Mayberry. J. (1983). The Van Hiele levels of geometric thought in undergraduate preservice teachers. *Journals for Research in Mathematics Education,* 14(1), 58-69.

Riley. K.J. (2003). A investigation of prospective secondary mathematics teachers' conceptions of proof and refutations. *Dissertation Abstracts International.* 64(03). 836.

Usiskin. Z. (1987). Resolving the continuing dilemmas in school geometry. In M.M. Lindquist and A.P. Shulte (Eds.), *Learning and Teaching Geometry, K-12: 1987 Yearbook* (pp. 17-32). Reston, V.A.: National Council of Teacher Mathematics.

Van Hiele. P.M. (1984). The child's thought and geometry: In D. Fuys, D. Geddes and R. Tischler (Eds.), *English translation of selected writings of Dina Van Hiele-Geldof* and *Pierre M. Van Hiele* (pp. 243-252). Brooklyn. NY: Brooklyn College. School of Education.

Van Hiele. P.M. (1984). English Summary. [The problem of insight in connection with school children's insight into the subject matter of geometry.] (Unpublished doctoral dissertation, University of Utredht, 1957). In D. Fuys, D. Geddles and R. Tischler (Eds.), English translation of selected writings of Dina Van Hiele-Geldof and P.M. Van Hiele (pp. 237-241). Brooklyn, NY: Brooklyn College, School of Education.

Van Hiele. P.M. (1986). *Structure and Insight.* Orlando: Academic Press.

Van Hiele-Geldof, D. (1984). Didactics of geometry as a learning process for adults. In D. Fuys, D. Geddles and R. Tischler (Eds.), *English translation of selected writings of Dina Van Hiele-Geldof* and *P.M. Van Hiele* (pp. 215-233). Brooklyn, NY: Brooklyn College, School of Education.

Van Hiele-Geoldof, D. (1984). The didactics of geometry in the lowest class of secondary school. In D. Fuys, D. Geddes and R. Tischler (Eds.), *English translation of selected writings of Dina Van Hiele-Geldof* and *P.M. Van Hiele* (pp. 1-214). Brooklyn, NY: Brooklyn College, School of Education.

Wirszup, I. (1976). Breakthroughs in the psychology of learning and teaching geometry. In J.L. Martin and D.A. Bradbard (Eds.), *Space and Geometry. Papers from a research workshop* (pp. 75-97). Athens, GA: University of Georgia, Georgia Center for the Study of Learning and Teaching Mathematics.

28

Empowerment of Teachers in Tribal Education

B.C. DAS

The National Policy on Education, 1986, and the Constitutional Fundamental Right to Free and Compulsory Education envisage the universal elementary education for all children in the age group of six to fourteen years. The expansion of elementary education has been the foremost attempt of the Government of India during the 1990s, which led to declare the Universalization of Elementary Education as the National Goal in the Ninth Five Year Plan (1997-2002). Therefore, providing quality elementary education has been dominated the agenda of related policy exercises and recent intervention strategies. As a part of these initiatives, *ab initio,* Indian insight into quality primary education gave birth to the district specific home grown idea i.e., District Primary Education Programme (DPEP). Further, this programme has been extended its debut in the form of *Sarva Shiksha Abhiyan* bringing the entire country under its massive operation with a view to achieve the goal of universal primary education. Initially, the District Primary Education Programme focused on improvement in primary education in rural and tribal belt of the country on priority basis. The DPEP/SSA interventions in tribal education aimed at overhauling various problems of primary education: poor attendance, dismal quality of learning achievement and poor participation of girls and tribal community. It also initiated a viable mode of monitoring to check the teacher absenteeism as well as launching a tribes – friendly attitudinal training for non-tribal teachers working in the schools of tribal belt. The state of Orissa having acute problems in education of tribes needs to be studied in relation to teachers' empowerment and schooling process at primary stage.

School Community Interface

The tribal community of a fifth scheduled state like Orissa by virtue of the Panchayat Extension to Scheduled Areas Act, shortly known as the PESA Act, 1996, is supposed to have participatory involvement in all development activities including primary education. Quality parameters of primary education focus on the quality teaching learning activities and a participatory school management involving the teachers and the community. Since the literacy rate and education level of the tribal community are found low, the degree of community participation in school management is assumed to be low. Therefore, the role of teachers working in tribal area schools remains important in managing the school involving the tribal community as well as enhancing the quality of teaching learning activities in school. But, it has been observed that working in tribal schools and that are in interior tribal pockets of hillsides not to the liking and interest of the teachers particularly the non-tribal teachers (Bhargava, 1989, Biswal, 1991 Pal, 1995). Further, most of the teachers working in tribal area in Orissa are non-tribal (Ekka, 1990, Panda, 1992, DPEP Report, 1995, Sahoo & Das, 2006). Hence, a need based teacher empowerment intervention in the field of tribal education in Orissa is imperative.

Need for an Attitudinal Change

'The people (indicating teachers and any other government officials) doing their job in this interior tribal pocket shed tears twice: once during their joining and again during their leaving'. This concern was poignantly expressed by a CRCC of Sai-surni in Thuamul Rampur block of Kalahandi District, who has been serving there for 14 years. He is an outsider there. He belongs to a remote district of Orissa's coastal belt. To my further question that

why do the government servant weep during their joining and leaving, he said, *'it is again a context specific phenomenon, which has the link to the case of missing teachers'*. The researcher in the course of his field study also found similar statements from the informants across the tribal districts of South Orissa.

It has now become a known fact that most teachers serving in tribal area stay in the district or block headquarters. They have least concern about their school and the education of the tribal community. They remain busy in other works and do school duties according to their sweet will (Das, 2006). Therefore, the need is about an attitudinal change. DPEP/SSA Orissa, felt that unless the attitude of teachers is changed and a new vision towards tribal children, community and culture is developed, the situation will not improve from its existing condition. An attitudinal Training Strategy was chalked out on the basis of following assumptions.

1. There is a visible socio-economic and educational disparity among the tribal and non-tribal community.
2. The tribal children are the first generation learners.
3. The children do not have study orientation at home since their parents are non-literates.
4. The tribal children have little hope of competing with the non-tribal children due to their ethnic prejudices and low level of aspiration.
5. Most of the teachers working in tribal belt are non-tribal and possess their own prejudices, beliefs and assumptions on tribal community, culture and children.
6. The teachers have ethnic biases, least knowledge on tribal culture and society and inability to relate knowledge to the children in their language and socio-cultural contexts.

The training package intends to:

(i) modify their personal beliefs and assumptions in the positive directions;
(ii) remove their existing prejudices;

(iii) bring out a change in their conventional teaching practices; and

(iv) improve their relation with the tribal community and adopt a participatory role in involving them in school management.

Along with attitudinal training package for the tribal area teachers, the DPEP/SSA also provided in-service training on Activity Based Classroom Transaction (ABCT) subject specific competency development and community involved school management practices.

The present study examines the teachers' participation in different contextual realities of teaching learning activities and school management in the tribal belt of Orissa.

The objectives of the study are:

1. To study the dimensions of intervention strategies for (i) teachers' attitudinal change and practice and (ii) participation in classroom transaction and school management activities.
2. To study the availability of teachers in schools in relation to students' enrolment and attendance.
3. To study the teachers' participation in relation to teaching learning activities and management of school.
4. To study the constraints as faced and perceived by the teachers and education functionaries.

Methods and Procedures of the Study

Eighteen primary schools were selected for this study. The purposive sampling method was adopted in selecting the schools from three tribal districts such as Rayagada, Gajapati and Kalahandi where the District Primary Education Programme followed by *Sarva Shiksha Abhiyan* were in operation. The selection of schools have been based on the following parameters purposefully:

Different categories of schools

(a) New Primary Schools started by DPEP
(b) Old Primary Schools
(c) Residential *Sevashram* Primary Schools

Development of Villages

(a) Village of underdeveloped category.
(b) Village of moderately developed category.

Accessibility of Schools

(a) Easily accessible schools
(b) Poorly accessible schools

Concentration of Tribal Population

(a) Rayagada District having the tribal concentration of 56 per cent.
(b) Gajapati District having the tribal concentration of 51 per cent.
(c) Kalahandi District having the tribal concentration of 31 per cent.

Alongwith 18 primary schools, available teachers (34) and education functionaries (42) constituted the sample for the present study. The study was conducted in three phases of field visit in order to observe the changing developments in availability of teacher and their participation in teaching-learning activities and school management.

Besides the field study experience, the data were collected by using a school information schedule, a classroom observation schedule as well as separate interview schedules for teachers and education functionaries.

Analysis and Interpretation of Data

The analysis and interpretation of data have been done objective-wise.

Dimensions of Intervention Strategies for Teachers'

Attitudinal Change and Participation

The data related to dimensions of intervention strategies for teachers' attitudinal change and participation were collected from 42 education functionaries working at different level i.e., from the Additional Director, Teacher Training, DPEP to cluster resource centre coordinators along with 34 available teachers. The data were analysed using content analysis technique component wise:

(a) Intervention Strategies for Teachers' Attitudinal Change and Practice

Different intervention strategies for attitudinal change and practice as perceived by the education functionaries and teachers were clubbed under following dimensions.

(i) Strategies Related to Tribal Languages

- Workshops at state, district and block resource centre level were organized for the trainers and teachers to share the interaction and development about the tribal languages of the locality.
- Bilingual (Oriya and Local tribal languages like *Kui* for Rayagada and Kalahandi and *Saora* for Gajapati Districts) Charts related to day-to-day behaviour, local and behavioural objects etc. were developed and provided to each school for improving teachers knowledge of tribal language.
- A bilingual (Oriya and local tribal language like *Saora*) primer called *"Errai, Errai"* was developed for Class-I students by which teachers were given encouragement to gain mastery over the tribal language.
- Teachers were encouraged to talk in tribal languages while interacting with the tribal children as well as the tribal community.
- Teachers were given instruction to learn the tribal language in the tribal setting of their work field.

- Teachers were given encouragement that learning tribal languages will strengthen their language resource and will help in rapport establishment with the tribal community.

(ii) Strategies Related to Tribal Culture

- Teachers were enabled to question/re-examine their beliefs, assumptions and prejudices about the tribal culture of their work field.
- Teachers were encouraged to identify various cultural components of tribal community: the identification and collection of meaningful folklores, tribal dictums, folk dances, folk songs and music and see their utility in teaching-learning process.
- Teachers were motivated to remove their ethnic stereotypes, prejudices and presumptions about tribal traditional festivals and observations and to develop a positive attitude towards the tribal culture.

(iii) Strategies Related to Tribal Children and Classroom Practices

- Teachers were made sensitized about the nature and potentiality of tribal children.
- Teachers were enabled to explore various skills at the interface of language resource of tribal children and the medium of instruction at school.
- Teachers were exposed to know the process in which the tribal children learn the language and understand the new knowledge in their social context.
- Teachers were exposed to use the tribal language and cultural components in the learning process of tribal children.
- Teachers were oriented to develop Teaching Learning Materials (TLMs) using local resources/materials.
- Teachers were given a rigorous orientation regarding the skills of identifying and using the required informations, skills and transaction process and making the school motivating to the tribal children.

(iv) Strategies Related to Tribal Parents and Community

- Teachers were oriented to understand their role as the nation builder and social reformer.
- Teachers were oriented to understand the backwardness of the tribal community.
- Teachers were made felt that the upliftment of tribal community is in the hands of the teachers. This is because of the fact that education is the key to development.
- Teachers were oriented to understand the low education level and simplicity of the tribal parents.
- Teachers were oriented to make the tribal community members conscious about the future of their children and understand about the fact of 'economic returns to elementary education'.
- Teachers were oriented to make the tribal parents feel about their village schools and participate actively in school functioning and management : attending the meetings of PTA/VEC/MTA and taking part in school level decision making, participating in school gardening, school festivals, monitoring their child's study at home and school, sending children to school and asking the teacher about their child's activities and progress etc.

(b) Intervention Strategies for Teachers' Participation in Teaching-Learning Activities and School Management

The specific interventions for teachers' participation in teaching-learning activities and school management as perceived by the teachers and education functionaries were categorized into following dimensions:

(i) Annual In-service Training
(ii) Specific Orientation on Activity Based Classroom Transaction (ABCT)
(iii) Development of Teaching Learning Materials (TLMs)
(iv) Development of Activity Banks (ABs)

(v) Orientation of utilizing local resources/materials in development and utilization of TLMs and ABs.
(vi) Annual Teachers' Grant (TG) of Rs. 500/- per teacher for the development of TLMs.
(vii) Training related to community involved school management.
(viii) Training on micro planning/school mapping exercise.
(ix) Orientation on the concept of devolution of power to community and community ownership of school.
(x) Special training on gender sensitization and equity focus.

Availability of Teachers in relation to Students' Enrolment and Attendance

Teachers are the arch-point in schooling process. The concept of school or schooling remains incomplete without teacher and students. The process of teaching learning in school takes place only when the teachers and students are engaged in teaching learning activities in a participatory environment. Availability of Teachers in the primary schools of the study area were analysed according to the availability of teachers appointed by the government and the availability of teachers on duty as per observation. Further more teachers' availability was analysed in different contexts like development of village, nature of school, access to school and area of tribal concentration. The availability profile of the teachers has been presented in related Tables respectively.

It is evident that the appointment of teachers in tribal area primary schools is adequate in relation to the government norms of student teacher ratio i.e., 1:40 both in underdeveloped and moderately developed villages (STR[1]). The appointment of female teachers is found very low (19.04%). It consists of a very negligible number of tribal female teachers. The tribal teachers consist of only 20.58% of the total teachers. The para teachers or the *Swechha Sevi Shiksha Sahayaks* (SSS) are found 21.42 per cent of the total teachers and it was seen that their number is high in schools of underdeveloped villages where the posts were vacant for a long period before their appointment. The average number of teachers per school is 2.3 in underdeveloped and moderately developed villages. But the extremes behind this average reveal the management of many schools by single teacher (Table 28.1).

With regard to the functional availability of the teachers, the issue of development imbalance awaits attention. It is evident from the wide gap between STR[3] existing in schools of underdeveloped and moderately developed villages. The teachers are found missing in more numbers in under-developed villages than in moderately developed villages. Further, this issue is witnessed from the phenomena when STR[2] is compared with STR[3]. This can be attributed to the nature of community awareness and participation. The teachers working in schools of moderately developed villages may have fear of community complaint and consciousness. It has been observed that most of the under-developed villages have neither well communicated with all weather road nor the people living there found mobilized in raising voice about the absentee teachers. The teachers confront communication barriers to reach those schools.

Going into the categories of availability of female teachers made by appointment, the study found that it is 28.57 per cent in the case of old primary schools, 11.11 per cent in the case of residential *sevashram* primary schools and 20 per cent in respect of new primary schools. No new primary schools are found with placement of tribal teachers, which raises a matter of concern specially, in the context of tribal belt. In the case of old primary school and residential *sevashram* school the placement of tribal teachers are found 21.42 and 27.77 per cent respectively. No female tribal teacher is found in the case of old primary schools. Out of total teachers, the SSS/para teachers are found in more numbers in new primary schools (40 per cent) in comparison to the old primary schools (14.28) and residential *sevashram* primary school (16.66). The average number of teachers per school is 2.3, 1.6 and 3 for the categories of old, new and residential primary schools respectively. Though the placement of teachers is adequate (STR[1]) according to government norms (1:40), many residential *sevashram*

Table 28.1: Availability of Teachers in the Context of Village Development

Context	Teachers			Ave. No. of Teachers per School	Tribal Teachers			SSS/Para Teachers			Teachers on duty as per observation (in%)	STR' (in%)	STR² (in%)	STR³ (in%)
	M	F	Total		M	F	Total	M	F	Total				
UDV	16 (80.00)	04 (20.00)	20 (100)	2.2	03 (18.75)	—	03 (15.00)	07 (43.75)	01 (25.00)	08 (40.00)	33.38	31.72	17.00	29.31
MDV	18 (81.81)	04 (18.18)	22 (100)	2.4	04 (22.22)	01 (25.00)	05 (22.72)	01 (5.55)	—	01 (4.54)	76.00	26.15	17.44	23.00
Total	34 (80.95)	08 (19.04)	42 (100)	2.3	7 (20.58)	01 (12.5)	08 (19.04)	08 (23.52)	01 (12.5)	09 (21.42)	54.69	28.93	17.22	26.15

Note: Number in the parentheses indicate percentage
UDV—Underdeveloped villages
MDV—Moderately Developed Villages
STR—Student Teacher Ratio
STR¹—Ratio of Students Enrolled per Teacher (as per provision)
STR²—Ratio of Students Attended per Teacher (as per provision)
STR³—Ratio of Students Attended per Teacher (On duty)
N.B.—State Norm of STR is 1:40

primary schools are running with two teachers and sometime one remaining absent (Table 28.2).

The case of the missing teachers is found higher in old and new primary schools than the residential *sevashram* primary schools (STR[2] & STR[3]). This may be due to the teachers' accountability related to running hostel and the minimum facilities available for teachers' stay in residential *sevashram* primary schools. Further, it is also witnessed that most of the residential *sevashram* primary schools (66%) are situated with the connectivity of all weather road, transport and electricity facilities (Table 28.2).

Accessibility in this study is indicated with the connectivity of all weather roads, transport, electricity, health and other facilities. An Easily Accessible School (EAS) is supposed to have most of the above facilities whereas a Poorly Accessible School (PAS) is construed to have least of the above facilities. It is witnessed in this study that easily accessible schools are found with more number of teachers (2.6) including female teachers than the poorly accessible schools (2). Tribal teachers are found higher (20.83) in easily accessible schools in comparison to poorly accessible schools (16.66%). However, the appointment of para teachers are witnessed more (27.77%) in poorly accessible schools. This is because most of the new primary schools are opened in poorly accessible unserved area and the SSS/para teachers were made available in those newly opened schools (Table 28.3).

A silver lining is that teacher absence is considerable lower (33.29%) in easily accessible schools with most of the facilities, a potentially cardinal pointer to the importance of working conditions. Another finding is that the teachers of the road side schools which have approaching possibility of on the way visit by the supervision and monitoring personnel, are found less likely to be absent than other schools. Poorly accessible schools suffer a lot of teacher absenteeism (57.33%) because of least connectivity of facilities and lack of community monitoring. The supervision and monitoring personnel remain away from gazing at these schools of poorly accessible hill pockets. It has been observed that many poorly accessible schools very often

Table 28.2: Availability of Teachers in the Context of Nature of School.

Context	*Teachers*			*Ave. No. of Teachers per School*	*Tribal Teachers*			*SSS/Para Teachers*			*Teachers on duty as per obser-vation (in%)*	*STR'* *(in%)*	*STR²* *(in%)*	*STR³* *(in%)*
	M	*F*	*Total*		*M*	*F*	*Total*	*M*	*F*	*Total*				
OPS	10 (71.42)	04 (28.57)	14 (100)	2.3	03 (30.00)	—	03 (21.42)	01 (10.00)	01 (25.00)	02 (14.28)	50.00	24.91	9.37	11.52
RS	16 (88.88)	02 (11.11)	18 (100)	3.00	04 (25.00)	01 (50.00)	05 (27.77)	03 (18.75)	—	03 (16.66)	64.06	41.56	35.13	53.11
NPS	08 (80.00)	02 (20.00)	10 (100)	1.6	—	—	—	04 (50.00)	—	04 (40.00)	50.00	20.33	7.15	13.83
Total	34 (80.95)	02 (19.04)	42 (100)	2.3	7 (20.58)	01 (12.5)	08 (19.04)	08 (23.52)	01 (12.5)	09 (21.42)	54.69	28.93	17.22	26.15

Note: Number in the parentheses indicate percentage
OPS—Old Primary School
RS— Residential *Sevashram* Primary School
NPS—New Primary School
STR—Student Teacher Ratio
STR¹—Ratio of Students Enrolled per Teacher (as per provision)
STR²—Ratio of Students Attended per Teacher (as per provision)
STR³—Ratio of Students Attended per Teacher (On duty)
N.B.—State Norm of STR is 1:40

Table 28.3: Availability of Teachers in the Context of Access to School.

Context	Teachers			Ave. No. of Teachers per School	Tribal Teachers			SSS/Para Teachers			Teachers on duty as per obser-vation (in%)	STR' (in%)	STR² (in%)	STR³ (in%)
	M	F	Total		M	F	Total	M	F	Total				
EAS	18 (75.00)	06 (25.00)	24 (100)	2.6	04 (22.22)	01 (16.66)	05 (20.83)	04 (22.22)	—	04 (16.66)	66.71	34.36	20.98	36.49
PAS	16 (88.88)	02 (11.11)	18 (100)	2	03 (18.75)	—	03 (16.66)	04 (25.00)	01 (50.00)	05 (27.77)	42.67	23.51	13.47	15.81
Total	34 (80.95)	08 (19.04)	42 (100)	2.3	07 (20.58)	01 (12.5)	08 (19.04)	08 (23.52)	01 (12.5)	09 (21.42)	54.69	28.93	17.22	26.15

Note: Number in the parentheses indicate percentage

EAS—Easily Accessible School

PAS—Poorly Accessible School

STR—Student Teacher Ratio

STR¹—Ratio of Students Enrolled per Teacher (as per provision)

STR²—Ratio of Students Attended per Teacher (as per provision)

STR³—Ratio of Students Attended per Teacher (On duty)

N.B.—State Norm of STR is 1:40

remain under lock and key. This kind of schools consequently cause low attendance during the occasional arrival of the teacher which make the average STR^{3} poorer to STR^{1} even in the context of high teacher absenticism in the schools of poorly accessible area (Table 28.3).

It is witnessed that teachers availability is more in Rayagada followed by Gajapati and Kalahandi. Summatively or separately it spells adequacy (STR′) with reference to the state norm of student teacher ratio (1:40). The least availability of female teachers in Kalahandi and Gajapati becomes a matter of concern. However, the percentage of placement of female teachers is 41.17 in the case of Rayagada district. The study also found another finding of regional disparity related to the placement of tribal teachers. The tribal teachers constitute 11.76 per cent in Rayagada, 16.66 per cent in Kalahandi and 30.76 per cent in Gajapati district. It has been observed that the availability of para teachers/*Sweccha Sevi Shiksha Sahayaks* shows need based variation (8.33% to 29.41%) in respect of different regions of tribal concentration (Table 28.4).

The issue that raises the strongest concern is regarding the case of the missing teachers. The low degree of teachers' availability on duty and participation (33.39 per cent) in actual school environment specially in Kalahandi district is in alarming state. For instance, many primary schools (33%) in this district have been witnessed under lock and key. This may be due to engagement of teachers in their other business keeping commissional contact with the supervision and monitoring personnel. This state of affairs is comparatively lower in Rayagada and Gajapati districts (STR^{2} and STR^{3}). Another significant finding is that the teachers absentecism consequently reduces students attendance in these primary schools across the districts (STR^{2} and STR^{3}).

Teachers' Participation as Perceived by the Researcher

Teachers' participation was observed in relation to teaching learning activities as well as school management. Significant observations have been indicated aspect-wise.

Table 28.4: Availability of Teachers in the Context of Concentration of Tribal Population

Context	Teachers			Ave. No. of Teachers per School	Tribal Teachers			SSS/Para Teachers			Teachers on duty as per obser-vation (in%)	STR' (in%)	STR² (in%)	STR³ (in%)
	M	F	Total		M	F	Total	M	F	Total				
Rayagada	10 (58.82)	07 (41.17)	17 (100)	2.8	01 (10.00)	01 (14.28)	02 (11.76)	04 (40.00)	01 (14.28)	05 (29.41)	69.5	31.41	19.87	35.24
Gajapati	12 (92.30)	01 (7.69)	13 (100)	2.1	04 (33.33)	—	04 (30.76)	03 (25.00)	—	03 (23.07)	61.17	20.70	19.16	19.13
Kalahandi	12 (100)	—	12 (100)	2	02 (16.66)	—	02 (16.66)	01 (8.33)	—	01 (8.33)	33.39	34.69	12.63	24.08
Total	34 (80.95)	08 (19.04)	42 (100)	2.3	07 (20.58)	01 (12.5)	08 (19.04)	08 (23.52)	01 (12.5)	09 (21.42)	54.69	28.93	17.22	26.15

Note: Number in the parentheses indicate percentage
STR—Student Teacher Ratio
STR¹—Ratio of Students Enrolled per Teacher (as per provision)
STR²—Ratio of Students Attended per Teacher (as per provision)
STR³—Ratio of Students Attended per Teacher (On duty)
N.B.—State Norm of STR is 1:40

(a) Teaching Learning Activities

Teaching-learning activities as observed have been interpreted component-wise :

(i) Motivating Children's Attendance

It has been observed that children's participation in schooling process is having its intricate link to teachers' regularity and parental compulsion on children for domestic works like sibling care, cattle herding and assisting in field works and so on. Children's participation in school can be observed in terms of their attendance rate from Table 28.5.

Table 28.5: Context-wise Attendance Rate of Children in Primary School

(in per cent)

Context	*Village Development*		*Nature of School*			*Access to School*		*Total*
	UDV (N=9)	*MDV (N=9)*	*OPS (N=6)*	*RS (N=6)*	*NPS (N=6)*	*EAS (N=9)*	*PAS (N=9)*	*N=18*
Rayagada	62.25	72.61	68.50	74.76	59.03	64.57	73.15	67.79
Gajapati	69.23	75.31	62.48	86.49	67.84	76.30	64.21	71.69
Kalahandi	20.73	53.45	30.05	72.15	9.07	54.52	33.60	39.08
Total	50.74	67.12	53.68	77.80	45.32	65.13	56.98	59.52

Pupils attendance is found more (67.12 per cent) in moderately developed school village than underdeveloped village (50.74 per cent).

The residential *Sevashram* School is found having better potentiality to motivate the children (77.80 per cent) in comparison to old primary school (53.68 per cent) and New Primary School (45.32 per cent).

Students' participation is found better in easily accessible primary schools (65.13 per cent) as compared to poorly accessible schools (56.98 per cent).

Students are found more motivated in Gajapati (71.69 per cent) followed by Rayagada (67.79 per cent) and Kalahandi (39.08 per cent).

Provision of 40 seat hostels for girls in Residential *Sevashram* Primary School has motivated them towards schooling. But this kind of provision has not been provided to Gajapati District as this district doesn't come under the jurisdiction of KBK plan like Kalahandi and Rayagada district. On the basis of the above observations it can be said that the teachers, parents and the facilities like the free hostels, food, dress and learning materials may be key determinants in motivating the children towards school in tribal area. Among these the teachers' role remains most important in motivating the children for schooling. Hence, to improve the situation further, the teachers need continuous empowerment.

(ii) Classroom Transaction

Making a paradigm shift from the conventional pattern to a child centred, child friendly and joyful learning through Activity Based Classroom Transaction (ABCT) is one of the major goals of the ongoing interventions in primary education. For this the teachers have been provided training on ABCT development of TLMs and Activity Bank.

It has been observed that:

- Textbook method dominates the classroom communication. Most of the teachers are indifferent to the practice of ABCT.
- TLMs are found limited to charts flash cards, pictures and maps. Their utilization level observed is below the minimum level.
- Chalkboards in most of the schools are found with pre-writings of some multiplication tables or words etc. This writing in most of the schools do not replace the other writings even for months indicating thereby the constant irregularity in the utilization of chalkboard in classroom practices.
- Most of teachers (80%) are observed using the textbook language and least concerned about the use of tribal language in the class.

- Home works are rarely given to the students.
- Most of the residential *Sevashram* schools (66%) are found with remedial teaching and guidance to the students.

(iii) Co-curricular Activities

An average number of primary schools have jumping ropes and ring balls only. A few schools have play-ground. Teachers are found reluctant to take classes of co-curricular activities. Instead the children play in small groups without any help and direction from their teachers.

(b) School Management

Teachers working in the primary schools of tribal villages have been provided orientation for taking initiation in mobilizing the community to participate in school management. Parents Teacher Associations (PTAs), Mothers Teachers Associations (MTAs) and the Village Education Committees (VEC_s) have been constituted to monitor and participate in the schooling process and management of school. But the members of the above bodies are observed (75%) not to be very active and bothered about the said purpose. Only some (22%) VEC members are seen active during the inflow of school improvement grant (SIG).

- Teachers are observed showing receptive attitude to the community members who visited the school spontaneously.
- An average number of teachers (45%) keep on contact with the Village Education Committee Members.
- A few teachers (20%) are able to establish rapport with the community members.
- Community participation like *'Vidyalaya Pravesotsva'* (School Entry Day), which was instituted on 23rd July, 1998; a traditional approach of *'Musti bhiksha'* (collection of alms) for school corpus fund and the

awareness campaign during the initial years of DPEP operation have been initiated by the teacher and education functionaries. These activities are found tempo-central. At present such activities are not in continuation.

- Teachers normally do not ask the parents to send their children. Rather, some of the children come to school at the arrival of their teacher.
- It has been observed that both the teachers and VEC member do not want the regular meetings of VEC/PTA and MTA. This kind of situation make teacher maintaining the formal records only. This phenomenon has an intricate link with the parental indifference and their unavailability due to wage labour and field works.
- In the case of new and old primary schools, the teachers found vulnerable in managing the mid-day-meal being afflicted by the irregular supply of food materials as well as the cook problem caused by no remuneration.
- Well maintenance of school records is seen during DPEP Operation and after. Most of the old primary schools even have no records of some of the preceding years of DPEP Operation.

The captured observations related to teachers' participation in institutional planning and community involved school management spell a lot about the indifference attitude of both the teachers and the community members towards an effective school management. Lack of teachers' initiatives has link with many problems and constraints that teachers face in relation to the practice of community involved school management in the tribal belt.

Constraints as Faced and Perceived by the Teachers and Education Functionaries

The teachers and education functionaries perceived a number of constraints on the way of their normal functioning in the tribal belt, which have been categorized as the following:

- Lack of all weather roads, transport and communication facilities.
- Lack of residential facilities.
- Lack of electricity.
- Lack of market facility
- Fear of malaria prone climate
- Lack of health facilities
- Lack of knowledge of tribal language and culture
- Existing prejudices among teachers about the tribal community.
- Lack of interest and attitude to do job in interior tribal belt
- Less possibility of early transfer
- Lack of better educational environment for their children
- Lack of special incentives for serving the tribal belt.
- Poorly paid remuneration to SSS/Para teachers. They are being treated as second category teachers which fans the members of discontentment and lack of will and attitude to work. The situation was found detrimental to quality teaching learning activities.
- Lack of entertainment environment
- Less opportunity for their socio-economic upliftment.

Conclusion and Implications

This study has many seminal implications for teachers' participation, in service teachers strategies, monitoring and supervision, community support to schools management, child centred learning environment, need based curriculum development and a holistic policy making exercise to bring up a perceptible change in educational development of the tribal community.

The study suggests the following areas of teachers' empowerment:

- Developing sensitivity of teachers towards school situation in the context of internal and external forces operating therein.

- Developing affective attributes : care, affection, self-identification and involvement in school system in the context of socio-ethnic and cultural environment of tribal schools.
- Developing abilities to co-relate structured curricular guidelines with flexible approaches to be adopted in real school situation.
- Developing holistic situation specific decision-making abilities of teachers in the tribal schools.
- Developing a receptive and follow-up attitude among teachers towards academic as well as management support rendered by the supervision and monitoring personnel.
- Developing own progress of ethical maturity in professional development and self-practice of managing the tribal school with initiating active involvement of the tribal parents and community leaders.
- Developing teachers' ability to organize content specific activity based classroom transaction.
- Developing teachers' competencies in utilizing local resources/materials for development of teaching learning materials and activity banks.
- Developing teachers' abilities in preparing and utilizing Information and Communication Technology (ICT) based teaching learning materials.

The in-service training strategies can be organized on the above- suggested areas of teachers' empowerment in the tribal area. The other implications of the study are :

- The intervening organizations should extend adequate physical and infrastructural resources support to each school including ICT based facilities.
- The supervision and monitoring personnel should adopt participatory approach to monitoring and supervision of the school activities.
- The education functionaries and the teachers must extend efforts to facilitate a decentralized and

community owned school management. Thus, an effective form of local ownership can be developed to substantiate the schooling process and school management.

- A regular practice of community involved school meetings through Village Education Committee (VEC), Mothers Teacher Association (MTA) and the Parents Teachers Association (PTA) can be of great help in empowering teachers for better turn out of the school.

REFERENCES

Biswal, G.C. (1991). 'Needs and Problems of Tribal Community in Orissa with regard to Education: An Indepth Study', unpublished Ph.D. Thesis, Vadodara : MS University.

Bhargava, S.M. (1989), Survey of Educational Facilities for weaker section of the society namely Scheduled Tribes of Orissa, Independent Study, New Delhi: NCERT.

Das, B.C. (2006), 'A Study of DPEP Intervention in Tribal Education and its Effectiveness in Orissa', Unpublished D.Phil. Thesis, Department of Education, Allahabad : University of Allahabad.

Das, B.C. (2009). Tribal Education: Trends and Future Scenario, New Delhi: Regal.

DPEP Report (1995), DPEP Report, Orissa Primary Education Programme Authority Bhubaneswar.

Ekka, E.M. (1990). 'Development of Tribal Education in Orissa after Independence', Unpublished Ph.D. Thesis, Utkal University, Bhubaneswar.

Pal, G.C. (1995). 'Dropouts: An Observational Analysis', *The Primary Teacher*, Vol. Xx(4) pp30-35 October, New Delhi : NCERT.

Panda, B.K. (1992). 'A Sociological Study of the Functions, Organization and Impact of Tribal School in the Koraput Tribal District of Orissa', Unpublished Ph.D. Thesis, Jamia Millia Islamia, New Delhi.

Sahoo, P.K. and Das, B.C. (2006). Primary Education in the Tribal Belt of Orissa, In Rath, G.C. (Ed) *Tribal Development in India*, pp 258-278, New Delhi/Thousand Oaks/ London : SAGE.

V

Quality Assurance

29

Futuristic Challenges to Quality Assurance in Teacher Education

SHYAM B. MENON

This paper attempts firstly to define the limits of the quality discourse in teacher education by articulating its assumptions in terms of what may be considered as some of the basic characterizations of teacher education. Further, it paints a picture of diversity of systems and processes involved in teacher education in India today, thereby attempting to bring out the challenges in arriving at formulations of quality indicators which are applicable to a variety of situations and are, at the same time, sensitive to the specific needs and functions of each of those. The paper then makes an effort to predict the broad future trends that may unfold with regard to teacher education systems and the challenges that they are likely to throw up for quality assurance.

Assumptions

It is useful to set limits to the notion of quality in teacher education right at the beginning. Any discussion on quality in relation to teacher education must, in my opinion, accept as its basic assumptions the following characterizations of teacher education:

First, it must be recognized that teacher education is not an autonomous entity. Its purpose is to cater to the needs of school education. In that sense, teacher education is a second order phenomenon; its structure and the processes it inheres are determined substantially by the characteristics of the primary phenomenon, school education, the role it earmarks for teacher and the competencies it takes to play that role effectively. Therefore, quality of teacher education is circumscribed by the expectations of school education. On the other hand, teacher education at its best is potentially the source of new ideas related to school. Quality of teacher education is thus not to be understood merely in terms of its effective performance of the role expected of it by school education, it would also be about the extent it is able to influence philosophies and practices of school.

Induction into teaching as a profession has two prerequisites: one, mastery over an area of knowledge that forms the substance of school curriculum; and two, internalization of certain basic competencies that are integral to its effective transaction. While teacher education ordinarily presumes the former, that is mastery over the content, in an aspirant even before s/he enters the system as a student teacher, it has as its primary focus the development of the latter, that is competencies related to curriculum transaction. However, quality discourse in teacher education cannot overlook the content component. It is material therefore to take as an assumption in the quality discourse a second characterization of teacher education, viz., that it is not a stand-alone system and is appropriately perched atop the edifice of general education at the secondary level or a system of liberal education in a specific area of knowledge at the tertiary level. In other words, teacher education builds on, or is integrated with, a system of secondary or tertiary education, which aims at imparting the basic knowledge adequate to transact the content of school curriculum and a world view and value system characteristic of an 'educated adult'.

Finally, what is ordinarily referred to as teacher education is the initial teacher preparation leading to certification, whether a degree or diploma, based on which teachers are recruited in school systems. However, it is now being increasingly recognized that the initial teacher preparation only serves to equip the professional aspirant with the basic skills and competencies. These basic abilities need to be polished and updated regularly on an ongoing basis throughout one's professional career, much in the manner in which more established professions like medicine expects its practitioners to go through alternative trajectories of continuing professional education. School systems that take quality seriously do have structures and processes built into them for the continuing professional development of their teachers. Thus, teacher education includes not only the initial preparation, but also the continuum of professional development of practitioners.

In sum, before we begin discussing on quality issues related to teacher education, we must assume that such discussion cannot be independent of quality issues related to school, that it cannot be seen unrelated to the quality of feeder systems of general secondary education and liberal tertiary education, and that it has to take a comprehensive view comprising the initial teacher preparation and the continuing professional development.

The Growing Diversities

The teacher education scene was fairly straight-jacketed in India till the nineties. There were only two major streams of teacher education, both of the nature of initial teacher preparation: The first was a two year programme after twelve years of schooling lading to a diploma, qualifying teachers for elementary education. The other was a one-year B.Ed degree programme after a graduation or a postgraduation, qualifying teachers for secondary and senior secondary levels, respectively. When the statutory authority for accreditation and maintenance of standards in India, National Council for Teacher Education (NCTE), was established through an Act of Parliament in 1993, it was considered that their primary focus would be on the above two streams. The norms and guidelines that the NCTE formulated as instruments for accreditation and assurance of a minimum acceptable quality were largely on the basis of input parameters in terms of infrastructure, size and qualification of faculty etc. However, today we find ourselves in a situation where there is tremendous variety of programmes of teacher education across states, particularly those preparing teaching personnel for primary education, which imposes an enormous challenge on quality assurance in teacher education. India has witnessed a remarkable expansion of primary schooling since the early Nineties largely through the centrally sponsored schemes under Education for All (EFA). The District Primary Education Programme (DPEP) has been perhaps the most ambitious, comprehensive and extensive of such programmes. As a part of providing for access to primary education among the unreached, both geographically as well as socially, several alternative school systems have been established in many states, the Educational Guarantee Schemes of Madhya Pradesh and Uttar Pradesh and *Shishu Shiksha Kamasuchi* of West Bengal, to name a few. In Gujarat, there are different alternative school systems, each with distinct characteristics designed to address the needs of a specific target group. These differ sometimes from district to district. There is a specially designed system of alternative schooling for children of migrant labour in one district, a non-residential bridge school in another and a special alternative school for children of saltpan workers in a third. Most of such schemes are essentially about providing the minimum basic conditions for primary schooling *inter alia* through a cadre of para-teachers, who have a stipulated minimum educational qualification, which vary from state to state and system to system even within states, and who are inducted and trained through training programmes whose structure and duration again vary from state to state and system to system. Most of such programmes have a built-in component of in-service training and continuing professional support for teachers. These programmes together deal with a sizeable proportion of teaching personnel in the primary school systems in India today.

The alternative schools and the system of para-teachers may well become a regular feature, particularly so long as budgetary allocation to education does not increase substantially. With the *Sarva Shiksha Abhiyan* emerging as the new initiative aiming at Universal Elementary Education (UEE), there are clear indications that alternative structures of schooling and cadres of para-teachers are likely to be a feature at the upper primary level of schooling as well. With UEE within reach, when pressures of numbers begin to hit the secondary schools, one could safely predict that similar strategies of alternative schools and para-teachers might proliferate even to the secondary school systems in several states in the foreseeable future.

It is thus clear that the diversity we see today in teacher education systems in India is not an ephemeral or a passing phenomenon; it is here to stay. The expansion and diversification of private sector in school education is also indicative of increasing diversities in teacher education. Some private universities are already involved in designing specific teacher training programmes, some through the distance mode, largely focusing on the growing private sector in school education, particularly aimed at the nascent phenomenon of international schools. Such programmes are also likely to attract those teachers aspiring to compete in job markets in the developed countries. The quality discourse in teacher education must therefore reckon with training systems and strategies, vastly diverse in terms of duration, substance and relative emphasis in training, location, level of education at which the training is perched and mode of certification. It would thus be increasingly difficult to define quality indicators in teacher education in terms of input parameters alone, cutting across the vast range of systems, institutions and strategies.

What the Future holds

Based on our understanding of these emergent trends in school education in India, one could venture to gaze into the crystal ball and make some fairly modest predictions about the future or futures that await(s) teacher education.

From what we saw in the previous section, it could be extrapolated that the State-initiated programmes for expansion of schooling will continue to look for alternative systems of schooling and alternative cadres of teachers. The growth and diversification trends in private sector of schooling also prompt us to predict increasing heterogeneity in the cadre of teachers. What follows logically is the prediction that school systems will tend to have increasingly heterogeneous cadres of teachers with a wide variety of educational backgrounds, trainings, orientations and so on.

School curriculum is becoming increasingly complex. Many new areas of knowledge are getting integrated into it. The methodology of curriculum transaction is also undergoing transformations. This is all the more the case with those school systems, which are pace setting and are 'market leaders'. In this context, we are likely to experience an increasing rate of obsolescence in teacher competencies, and therefore, a more pronounced need for continuous professional development of teachers and for provisions for periodic assessment of teacher competencies.

The emphasis in periodic in-service training and ongoing technical resource support for professional development of teachers, which we have begun to see in some of the recent alternative school systems, is likely to be mainstreamed and institutionalized. There is enough evidence to suggest a definite shift from an exclusive focus on initial teacher preparation to an integrated and inclusive perspective of initial preparation and continuing professional development of teachers.

With all these above developments, and with a liberalizing economy as backdrop, it is most likely that along with single-entry, single-exit programmes of teacher education with relatively rigid designs, there will also be those with more flexible designs, with provisions for multiple entries and multiple exits and for bridges with other courses and with continuing professional practice. In conjunction with this development, the distinction between face-to-face (formal) mode and distributed (open and distance) mode of teacher education will become increasingly blurred. The insularity of conventional institutions *vis-a-vis* open and distance education institutions offering teacher education programmes is likely to diminish. Multimode, multi-site and modular programmes of teacher education may come into vogue.

The Challenges for Quality Assurance

These emerging and futuristic trends in teacher education will have a bearing on considerations related to quality and quality assurance of teacher education. These developments are likely to throw up a number of very specific challenges for quality assurance in teacher education. Our existing notions related to quality assessment and the indicators used for this will need major transformations. We will need to go beyond the first generation indicators which are based on input parameters and move towards those which are applicable to a variety of situations with a wide range of diversity in each input parameter, and are, at the same time, sensitive to the specific needs and functions of each of those. It will need to be based on definitions of specific competencies associated with effective practice of teaching, and of the training experiences and processes that facilitate the development of these competencies. In other words, the focus of quality assessment will then shift from inputs to processes and outputs.

We will need to recognize that just like there could be different notions about 'good' classroom teaching and 'effective' professional practice by teacher, there could well be alternative philosophies, and divergent notions emerging from them, related to 'good' or 'effective' teacher education. This will call for flexibility in approaches to and methodology of quality assessment in teacher education. Quality guidelines will then need to be so formulated as to enable alternative and creative designs for programmes of initial preparation and continuing professional development of teachers.

The systems of accreditation and maintenance of standards may need to broaden their domain, which is at present focused on teacher education programmes and institutions, and include within it *teacher* as well. A need is perhaps increasingly felt now for a system of professional accreditation and renewal of accreditation of practicing teachers, in other words, a system of licensing practitioners. If there is greater clarity about competencies associated with effective teachers and a valid methodology of assessing them in aspirant teachers and practicing teachers, an accreditation system could then shift its focus from teacher education to teachers, in which case they could adopt greater flexibility in accommodating a range of alternative and creative designs for teacher education programmes and systems. For this to happen, new instruments, methodologies and systems for periodic assessment of teacher competencies need to be researched and developed.

30

Quality Issues in Teacher Education

SUBHASH GAKHAR

Confronted with quality standards, primarily due to expansion in Indian higher education system, the emergent questions of quality nurturing and assurance are being discoursed critically. This paper particularly discusses quality improvement related to teacher education

The attribute of nurturning or sustaining is bound up with the idea of quality and the idea of standards. Quality and standards are of course interlinked; one cannot have one without the governing function of the other. Quality is governed by standards, and standards in turn are determined by the prerequisites of quality.

In the educational domain (including of course teacher education), quality and standards pertain to the domain of objectives, to knowledge, to the domain of methods, skills and application, evaluation and importantly the domain of sensitivity by which knowledge and methods are transfused into that unique and amazing phenomenon—the teaching-learning process. Moreover, nurturing in terms of quality and standards cannot be realised, other than in the degree in which it is embodied in the "product" i.e. pupils. So both "process" and "product" are determinants in equal measures of quality or excellence in education as much as in teacher education. It is the final "product" the pupil, the educated—in whom excellence, or the absence thereof, and standards, or the lack thereof, are defined.

Teacher education by a self-imposed definition is seen and treated by teacher educators as a sub-system of the education that is concerned first and foremost with the important task of preparing teachers professionally. Given this one is easily tempted into thinking that quality and standards in teacher education should be identified by some of the factors involved in the process of professional training. Preparation of teachers, important as it is in its own right, is nevertheless an intermediate link in the process. One must see teacher education in a wider context and as a continuum that starts from teaching-learning from the preparation of teachers and other educational personnel to the study site, in the class rooms or on-the job.

Keeping this continuum in mind, one should take note of the thoughtful concerns expressed in our country. First is the concern that teacher education is functioning in an environment (partly self-created) that is remote from the realities of the classrooms, or the persistent problems of the education system. Another concern is that teacher education is slow to change and slower to respond to changes and challenges of socio-economic environment, or those that occur rapidly in the education system even while the socio-economic and the education systems are being overwhelmed by problems around new thinking and initiatives.

If teacher education systems are indeed becoming remote from problems, a search for quality and standard may well lead them into even greater remoteness unless the definition and search for excellence are seen in the wider educational and socio-economic context. It is of critical importance that the linkage of teacher education and the final educational product, namely the pupil, the educand, is reestablished in order to define sensitively what constitute excellence quality and standards in teacher education.

Generally speaking, excellence refers to high quality education at the hands of an educator or as organised by an institution. Applying this to teacher education institutions, we would draw the inference that the excellence of teacher education would be assessed according to the purpose and objectives, concept innovation used, curriculum, student teaching and preparation of teachers of a given teacher education programme.

Quality and Objectives of Teacher Education

The objectives need to be stated in terms of knowledge, skills, attitudes and interests. These must include both personal as well as professional aspects so as to adequately ensure a teacher's education as well as training. Further, a pertinent aspect of viewing excellence in relation to objectives of a Teacher Education Programme is the relevance of the objectives. More than anything else this has to be ensured.

In recent years many countries and especially those in the third world have taken a fresh and more critical look at the role of education within the context of overall national development. New concepts of education have evolved, both formal and non-formal and these have often been formulated in forthright terms settings the national educational objectives. In India, the goals of education follow the national goals of development set for the country. Among other things they include: to accelerate the process of modernization through computers, communications technology and so on and to make education a powerful instrument of socio-economic and cultural transformation necessary for the realisation of the national goals. It is imperative further that the teacher has to assume greater responsibiity so as to 'initiate action for the transformation of society as an agent of social change and thereby help in achieving the goal of national development.' Thus the success in carrying out educational reforms and acceptance of the new role by the teacher depends on the quality of teacher which, in turn, depends largely on the quality of Teacher Education. All this has implications for clearly formulating the aims and objectives of Teacher Education as relevant to the needs of the society. Ensuring relevance of objectives is thus the first step in any programme of promoting excellence in Teacher Education.

A set of board objectives that may be central to any teacher education programme in India regardless of the structure and stage or level may be as follows:

(i) to develop concepts and acquire understanding of those areas and aspects of knowledge which have professional significance;
(ii) to develop an understanding of educational theory which will inform professional judgement and actions;
(iii) to develop technical skills necessary for the achievement of professional competence on the basis of accepted principles of learning and teaching.
(iv) to develop understanding of the relationship between logical and psychological aspects of the teaching-learning process at a given stage of human development;
(v) to develop skills to organise institutions as educational, cultural and social centres for the community;
(vi) to develop faith in democratic and secularistic values e.g. self-reliance, dignity of labour and provide experiences and skills in organising community living based on these values and to act as a link between institution and community;
(vii) to possess warm and positive attitude towards growing children;
(viii) to develop communication and psychomotor skills and abilities for interacting with students in order to promote learning inside and outside the classroom;
(ix) to keep abreast of new knowledge and methodology of teaching; and
(x) to undertake Action Research.

Quality and Emerging Concept of Teacher Education

An expanded function of education in India when it is directly linked to national development requires a broadening and deepening of the teacher's own knowledge and understanding. It also requires that the teacher sees himself not as a prime source of knowledge but as an organiser of learning and learning experiences. This calls for a change in the concept of teacher education reorienting the teacher education curriculum both for enhancing the teacher's educability as well as his contribution to development. While there is a growing awareness that education can make important contribution in respect of the national development programme, the curricula of teacher training institutions have yet to be accordingly revised. Teacher education thus will have to find an entirely different focal point in planning and implementing various aspects of its programmes.

The curricula would necessitate courses on national development, and activities which will assist teachers in developing a clear understanding of the national educational goals of development. Likewise, the methods of teacher education will have to undergo a new orientation as they will be affected by the new objectives of education for development. In-service programmes for teachers and teacher educators would require to be planned in the context of knowledge and skills required for the new challenge of development. The UGC introduced a centrally funded scheme of Academic Staff Colleges (ASCs). Here specially designed programmes in teaching methodologies, pedagogy, educational psychology for new entrants may be designed.

Quality and Standard through Innovations

Some of the important areas in which innovations have been attempted with a considerable degree of success may include:

(a) Improvement in student teaching through micro-teaching techniques, introduction of internship in teaching programmes, organisation of joint supervision.

(b) Improvement in the methods of teaching by introducing approaches such as team-teaching, workshop on models of teaching, seminars and discussions, systematic evaluation as an integral part of teaching-learning process, etc.

(c) Introduction of alternative programmes like the four-year integrated teacher education programmes.

(d) Planning and organisation of professional orientation of teachers of higher education.

(e) Planning and implementation of strategies in respect of non-formal education by teacher educators.
(f) Devising programmes of staff development through continuing education of teacher educators.

It may be necessary to include the understanding of the processes of innovation as an inegral part of the system of teacher education. For this purpose, it may be worthwhile to derive this understanding from actual situations at the grassroot level. This will better prepare the teacher educators and others in the field of creating, planning, implementing and evaluating innovative programmes.

Quality in Teacher Education Curriculum

Practically all the Review Committees and Commissions on education have made recommendations for improving not only teacher education curriculum but also various other aspects like its linkage with the main stream of university education, admission procedures, teaching methods and so on. All this has been adequately highlighted in the NCTE document entitled Teacher Education Curriculum: A Framework. By and large the course components of the existing teacher education programmes in India could be categorised as: (i) theory courses; (ii) practice teaching; and (iii) some practical work. If one were to look back into the theory courses taught several years ago and compare it with that taught presently, it may be found that in most cases there are practicaly no changes. Many ideas in the field of education have become outdated and may have at best an historical importance. This is equally true in respect of the practice teaching aspect of teacher education. The approach with which classroom teaching is viewed should be changed. Better techniques of the training in teaching should be constantly under experimentation in different parts of the world. The teacher educators would do well to keep track of the findings and results of these experiments in their efforts to modify the curriculum in teacher education not only in theory courses but also in respect of the hitherto neglected aspect of practice teaching.

Changes in the school curricuum have of late been contemplated by introducing what has been termed as Socially Useful Productive Work. But are our teachers capable of handling this new subject area? Are they themselves aware of the needs and aspirations of the community around? The teacher education programmes should incorporate in its curriculum that aspect of providing for the teacher trainees to work with the community. Some attempts have recenty been made at improving the teacher education curriculum. There is a general consensus that the NCTE curriculum attempts to bring out the teacher education from its age-old shackles putting it on a more progressive path. It has accepted 'flexibility' and 'integration' as its base points. Flexibility is referred to as; (i) mobility of entry and exit of a teacher trainee at different stages of teacher preparation and also mobility from one discipline to the other; (ii) flexibility for relevance to develop 'teacher education modules' catering to the needs of the states and the local communities within each State; and (iii) flexibility with regard to the continuity between pre-service and in-service education of the teacher.

The national goals of education are achieved through the cumulative efforts of teachers at all stages, from the pre-primary to the collegiate. This implies a teacher education curriculum model which would run similar for the different stages with common components though providing for certain modifications as per the needs of a given stage. In the broader sense, the teacher education curiculum would comprise; (i) Pedagogical Theory; (ii) Working with the Community; and (iii) Content-cum-Methodology of Teaching School Subjects and Practice Teaching. While the pedagogical theory has to clearly reflect our national ideology and the problems and issues faced by our society, it is further necessary that the intending teachers should be thoroughly familiarised with their complex socio-economic environment through actual work situations in society. The rationale for introducing "Working with the Community" in the teacher education programme is two-fold. Firstly, theoretical knowledge based on the pedagogical courses needs to be reinforced and validated by means of actual life situations in community. Secondly, that only through practical training based on participation in community work could a trainee develop insight into, sensitivity to, and attitude towards common social problems.

The theoretical aspects that should go into the curriculum may be broadly classified into core subjects and special subjects. The former were those which are consirdered to be highly essential so as to ensure mastery over the teaching process. The cultural aspects of the community in which the teacher works and the related social, geographical and other aspects also influence the teaching process to a certain extent. Hence the core subjects could be considered to contain the knowledge of the cultural and social aspects of a given community. This is where the teacher education curriculum requires flexibility. The content and methodology courses in teacher education need to be integrated. This is not an easy task however. The NCERT has provided guidelines for developing such an integrated curriculum hoping that such a curriculum for content-cum-methodology would help integrate content and method in such a way that the dichotomy that has existed between them for such a long time will finally disappear.'

Summing up, a curriculum howsoever reformed, can never be final in its form. It is a continuous process of thinking, modifying and evaluating. New ideas do emerge as a result of thinking, discussion and experimentation.

Quality of Student Teaching and Practical Work

This could preferably be done in three stages. In the first stage the trainees should learn different component skills of teaching. This may take say two to three weeks time. At this stage the micro-teaching technique is found to be highly economical in terms of time and effort. Together with the idea of micro-teaching goes the idea of simulation.

The second stage of the teaching practice should comprise the teaching at school for one to two months. Once the trainee has been well groomed during the first stage, the ideas and skills in teaching would assimilate further in school situation.

At this stage, the teacher educator or the supervisor should consider the totality of the teaching process looking to the most efficient form of combining the different components of teaching.

The final stage in the teaching practice should be the internship in schools. This is to make them familiar with the total picture of a school. This is intended to give them a feeling of how a teacher's life in a school would be what may be his/her expectations from the pupils, fellow teachers, head of the institution, parents, and community at large. This stage could be compared to that of a house surgeon in the medical profession or a junior lawyer in the legal profession.

'Working with the Community' and 'Socially Useful Productive Work' are yet other aspects of the teacher education curriculum which should be properly understood and sincerely implemented. Needless to say that 'Socially Useful Productive Work' and 'Working with the Community' when included in the teacher education curriculum would ultimately result in linking the school with the community. All this would go a long way in making theory and practice of education both realistic as well as challenging.

Quality and the Preparation of Teachers

Along with content and transactional or pedagogical skills, teachers need managerial skills and competence. There are *five* main *commitment* areas:

(i) **Learners:** Love for the learners, readiness to help for learners, concern for their alround development.

(ii) **Society:** Awareness and concern about the impact of teachers' work on the degree of advancement of families, community and nation.

(iii) **Profession:** Internal acceptance of the role and responsibility of the teachers' profession.

(iv) **Excellence:** Care and concern for doing everything in the classroom in the school and in the community in the best possible manner.

(v) **Basic Human Values:** Genuine practice of professional values such as impartiality, objectivity, honesty, national loyalty etc. with consistency. Teacher must have the quality of *'Satwa'* which is indicated by knowledge, wisdom and enlightenment. In other words *'Satwa'* implies harmony.

There are five important areas where the teacher should perform well. These are:

(i) **Performance in Classroom:** Teaching-learning, evaluation and management techniques.
(ii) **School Level Performance:** This includes organisation of morning assembly, celebration of national day etc.
(iii) **Performance in Out of School Activities:** Field visits, tour, community survey etc.
(iv) **Performance related to Parental Contact:** Enrolment and retention, regularity in attendance etc.
(v) **Performance related to Community:** including joint celebration of certain events by the community, encouraging community involvement in school functioning.

Besides, teacher education programme must include certain aspects to enable the teachers to master the content and curricular competencies, management and evaluation competencies and willingness to perform.

It is important that for nurturing good quality and standard, there must be provision for: (i) Induction training to the newly recruited staff to know about the culture, practice and programme of the institution. (ii) On the job training one of the ways is attachment to senior teachers who guide the new entrant in all areas of functioning. Othr methods are staff workshops, job allocation, followed by observation. (iii) Participating in training programmes such as taking advantage of formal in-service programmes offered by NCERT, SCERT, SIET etc. by attending seminar, conferences etc. (iv) *Open and Distance Education:* There are post-graduate programmes in content and pedagogy related issues in education. Similarly there are education channel like *Gyan Darshan*, journals, books, self-instructional material and internet.

At present professional preparation is generally done once to last a life time. The recurring training and re-training of educational personnel (teachers and all others concerned with the education of young people) throughout their working life should be an indispensable function of teacher education. Teaching like learning is lifelong, and so its renewal and recharging be. The search for quality in teacher education as a spring of generative knowledge and practice may remain elusive as long as lifelong learning for teaching does not become an integral part of the way we begin to see the country's education quest. This also implies that teacher education should be at the cutting edge, of new knowledge, insights and innovations. It has to be a fountain head of renewing energy for the education system.

There is one more function of excellence seeking teacher education system, which needs special attention. This is for the teacher education system to act intellectually and professionally as a watch-dog, no less, of quality and standards in the education system as a whole. Teacher education system cannot be excellent if the rest of the system is one the downward path. The watch-dog function means, the monitoring the performance of the education system for quality and standards and making known the results, loud and clear. In our country we are at the crossroads where the attitude of 'let business be as usual' will be a grave disadvantage to the educational cause and a dereliction of duty on the part of teacher educators.

At post-primary levels, failure rate at each grade level have increased and achievement levels are on the decline. The result is that quality and standards are slowly pulled downward, pulling down with it the related systems notably teacher education. Think what the performance of this character will do the future of millions and millions of young people who will have to wrestling, with little endowment given by the present education system, with the in rushing problems of the morrow which is as unlike the present as one can imagine.

The search for high quality and standard in teacher education, lies not in the secluded hypaths but in the highways crowded with real problems of young people and their dreams and aspirations straining to breaking point.

For this every institution should:

- identify and encash on its strengths and strengthen them further.
- identify and initiate deliberate action to reduce weakness.
- identify the opportunities, exploit them and convert them into strengths.
- identify the apparent and potential *threats* and try to eliminate or reduce their intensity.

In addition to the above in this process training, research as well as wage policies and social and official recognition are indispensable ingredients.

In regard to qualitative improvement of teaching vis-a-vis teaching-learning situation we ought to ask ourselves some crucial questions. They relate to whether children learn as much as we teach, and whether they enjoy learning, whether they find it meaningful. Teachers should, therefore, be mindful of the possibility of too much emphasis on the refinement levels of teaching without proper reference to the child. However, in spite of the accumulation of research findings over the years, it has not yet been possible to lay down in specific detail what exactly needs to be taught and how it could be taught effectively. The instructional and assessment methodologies continue largely to perform the functions of selecting able pupils and eliminating those who do not measure upto the pre-determined standards.

This has resulted in widening the functions and role of the teacher. This refers to the teacher's role in working with community around the school. But this role does not necessarily mean that instead of working with the students or in addition to his work in the school a teacher has necessarily to render some kind of social service to the community as an isolated activity. What is implied is that teachers have to show a special concern about the contribution of education to development goals. This includes the analyses of social problems and re-thinking the basic values and structure of society. It includes the study of critical issues involved in the country and direction of development. Thus the new role of the teacher includes imparting of education to young people with the understanding, attitudes, critical abilities and skills required to make the most appropriate contribution to the rapid development of the country.

This new style of the teacher is one whose high sound of productivity (Methodology) will in most cases require the use of new technology. Programmed instruction, team teaching, computer assisted learning, use of internet and various instructional aids should increasingly be used as tools of the trade.

To be able to bring about quality in higher education, teachers must put their own house in order. They must introduce such innovations as would transform schools, colleges, and universities into dynamic, creative, self-reforming organisations capable of responding to the developmental needs of the country. Teacher's role today, under the stress of change and in the context of knowledge becoming obsolete in a very short time, cannot be what it was before in a more placid era. Today the teacher has to be a senior partner with the student taking part in the joy of the pursuit of learning and of the adventure of seeking the acquisition of new facts, new ideas, new skills and new techniques relevant in to-day's context. It is now impossible for the teacher to function successfully unless he keeps him/herself abreast of the latest advances in own field of speciality, the latest development in the methodology of teaching, and the latest changes occurring in the social order as also in the aspirations, attitudes and requirements of his/her pupils. Needless to say that quality institutions can play an important role in the development of teachers in the desired direction. If the 'essence of a programme of teacher education is 'quality', it is needless to say that the institutions charged with the responsibility of teacher preparation have got to be quality institutions.

The problem of teacher supply and demand is directly related to the quality of educational institutions and in fact to the overall quality and standards in education. The dearth of good teachers continues to be felt. Education, being a producer and consumer of high level manpower should 'recoup enough of its own best output to reproduce a good further crop.' Thus if there is to be an improvement in respect of quality in the teacher education institutions, there must be an increase of input in them of competent staff and of potential intending teachers.

Again, most teacher education institutions are so often isolated from research organisations and there is not much of quality research conducted by them. Obviously, making teacher education a part of mainstream of national education and improving the quality of teacher education institutions is inescapable if a serious attempt is not to be made for improving the quality of education in general.

Conclusion

Teacher education thus needs to be continuously modified with a view to playing its role in qualitative improvement of higher education. It is to be stimulated by pedagogical research and made intellectually richer and more challenging within the orbit of national education. Further, it needs to be extended far beyond pre-service training into a system for continuous professional renewal and career development of all teachers. Teacher education institutions should also be in close touch with the community around making sure that their work is relevant to the needs of the schools in the community. In addition, they must maintain equally close ties with schools and classroom teachers on the one hand and innovative institutions on the other so that they are not isolated from new ideas on curriculum or educational enquiry, and more importantly feel themselves as equal partners with other educators in the national sytem of education.

To sum up, for nurturing good quality and standard in teacher education programme, good quality in terms of content, pedagogy, management and evaluation is needed. Teacher's programme has to be effective, efficient, meaningful and result-oriented. There should not be any wastage of human resources. Every one should get good marks and work upto the optimum level. We must be conscious about the dimensions of social capital i.e. human relationship. There must be total understanding, commitment, involvement and acceptance of each other members. Every one should believe in action and there should not be any slackness. Every teacher educator should have vision, should move together for a common mission.

Thus reform on such lines as these would carry with it exciting possibilities for attracting more of society's best talent in terms of both staff and students into the institutions of teacher education. This would in turn lead to overall nurturing high quality and standard and improvement of higher education.

31

Improving Quality in Teacher Education

M. VARMA

Quality improvement in educational systems without thinking to reform professional education of teachers is just like thinking about a circle without having the concept of the center. With rapidly changing national and international economic, technological and socio-political scenario, the perspective of teacher education in 21st century has completely changed, which has necessitated the educational planners to think about qualitatively reforming teacher education at massive scale throughout India and also without suffering a time and socio-cultural lag.

Perspective and Future Vision

Indian teacher education has travelled a long way. Starting from British style normal schools, passing through NCERT-Regional College of Education phase to NPE1986 suggestion of DIET, CTE, and IASE structure, followed by coming up of statutory control of NCTE and finally reaching the present stage of accreditation concept of NCTE-NAAC. But this journey has somewhere ignored the national and international social perspective and future vision of teacher education and consequently suffered in quality.

But the present professional education of teachers in India is theory oriented, isolated from the community, stereotyped, impractical and has no or little scope development of affective domain of teacher i.e. empathy, respect for individual, and positive attitude towards teaching profession, children, society and values. It shows little scope for innovations and social sensitivity and is generally ill suited to the needs of school and learner. The perspective of teacher education in 21st century has completely changed. The teacher in near future will be expected to function in the context of rapidly changing socio-cultural, political and techno-economic scenario, onset of information revolution, value crisis, increasing complexities in society and classroom.

Strong Will for Quality Improvement

Numerous suggestions to overhaul Indian Teacher Education by many Commissions and Committees are accumulating but the quality improvement still remains an unrealized dream. One reason for this is that there always remained a mismatch between efforts of improvement and the vastness of the nation and it's geographical, economic, social, religious, political and linguistic diversities. *Secondly,* a vigorous and sustained implementation of the reforms has always been lacking. Education Commission rightly observed, " *the report of a commission is not a substitute for action. The responsibility of implementing the report is primarily that of the Government* "(Report of Education Commission 1964-66). A strong political will and a cautious social vigilance are the requirements for the quality improvement.

Since education is now in the concurrent list of the constitution of India, it has become easier to convert into reality the vision for new teacher education for the whole country and to implement the same through an act of Parliament. This will help in percolation of reforms into all regions of India. Supported by strong political commitment and will following measures may improve the quality of teacher education in India.

Admission Procedure and Standards

An objective procedure need to be developed for admitting in the courses of teacher education, right persons having taste and aptitude for teaching. For this purpose, a policy with a national vision is required

Secondly, admission procedure in various teacher education courses needs to be made uniform throughout the nation. The NCTE has already taken up this task but this need to be done fast without loosing time. This is possible by centralizing the admission on the model of IGNOU.

Thirdly, regional and state variations in standards of teacher education programmes also need to be minimized.

Efficient and Effective Curriculum Transaction

A course in Teacher Education should aim at transforming an educated person into a vibrant teacher with all the professional skills, attitudes and commitment. For this purpose an element of rigour and hard work needs to be introduced in teachers' training. Effective and efficient transaction of curriculum needs to be planned and implemented simultaneously throughout the country in an innovative way ensuring the use of non-conventional pedagogy. Establishment of a National University of Teacher Education can better ensure the quality improvement. Universities of Teacher Education have done good job in Japan.

Need for a National University for Teacher Education

Experience shows that the government agencies have generally not been able to perform the task of teacher education with a commitment and professional attitude. Political changes also affect them directly. This task may be better performed by a university because the universities, by their very nature, are autonomous bodies and are independent in taking the academic decisions and sticking to their traditions for the long period of time. History shows that the universities have retained their basic character for the last almost one thousand years. *The primary purpose of the university is to provide an environment in which faculty and students can discover, examine critically, preserve, and transmit the knowledge, wisdom, and values that will help to ensure the survival of the present and future generations with improvement in the quality of life* (Kneller, 1971).

Secondly, the university with a national vision is required to take care of the task of teacher education throughout India so that it may produce not only good teachers with a high level of professionalism but also citizens with a national vision, character and attitude.

Thirdly, in order to reform and modernize teacher education throughout India within a short period of time establishment of a National University of Teacher Education by an Act of Parliament is the need of the hour which is possible only when there is a strong political will to reform this sector.

Features of Proposed National University for Teacher Education (NUTE)

The NUTE should be an autonomous body and an apex institution for teacher education directly under the control of Parliament with its headquarters at New Delhi, constituent campuses in northern, southern, eastern, western and central regions of India and an all India jurisdiction. All the DIETs, CTEs and IASEs need to be affiliated to this university. The university and college departments of teacher education may be provided academic affiliation to NUTE. This national institution should also be empowered to set up, and run Academic Staff Colleges exclusively for in-service professional enrichment of teacher educators throughout the nation.

The NUTE should be a state of art modern university having tremendous capacity and capabilities so that it is able to reform teacher education in this vast country at a massive level without suffering a time, or socio-cultural lag. It should be able to provide teacher education through modern technology based on electronic communication, computer and internet.

There should be inbuilt quality improvement and maintenance mechanism in it. It should also enter into memoranda of understanding with the best teacher education institutions and teacher educators of the world to bring in their inputs and should, at times, get accredited by the international agencies. Best of the great educationists, thinkers and institutions of India and world should be involved with the affairs of this university through modern technology.

The NUTE should be capable of providing teacher education for all levels and types, formal as well as open/ distance modes. It should not only show excellence and make a niche of its own but should play a role in improving existing teacher education institutions and accrediting them. Some of the powers of NCTE and NAAC need to be delegated to this proposed national university.

All important and great national institutes (IIMs, IITs, NCTE, NUEPA, NCERT, IGNOU, NID, NIRD, NIMH, Central and State Boards of secondary education) should have a say in the affairs of this university in the form of their inputs.

The NUTE should have following objectives:

1. The National University for Teacher Education shall in the exercise of its powers have jurisdiction over the whole of India and to the centers outside India.
2. The NUTE shall endeavor through education, research, training and extension to play a positive role in the development of teacher education in a multicultural, multi-lingual and highly varied Indian society.
3. To promote teacher education in a rapidly developing and changing society and to continually offer opportunities for upgrading knowledge , training and skills in the context of innovations, research and discovery in all fields of human endeavors.
4. To provide an innovative system of teacher education, flexible and open in regard to methods, pace of learning, conduct of examinations and operation of the programme with a view to promote learning and encourage excellence in teacher education.
5. The NUTE shall function in cooperation with the existing National Institute, Universities and Institutions

of higher learning and make full use of the latest scientific knowledge and new educational technology to offer a high quality of teacher education which matches contemporary needs.

Professional Growth of Teachers

1. The DIETs, CTEs, IASEs need to be better integrated to cater to the working school teachers' professional development and continuing education. Presently their efforts are insufficient. If all these institutions get attached with the proposed NUTE then they will be constantly receiving academic inputs and leadership and will be better equipped to undertake professional growth of teachers.
2. The professional growth of teacher educators is of more importance. Presently, IASEs and UGC Academic Staff Colleges in various universities are doing this job but establishment of Academic Staff Colleges exclusively for teacher educators may be more useful for their professional growth. The NCERT and the proposed National University of Teacher Education and its constituent campuses as well as the state capital headquarters of NUTE may establish such colleges for benefit of teacher's educators. All such colleges should remain under the direct supervision of NCTE.

Accreditation after providing a Model

Accreditation of teacher education departments and institutions may be beneficial but only under certain conditions. *First,* when there is uniformity in yardsticks of accreditation. *Second,* when there is uniformity in curriculum and modes of transaction in teacher education programmes throughout the nation. *Third,* when teacher education departments and institutions have some ideal model before them to follow. *Fourth,* when there is ample facility for professional growth of working teacher educators.

These conditions are hardly there in the present Indian educational scenario. The institutions do not have before them any model of excellence to draw inspirations from. The nation should establish a University par excellence for teacher education to work as a model for the whole country. Then the exercise of accreditation will become meaningful and will certainly help in quality improvement in teacher education.

REFERENCES

Delors, J. et.al. *Learning: The Treasure Within. (Report of the International Commission of Education for Twentyfirst Century.* Paris: UNESCO, 1996.

Good, H.. G. *A History of Western Education,* New York: The Macmillan Co. 1949 pp. 80-111.

Kneller, G.F. "The Universities" in George, F.(Ed.) *Foundations of Education.* New York: John Wiley & Sons, Inc. 1971 .pp. 553-71.

Monroe, Paul. *A Brief Course in the History of Education.* New York: The Macmillan, 1937 pp.138-45.

Mukhopadhyaya, Marmar. *Total Quality Management in Education.* New Delhi: NIEPA, 2001, p. 45-59.

National Council for Teacher Education. *Curriculum of Framework for Quality Teacher Education.* New Delhi: NCTE, 1998.

Sharma,A.P. *Development of Western Educational Thoughts,* New Delhi: Concept Publishing Company, 1997, p. 63-66.

The Indira Gandhi National Open University Act 1985 (No. 50 of 1985) & The Statute of the University. New Delhi, IGNOU, 1998, p. 2.

The New Encyclopaedia Britanica vol. 12 Micropaedia Ready Reference. Chicago : Encyclopaedia Britanica Inc. 1998, p. 164-190.

32

Professional Development Among Teachers

PURNIMA K.

Quality issues associated with any facet of education raises an awareness of the desperate situation existing in education system of the developing world. The most common characteristics that have been frequently traced out are : (i) a leap in the quantity of education available, and (ii) a steady deterioration in the quality of education available.

Schooling is now becoming a part of the broader value system with the consequence that enrollments are sky rocketing. Between 1970 and 1985, school enrollments in the developing world doubled and almost tripled (UNESCO, 1987.) Even so, the participation and performance rates of young people beginning school continue to be so minimal that up to 40 per cent of first grade children in certain countries fail and are expected to repeat the first grade. By the fourth grade, over half of the children in many developing countries have already left school. At the age of 14 years only 10 per cent of developing world children are literate in their native language (Fuller, 1990). It is unequivocal, though, that the working conditions in which teachers are expected to function what they are able to accomplish along with the teaching competence they possess. If teachers are to be more effective, their physical and social surroundings will require improvement. Teachers, in general, are willing to do what is necessary to improve, if the challenges put before them seem in the best interests of the young people with whom they work. Here the major responsibility lies with, the managers and policy makers to create a climate and provide the resources necessary to improve the quality of teaching learning system.

Climate Building for Quality

(a) Teachers' relation with the students is an ongoing process. The attitude of teachers is of prime importance if they are to strive for excellence. Good inspiration will encourage students to love learning. Teacher should respect the human dignity of children. The code for professional ethics need to be followed in this respect.
(b) Teachers should be aware of their rights and responsibilities. Knowledge about the service conditions would avoid a lot of unnecessary hassles. It is their duty to take the task of teaching very seriously, by introducing innovations and adopting appropriate methods of teaching suiting to the learners group with emphasis on practical work, seminars and workshops.
(c) Teachers are now emerging from an information society into a responsive society where the focus is on knowledge, spiritualism and responsibility. The teaching profession should not be merely an occupation but should be taken as a mission. The mission can be accomplished by self-assessment. Assessment can also be done by the head of the institute, students and by competent external bodies.
(d) Regular session of in-service teacher training programmes help in building confidence to use innovative techniques and information technology. They also help to upgrade subject knowledge and planning lesson for day-to-day teaching learning activities

Initiatives at Institutional Level

A commitment to teacher quality requires every school to re-think the nature of the management: what it is and what it needs to become. As the organisation of teaching and learning reflects the practical applications of a school's commitment to teaching and teacher development, so does the policy formation process signals a school's ability to adapt to changing circumstances within the context of its own values base. This refers to the school's process for identifjring priorities, planning, implementation and evaluation. This is often treated as an evolutionary rather than a bureaucratic process.

"Teacher Quality", the way being defined, is a consequence of deliberate action and commitment by individual teachers at the classroom and school level rather than as a result of the demand for enhanced teacher quality through external or top-down policy initiatives. The success of policy implementation is a function of the "goodness of fit" between the fundamental beliefs of teachers and the values of the school and the policy being implemented. The five key characteristics of the contexts of the schools that exhibit high levels of teacher quality are:

- A clear vision or moral purpose leading to the progress of the student: teachers believe they can and will make a difference to the life-chances of all their pupils.
- An investment in high quality teachers on the part of the school, it applies to recruitment and staff development programmes, as well as the resourcing of collaborative activities; the encouragement of "leadership" at all levels of the school.
- The school management must to ceate an infrastructure within the school, supportive of high quality teaching and learning it involves and commitment to school-based development planning, increased communication and broader involvement in decision making.
- A symbiotic relationship between the school and community, it involves pressure and support at all levels within a context of shared educational values.
- The individual teacher: "Teacher quality" springs from individual teacher's motivations and capacities. Gifted teachers create excellence in their teaching

environments; their confidence is underpinned by thorough preparation and deep understanding of the needs and interests of the students. Their collaboration with colleagues is usually for a specific purpose: from whom they can learn. They take in-service courses and engage in professional development. to the extent that teacher quality rests on individual initiative and skills. The policy implications include:

(a) Rigorous selection procedures which admit only high quality entrants to the profession;
(b) Pre-service teacher education, that is challenging and practice-based;
(c) A relatively high level of financial remuneration;
(d) Career progression that rewards excellence in teaching and keeps good teachers in the classroom.
(e) Challenging professional development opportunities that allow individual choice;
(f) A school organisation which fosters institutional autonomy;
(g) A policy environment that is enabling rather than constraining;

School Factors concerning Teacher Quality

"Teacher quality" springs from schools organized with infrastructures that support good teaching and collaboration among teachers: conditions being created specifically to support the teaching and learning process; at an organisational level to create roles, allocate responsibilities, and generate ways of working that reflect the shared educational values of the school.

To the extent that "teacher quality" rests on school level factors, the policy implications can be listed as:

(a) Pre-service education of new teachers which is, to a large extent, school-based;

(b) Decentralisation of management and budget at the school level;
(c) Specificity in policy directives with high levels of support and the opportunity to adapt and experiment in teaching;
(d) Creation of networks of the schools to exchange information and support;
(e) Opportunities for school in curriculum decision-making;
(f) The encouragement of self-evaluation and planning at the school level;
(g) Flexibility in provision of in-service teacher education and staff-development.

Teacher Quality Assessment

Teacher quality is also the result of coherent and well-tested policies relating pre-service and in-service teacher education, curriculum, student assessment and teacher appraisal. Educational excellence depends mainly on faithful implementation of these policies, Independent initiatives of individual teachers or schools in this respect must be praised. At the school level, school, administrators are to be increasingly held accountable for meeting centrally defined standards. Teacher evaluation systems should reflect central rather than individual values. Teacher education programmes nationally need to be widely scrutinized, and schemes for accreditation established. To the extent that teacher quality rests on central authorities, the policy implications should be:

(a) A broad and coherent range of complementary policy options;
(b) Teacher education that complements the direction of the reforms;
(c) A central inspectorate to monitor the progress of individual schools,
(d) An information system to generate public debate on education.

It is necessary to assess teacher quality so that policies to improve it can be rationally formulated. It is also necessary to recognize that no static, uniform definition of teacher quality is possible. Empirical research relating teacher's behaviour around characteristics to pupil's learning has shed light on the following features:

(a) Knowledge of substantive curriculum areas and content;
(b) Pedagogic skill, including the acquisition and ability to use a repertoire of teaching strategies;
(c) Reflection and the ability to be self-critical, the hallmark of teacher professionalism;
(d) Managerial competence. As teachers assume a range of managerial responsibilities within, and outside the classroom.

Making ICT User Friendly

Development in information and communication technology have offered possibilities for raising the quality of school education by introducing new instructional technology with the use of multimedia, learner centered pedagogy etc. The challenge is now to use the ICT for education; the change has to begin from the teacher education system. Teacher education will have to assume new responsibilities and come out of phobia of the machines and take it as userfriendly. For using the ICT in education, professional development in ICT of teacher educators and teachers is imperative. Every teacher educator must be able to handle internet, create database for his/her institution, putting of innovation of institutional home page, preparation of web page and creation of forums of chat etc. online conferencing between all like minded people, generations of software, preparing multimedia lessons on teaching learning, innovative practices in software and software pool for national distribution is pre]requisite.

- Teacher educators must focus on pre-service and in-service workshops to equip teachers in the use of the web technology, content creations and the like.
- Teachers must be made familiar with the net and given easy access to it.
- Teacher educators must explore the ways in which the Internet can benefit teacher education programmes.
- Microplanning for an effective use of technology to support teaching/learning and educational management.
- Orientation of teachers and students to look at the web as an information provider.
- Teacher educators should adopt multi-media approach, develop CD based course materials, and conduct online tests and grade the students.
- Opportunities to attend an online class/cyber class/ cyber seminar/digital subscribers lines. Teachers training particularly for non-formal education sector should be decentralised.
- Private partnership should be encouraged with spirit of co-operation rather than competition.
- Making Teachers ICT knowledgeable,
- Web-based curriculum and assessment related strategies must be promoted at teacher education level.

REFERENCES

Fuller, (1990). 'What investment raise achievements in the Third World', In Chapman (ed.) Improving Educational Quality: A Global Perspectives, New York: Career Greenwood.

UNESCO, (1987). Report on School Enrolment in Developing World, Paris: UNESCO.

33

Quality Assurance in Teacher Education

P. MALLICK

Quality has become the buzz-word of education in the 21st century. The development economists have rightly emphasized the importance of developing human capabilities through education for development. The information and communication revolution, knowledge economy and globalization are increasingly influencing the younger generation. In the context of global society, each and every country is seriously thinking of heightening the degree of quality in the system of education. Teacher education is an important area of concern in our educational system. The quality and efficiency of education depends on the quality of teacher. The standards of learning are influenced strongly by the teacher's capacity, understanding and skill. The upgradation of standards in our educational system is dependent on quality improvement of teacher education.

The quality of teacher education can be attained by input, process and output variables of the institution. If we want to analyze the institution as a system in totality we can have performance indicators with reference to input, process and output. Input indicators are concerned with the physical resources such as building, equipment, library, laboratory and playground and human resources like teachers, students, administrators and parents etc., and financial resources like budgeting, resource mobilizations in respect to availability, feasibility, economy and efficiency. Process indicators include the instrumental strategies and the way in which resources and factors are combined and used in order to produce the institutional output. Output indicators describe the outputs to be produced by the institution. These indicators determine whether objectives of a particular course of instruction are being achieved or not? These indicators are certainly useful to see whether the inputs have been transformed to outputs of expected standards through appropriate process or not?

Agencies of Quality Assurance

The National Policy on Education (1986) and Programme of Action (1992) recommended that excellence of institutions of higher education is a function of many aspects; self-evaluation and self-improvement. There should be a council to encourage self-assessment in institution and assessment and accreditation of the institution. The quality process, participation, achievement etc. must be constantly monitored and improved. The Ram Murthy Committee (1990) further emphasized that the quality of higher education should be improved in real terms not only to make it more relevant to our society but also to cater to the needs of competitive industry, indigenisation of technology including research and development therein and their application. The process of accreditation is now a full-fledged process known for academic evaluation with the sole purpose of improving the quality of higher education. The National Board of Accreditation (NBA) for technical education, and National Assessment and Accreditation Council (NAAC) for general education are the two significant initiatives of All India Council of Technical Education (AICTE) and University Grants Commission (UGC) respectively. Similarly, other agencies like National Council for Teacher Education (NCTE) Medical Council of India (MCI) and the Distance Education Council (DEC) of India and the Pharmacy Council of India (PCI) are already in existence for assessment of their respective programmes and institutions. The UGC initiated several schemes like Faculty Improvement Programme (FIP),

University Leadership Programme (ULP), National Education Testing (NET), Academic Staff College (ASC), Autonomous Colleges (AC) including National Assessment and Accreditation Council (NAAC) for quality assurance in higher education.

National Assessment and Accreditation Council (NAAC): The UGC setup the NAAC on 16th September 1994 to assess and accreditate the institutions of higher education with an objective of helping them to know their strength, weakness and opportunities through an improved review. The process of assessment involves preparation of self-study report by the institution, validation of the self-study report by a peer team on the basis of field visit and final decision of accreditation to be made by the NAAC Committee. The NAAC has been using a set up criteria with the following seven items to assess the institutions.

(i) Curricular Aspects : This is the first of the seven parameters stipulated by NAAC. It deals with the compatibility of the ongoing academic programme in the institution with its goals and objectives. This aspect includes goal orientation, initiation and design of courses, programme options, academic flexibility and feedback mechanism.

(ii) Teaching Learning and Evaluation : This is the most important parameter carrying highest weightage by NAAC. This aspect includes admission process, teaching-learning process, use of new technology, remedial courses offered, examination innovations, such as continuing evaluation, question bank open books system etc., recruitment of teaching staff, faculty development programmes, external evaluation, research and work satisfaction of the faculty, monitoring and rewarding the successful teaching, the research innovations are some of the variables considered in this section.

(iii) Research Consultancy and Extension : This aspect includes promotion and sustenance of research culture, research output, publications, consultancy activities, need based community extension activities, involvement of faculty and students, resource generation for broad based extension activities etc.

(iv) Infrastructure and Learning Resources : This aspect includes physical facilities, library, laboratory, computer center, sports, games and physical development programmes including health services, hostel and canteen facilities etc.

(v) Student Support and Progression : This aspects includes issues such as student profile, ratio of pass and drop-out, progression of students on employment including self employment, higher studies and specialization, noteworthy achievement of alumni, involvement of alumni and parents with the functioning of the college, student feedback on various activities including faculty performance, mechanism of grievance redressing, financial support to needy students, career counseling and job placement etc.

(vi) Organization and Management : It includes administrative mechanism, recruitment, progression, training and performance of the non-teaching staff, participation of students, faculty and staff in decision making at various levels, creation and utilization of management fund and the transparency in budgeting, accounting and auditing of financial resources etc.

(vii) Healthy Practices : Healthy practices is an open ended item that promotes academic ambience and initiatives for over all developments of the institutions. It includes linkage with industry, institutions and user sections in the neighbourhood as well as the national and international levels, educational and extension innovation, welfare activities, value based education etc.

The above seven points are assigned with different weight depending upon the unit of accreditation. The universities are given one kind of weightage system and the affiliated and autonomous colleges are weighted differently, ultimately to arrive at a single weighted average, to assign grades. This method is followed to avoid any problems in the inter institutional comparison of scores. In the case of teacher education institutions' detailed criteria have been worked out jointly by NAAC and NCTE by means of giving more weightage to process orientation of teacher education programmes. Assessment is done by the peer team comprising of experts from the field of teacher education.

Various attempts have been made to improve the status of teacher education in India. The National Policy on Education (1986) has suggested establishing District Institutes of Education (DIETs), Colleges of Teacher Education (CTEs) and Institutes or Advanced Studies in Education (IASEs) for providing Teacher Education at various levels. DIETs cater to the pre-service and in-service education of elementary school teachers at district level where as CTEs and IASEs are responsible for Teacher Education at the Secondary and Higher Secondary stages at state level. Besides these, University Departments and national level organization are also conducting in-service education programmes. It is very much essential to identify mechanism for ascertaining quality performance of these institutions in the context of objectives categorically set for each kind of institutions.

National Council for Teacher Education (NCTE)

The National Policy on Education (1986) recognized the continuity and inseparability of pre and in-service teacher education and recommended permanent educational mechanism. Initially the NCTE was setup by a resolution of Government of India in the NCERT. Later it became a statutory body responsible for the co-ordination and maintenance of norms and standards in teacher education since 1995. The main objective of NCTE is to achieve planned and co-ordinated development of the teacher education system throughout the country. The NCTE has taken number of steps for raising the quality of teacher education system with the following major responsibilities:

- Co-ordinating and monitoring teacher education and its development in the country;
- Providing guidelines for the content and methodology of education;

- Promoting and conducting innovation and research in various areas of teacher education and disseminating the results thereof;
- Taking all necessary steps to prevent commercialization of teacher education;
- Undertaking surveys and studies relating to various aspects of teacher education and publishing the results thereof;
- Making recommendation to the Central and State Government, Universities, University Grants Commission and recognized institutions in the matter of preparation of suitable plans and programmes in the fields of teacher education.
- Laying down norms for admission, method of selection of candidates, duration of the course, course contents, mode of curriculum, tuition fees and guidelines for starting new courses, providing instructional facilities, staffing pattern and staff qualification.
- Evolving suitable performance appraisal system, norms and mechanism for enforcing accountability, on recognized institutions.
- Formulating scheme for various level of teacher education and identifying recognized institution and set up new institution for teacher development programme.

Suggestions for Improvement in Teacher Education

The NAAC and NCTE play important role for bringing qualitative improvement in the teacher education programme. There is an urgent need to bring improvement in prevailing teacher education programme in order to develop quality and competence of the institution. The following suggestions have been provided for consideration of these bodies :

- Policy makers and teacher educators should strive to promote appropriate concerns to ensure quality teacher education system.

- For professional development of teachers, emphasis should be given on learning rather than teaching. At the same time professional responsibility has to be taken up willingly by the teachers themselves.
- Teacher education institutions have to be autonomous, self-supportive and accountable in all respect.
- Teacher education institutions should be innovative, creative and explorative in their approach for developing skills among students.
- Teacher education institutions should inculcate desirable values among students.
- Teacher educators and trainees should be trained to use appropriate methods and technologies for effective teaching learning processes.
- Each teacher should involve himself/herself in undertaking action research for qualitative improvements.
- Teacher education institutions should prepare professionally competent teachers to perform their roles effectively as per the needs of the society.
- The system of evaluation in teachers training must be based on continuous evaluation to make it more objective and transparent.
- Combined entrance tests should be implemented to ensure uniform standard.
- The training programmes of teacher training institutes should be more activity oriented rather than theory based.
- Teacher training institutions should be well equipped with good facilities and quality instructional materials.

REFERENCES

Ahrned, A. and Siddiqui, M.A. (2005). Need for Revamping Teacher Education Programme, *University News,* 43 (18).

Chakravati, I. (2004). Quality Control and Assessment of Performing Arts in Higher Education, *University News,* 42 (24).

Khanna, P. (2005). Changing Scenario of Higher Education, *University News,* 43 (07).

Mohanty, A.K. and Pani, A. (2005). Landmarks in the Development of Teacher Education in India, *University News,* 43 (18).

Sharma, R. (2004). *Assessment and Accreditation in Higher Education* (Ed), New Delhi : AIU.

Sharma, S. (2005). Rethinking Teacher Education, *Yojana,* Government of India, 49.

Singh, L.C. and Mishra, S. (2005). Quality Concerns in Teacher Education, *University News,* 43 (18).

Sungoh, S.M. (2005). Quality Issues in Teacher Education, *University News,* 43 (18).

Swain, S. and Pradhan, N. (2005). Quality Education in the present context, *EDUTRACK,* 5(3).

Upadhyaya, S.K. and Upadhyaya, V. (2005). Quality concern indicators of Teacher Education, *University News,* 43 (18).

Verma, R. (2004). Quality and Relevance in Education, *University News* , 42 (10).

Index